SUCCESS IS A TEAM SPORT

The Marshall Rauch
Family Story

NED CLINE

RAUCH FAMILY FOUNDATION, INC.

ISBN 1-878086-97-9
Library of Congress Control Number: 2004097926
Printed in the United States of America

Book design by Beth Hennington
Jacket design by Tim Rickard

Rauch Family Foundation, Inc.
1309 Union Road
Gastonia, NC 28054

Dedication

*To my parents and grandparents
for their love, devotion, and foresight in
bringing our family to the United States.*

Acknowledgments

For the three-plus decades I have known Marshall Rauch, I have always considered him one of North Carolina's finest and most visionary leaders. He has succeeded as a city councilman, state legislator, university official, private businessman, civil rights advocate, and philanthropist.

To say that Rauch and his family lead interesting lives and are committed to sincere appreciation for each other and their community is like saying homegrown tomatoes taste good: it's an indisputable fact. If the family's love and affection for each other could be bottled and marketed, it would fly off the shelves with record sales.

It was several years ago that Marshall Rauch first asked if I would be interested in a research and writing project to chronicle his family members' lives and history. It would be interesting and enlightening, he said, and he wanted it published not so much for the present, but for future generations as a factual history of the family's early struggles and later successes.

I initially demurred because I had just accepted a new assignment as a newspaper editor. I also needed assurances that he really wanted a book outlining the whole story, warts and all.

From my association with him in my role as a journalist and his role as an elected state senator and public university board member, however, I knew him as a man of incredible candor and integrity. The more he and I discussed a book, the more I became convinced it should be done.

Furthermore, it became abundantly clear in our conversations that he would willingly permit the review of the wounds as well as the recovery that would include personal and financial hardships and heartaches along with the incredible successes as a private businessman and public servant. It would be a story of perseverance and one with lessons for others to learn in dealing with their daily lives and offering services to others.

So, I set aside daily journalism to begin this project. It has been an immensely rewarding experience. I hope it will be a beneficial one for readers as well.

Marshall Arthur Rauch is a man of intelligence, charm, business savvy, strong religious faith, political instinct, vision, good humor, and just plain common sense. Too few people are willing to show the courage to take on the responsibilities, both private and public, that he has accepted. Even fewer would have been able to meet the challenges that fell his way as he progressed in business and public service.

His is, indeed, a story not just for now but for future generations.

I owe him a great deal of gratitude for his willingness to discuss the negatives along with the positives.

A big thank you is also in order to his wife, Jeanne, and their children, all of whom have opened their hearts and heads to help put the Rauch family story together. A word of appreciation is also due the family patriarch's many friends, business and political associates with whom I spoke and whose assistance was essential.

Gratitude also is owed those who assisted with fact checking and editing. A special word of appreciation goes to Jack Claiborne. He's a first rate retired journalist in Charlotte whose skills in editing a book are as sharp as those he used on newspaper editorial pages. He had keen eyes and reasoned suggestions for improvements. Multiple thanks are also due Mark Bernstein, who was the corporate attorney for Rauch Industries and remains one of Marshall's closest friends, and whose talent at working through tedious legal issues was more valuable than even he might realize.

I would also be remiss if I didn't say a word of gratitude to my son Jeff, who repeatedly rescued me from the pitfalls of my earliest days of dealing with the mysteries of cyberspace. Without him, this book might never have been finished, although in all probability I would have been.

This project has been a treat for me. I hope others will find it beneficial as they view the Rauch stories from the inside.

Ned Cline

Foreword

North Carolina has many splendid traditions. The finest among them is the notion founded in the spirit of the American Revolution that each of us should serve the commonwealth in some expression of responsible citizenship. It is this history of self-giving that has provided North Carolina with succeeding generations of citizen leaders who are builders, guardians of freedom, and servants of the people.

This book is about my friend Marshall Rauch. He and I come from the same county, Gaston. He is a person of deep religious faith, and his life and commitment of service have been nourished and sustained by ancient moral and spiritual teachings he learned as a boy. His adult years have been devoted to working hard in the interest of the state and its entire people.

Beginning with service as a local officer of government, then state senator, university trustee, and member of numerous boards and commissions, Marshall Rauch has led a life that exemplifies leadership and progress. All of us have benefited greatly from his diligence and his highly intelligent and energetic attention to everyday issues facing the people. Through it all, his wonderful wife, Jeanne, has been his sustaining strength and loving critic.

The book's author, Ned Cline, is a perceptive student and highly competent recorder of the human scene in North Carolina. His long tenure as an award-winning reporter and editor at the *Greensboro News & Record* and *Charlotte Observer* abundantly schooled him as a political biographer and interpreter of events that shape public policy. Writing this book was his pleasure, as these pages make clear.

This, then, is a book to enjoy. It tells the story of a warm human being, endowed with many natural gifts, all of which he has put in the service of others. To live so is to serve nobly.

William C. Friday
Former UNC System President

Table of Contents

All quotations in this biography are
from public documents and a series
of personal interviews by the author
with Marshall Rauch, his family,
business and political associates,
and his personal friends.

Chapter 1
The Phoenix

If this had to happen, we can at least be thankful it didn't happen when our grandfather was still with us. It would have devastated him to see a life's work in ruins.

Marc Rauch, commenting on the fire that destroyed Rauch Industries' largest plant in October 1994, weeks after the death of 98-year-old Nathan Rauch, the company's honorary chairman.

The fire spread quickly and relentlessly, fueled by autumn winds and thousands of shipping cases stacked to the rafters of the five-story warehouse that once was home for a cotton mill. Marshall Rauch could only watch helplessly. His early hopes of saving the building slowly turned to dismay as leaping flames lit up the October night. The searing heat and the charred red brick walls meant that Rauch Industries, his hard-won, family-owned enterprise, was literally going up in smoke and flames. At least a year's inventory and nearly a lifetime's investment of money and effort were perishing before his very eyes.

Despite heroic efforts, firefighters from more than twenty nearby communities gradually lost the battle to preserve the structure and its contents. They were lucky to save their own skins. Perhaps the only good news was that no lives were lost and there were no personal injuries, largely because families living nearby had been evacuated.

As the flames died and the dreadful night turned into day, the morning light revealed that little was left of the 670,000-square-foot edifice on the outskirts of Cramerton in the southwest corner of Gaston County, just across the Catawba River from Charlotte.

From a business perspective, the fire hit at the worst possible moment. As the world's largest manufacturer and distributor of Christmas ornaments, Rauch Industries produced merchandise all year but stored most of it until the beginning of the Christmas shopping season, when it was shipped to retail stores. The fire occurred in the week that major shipments were just beginning. Almost three-fourths of the year's production was destroyed. The loss totaled $44 million. Residents of Cramerton and south Gaston County had never seen anything to equal it and hoped never to see anything like it again.

As Marshall Rauch watched the old building go up in flames, fearing what the final outcome might be, his entire life raced through his mind. Worse than the physical and financial loss was the emotional damage. In the destruction of the warehouse, he felt a part of him being destroyed. He could not help but question his fate. Why was another devastating event crashing into his consciousness, especially so soon after the last painful experience of his father's death?

But Marshall Arthur Rauch also knew, perhaps better than anyone else, that he had been fortunate. He had been successful in business and public service beyond his wildest expectations. His thriving manufacture of Christmas ornaments was a venture he entered more by good luck than by design.

He had started out in a different enterprise. Then one day he received an unexpected phone call that changed his life. It was not odd, he insisted, that a faithful Jew should earn a living in manufacturing ornaments for a Christian holiday. His was a business enterprise instead of a religious one, and one that had helped him help others. It had enabled him to give time and service to his state and had allowed him to provide for his family and future generations.

He had much to be thankful for. His was a life—both public and private—built on love of family, respect for others, and faith in God and his fellowman.

His success had not always come easy. His good fortune frequently had been marred by crises that might have driven others to despair. The warehouse fire was just another adversity he would have to overcome. In the past he had never thought of quitting, even in the worst of times. As he stood watching the flames devour his warehouse, he knew that would be the case again.

His mother Tillie and his father Nathan had taught him never to give in to misfortune. It was a lesson he would not—could not—forget. His mind recalled earlier times when he had been challenged to overcome obstacles, ranging from military combat to costly relations with business associates to religious prejudice.

He had faced death during World War II as a combat infantryman in France. There he began taking his religious training and upbringing more seriously. On the battlefield he made a pact with God: his personal safety in exchange for greater devotion to Judaism and helping his fellowman. He survived the war without injury, and each year afterward his faith and good works had grown.

In the 1960s, ignoring the warnings of those who advised against getting involved, Rauch had led a successful effort to keep the peace and assure harmony in the desegregation of public schools and public accommodations in Gastonia. Despite the religious prejudice against him, he went on to win his first political campaign and was elected twelve times to the North Carolina State Senate. He rose to positions of power in the state legislature, working for twenty-four years to control government spending and enhance social justice.

In the 1970s, Rauch suffered personally and financially when a partnership with two business associates failed. When the venture collapsed, he was left to absorb about $3 million in debts. Two of the state's largest banks sued him, but not his associates, to recover their loans. Rauch personally satisfied the entire sum.

In the early 1990s, he planned to run for governor or U.S. senator from his adopted state, but those plans were thwarted by the appearance of newspaper stories about old environmental problems at his manufacturing plant. Following the publication of those stories, Rauch lost his last campaign for reelection to the North Carolina Senate and any hope of seeking higher elective office.

But the most painful recollection of all was his memory of the most recent loss. Just two months before the fire, the Rauch family had said a final farewell to his beloved father who died at ninety-eight after having been a participant in the family business he helped to establish more than forty years earlier with a $10,000 loan to his son.

When Nathan Rauch moved from his native New York to Gastonia in 1991 to be near his son and grandchildren, he became the honorary chairman of Rauch Industries. In addition to a private office and a secretary, he had a company parking space with his nameplate attached—even though he no longer owned or drove a car. The parking space symbolized the respect that members of the Rauch family held for the man who had meant so much to them.

Watching the fire that October night, Marshall Rauch felt tears well up in his eyes as he heard his own son, Marc, comment on the trauma that the fire would have caused his grandfather. If there was anything good about that devastating blaze, the son said, it was that Nathan Rauch, buried ten weeks earlier, had not lived to see it.

All those thoughts raced through Rauch's mind as he watched the fire consume his company's warehouse. But like so many other roadblocks, the fire would slow him only temporarily. It would make him more determined to rebuild and bounce back. As consuming as the fire was, it devoured only inventory and a portion of the company's manufacturing facilities, but it didn't destroy his determination to continue.

As fast as possible, and quicker than most people expected, he restored Rauch Industries to its former stature and even beyond. He built new warehouse facilities, recouped lost clientele, added new customers, and within two years of the fire sold the company for a sum that would make him and his family financially independent.

The way Marshall Rauch had rebuilt his business would have made Nathan Rauch proud, though chances are good the old patriarch would never have admitted it—certainly not to his son—because that was his way of pushing the family even harder to strive for success and progress.

"I know he loved me," Rauch said of his father, "but he could never quite say it. I greatly appreciate the many things I learned from him, but one thing I do differently from him is to let my family and friends know my true feelings. I hope my family continues to do that."

Marshall Rauch's success had enabled him to provide humanitarian services extending over several states. They ranged from offering interest-free loans to deserving college students to giving hundreds of thousands of dollars to institutions of higher learning. Those acts of generosity have been his way of making up for the fact that the war interrupted his own college education. They were also the result of his adherence to the creed of the twelfth century Jewish philosopher Moses Maimonides who challenged his followers to help the less fortunate.

No other benevolence, however, exceeded Rauch's act of kindness more than forty years ago when he invited into his own family a Christian teenager whose mother had died and whose father had abandoned him. That young man, John White, now a recently retired successful stockbroker is still part of the Rauch family. "He is our son," Rauch said.

Despite the repeated setbacks, Marshall Rauch's continued success will allow him to fund even greater philanthropies. Having rebuilt his business and sold it to others, Rauch is devoting the remainder of his life to expanding the charitable Rauch Family Foundation.

The Foundation's goal of $10 million would allow the distribution of hundreds of thousands a year to worthy individuals and charities. As foundation chairman, Rauch intends that this legacy of *tzedakah* (Hebrew for acts of kindness that benefit others) will continue through future generations of his family. Like the phoenix, the mythological bird that rose from its ashes, Marshall Rauch has risen and soared.

Chapter 2
Family Roots

*The genes that produced my brother Marshall and me came
from two completely different families. On one side was the
understated, reserved, and studious Rauch family. On the other side
was the more dramatic, flamboyant, and emotional Wohl family.*

Jacqueline Rauch Gottlieb, describing her grandparents who came
to America from Austria-Hungary near the end of the nineteenth
century with hopes for a better life for themselves
and future generations.

Jewish immigrants by the thousands poured into New York City
during the closing decade of the nineteenth century. Their goal
was to provide educational and economic opportunities for themselves and their children far beyond what they could expect in
their homelands, where religious persecution, wars, and crumbling
governments were the order of the day.

This was especially true for Jews living in what was then
Austria-Hungary. The wave of nationalism that had unified
Germany and Italy in the 1870s destabilized Eastern Europe.
Power-hungry nationalists exploited a vulnerable Austria in
forging a pact that made Hungary an equal partner with Austria
in a dual monarchy. The divided government and diverse
nationalities served to weaken that polyglot nation that included
the quarrelsome Balkan states.

The Balkans had long been a source of unrest. Ethnic and
religious groups there were more interested in asserting their
own independence than in helping to preserve a tottering
monarchy. Conflict in the Balkans was continuous and ultimately
touched off World War I.

Many Jews residing in Austria-Hungary watched those
developments with misgiving and saw themselves facing an
uncertain future as the nineteenth century came to a close. The

situation was bleaker than many were willing to endure. In a mass exodus, many of them sought something better in another land, specifically the United States.

The hope and determination those immigrants sought for themselves and their families increased dramatically as they sailed into New York harbor and caught sight of the Statue of Liberty.

Three of those new arrivals—all young and scared but hopeful—were Isaac Rauch and his brothers, Louis and Victor. A fourth was the equally young and frightened Esther Schoenberger. At different times, their parents had put each of them on ships headed for New York, convinced that despite their innocence and the hardships they might encounter their lives would be enhanced by the opportunities available in the New World.

Marshall Rauch doesn't disagree with his sister Jacqueline's view of the two sets of ancestors, but his assessment is more philosophical:

> They had the average struggling but happy life of Jewish immigrants. They realized, of course, the difference between life here [in the United States] and what they would have had in Austria-Hungary. That's a part of our family history that has been especially meaningful. It's hard to comprehend the magnitude of what my great grandparents, Kalman and Velka Rauch, did when they actually took their children and put them on a ship bound for the United States. They prayed that their sacrifice would prove worthwhile for their children and for generations to come. Our entire family is the fortunate beneficiary of what they did.

Isaac Rauch arrived in New York at Ellis Island about 1890 when he was about twenty-one years old. Victor, later nicknamed Willie, came two years later. Louis came in his early teens. Esther Schoenberger, who did not know the Rauch brothers until she came to America, arrived about 1893 when she was about nineteen.

It was anything but easy for each of them as they strove to earn and save pennies from their first jobs as sewing machine operators in sweatshops of the Manhattan garment industry. The working hours routinely stretched from 6 a.m. until 5 p.m. and sometimes even later. As difficult as the times were, life was clearly an improvement over what they had known earlier in Dukla, the brothers' home in Austria-Hungary. They saw a future that looked brighter than the past.

The brothers' parents, Kalman Rauch and wife Velka Seeder Rauch, clearly agonized over their decision to send their sons alone and virtually penniless to a strange country. Velka would never see her sons again because she never came to America. But the parents were extremely proud as first Isaac and Louis and then Victor, despite their youth and inexperience, worked and saved to establish themselves in New York City.

Kalman Rauch later migrated to America, never to return to his homeland. Many years later his sons, Isaac and Willie, returned to Dukla to have a monument erected at their mother's grave.

During their first years in New York, the three brothers saved what little money they had left after paying for basic essentials and were able to buy a used sewing machine, which they set up in their low-rent tenement. It was the beginning of what would become their own business, built on sacrifice, hard work, and personal integrity.

After saving for the sewing machine, Isaac and Willie slowly scraped together money for materials and began to make women's suits and coats in their home at night after they finished their twelve-hour work day in the garment district. Their dedication to quality and attention to detail won the favor of buyers. They attracted a small but growing market that eventually led to the establishment of their own factory and showroom under the name of Rauch Brothers.

Just as Isaac and Willie Rauch struggled to get established in the garment district, so did young Esther Schoenberger. She also took a job in the district and began to save. Within a year she met Isaac Rauch and fell in love. They were married in 1894. Esther was a seamstress at Rauch Brothers until Nathan, the first of their three sons, was born in 1895.

Nathan Arnold Rauch was Marshall Rauch's father. He grew

Isaac and Esther Rauch, paternal grandparents of Marshall Rauch, who were immigrants from Austria-Hungary prior to the 1890s

up to be a man of strong will and instilled in his son the values he had learned from his parents during their early trials in America and during the Great Depression of the 1930s.

Isaac's marriage to Esther set a pattern for his brother Willie, who went to the same family to find a wife. Shortly after Isaac married Esther, Willie married Esther's sister, Sarah, who had followed Esther to the United States from Ungvar in Austria-Hungary, in search of a better life.

The hard work of Isaac and Willie Rauch began to pay dividends in the first two decades of the twentieth century. As children came into the family and reached working age, several joined the family business at 512 Seventh Avenue, in the heart of the New York garment district. Brother Louis also became part of the company, as did members of the next generation.

Like other Jewish immigrants, Isaac and Esther Rauch insisted that their children get a good education before entering the family business. Albert Rauch joined Rauch Brothers straight out of college. A third son, Elias Rauch, passed up a place in the family business in favor of medical school and a career as a physician.

Their first son, Nathan, had a greater interest in chemistry and horticulture than in women's coats and suits. After obtaining both baccalaureate and master's degrees in chemistry at City College of New York, he joined the faculty of Columbia University until he was called into military service in World War I.

Marshall Rauch vividly remembers his grandfather Isaac and great uncle Willie and their successful clothing business. He also has memories of his great grandfather Kalman, who died at age ninety-four in 1932, when Marshall was nine. Despite the generation gap, Marshall established warm relations with his father's brothers and their families. Of them he said:

> I was always close to my uncles and their wives. Uncle Al Rauch and his wife Darcy were always a strong part of our family. When my sister Jackie had scarlet fever, I was sent across town to live with Al and Darcy and their daughters, Lois and Renee. When I was in the Army, Uncle Al came to visit me in Nebraska. I still appreciate that kindness. Al was a great piano player, too, one of the finest I've ever known. He could sit down anywhere, anytime, and play anything anyone wanted to hear. He had perfect pitch and could play without reading music.

Al Rauch's musical abilities came naturally, not from instruction. One family story is that Uncle Al once so enthralled a neighbor with his piano playing that the neighbor urged his parents to give him lessons. "Why waste a dollar on lessons?" was the reply. He already could play better than most teachers could.

Marshall Rauch had a similar relationship with his Uncle Elias (Ellie) and wife Miriam and their sons Bobby and Steve. He still maintains contact with his cousins. "I well remember in the middle 1930s when times were tough for my father and other members of the family," Rauch recalled. "Even though Uncle Ellie was a doctor, his family and my family moved into one small house. I realize now it was for economic reasons, a financial necessity. That's all we could afford, one house for everyone. But at the time I thought it was great because we were all together."

The extended Rauch family was supportive of young

The home in Woodmere, New York, where Marshall Rauch grew up

Nathan Rauch, Marshall's father, during military service as a chemist during World War I

Marshall during his formative years and that support instilled in him a desire to do the same for his own children. He recalled, "My father, both his brothers, and their families lived in the Woodmere neighborhood, a Long Island suburb of New York City, as my sister and I grew up. We grew up with our four cousins as a close family. My father and both his brothers, Ellie and Al, were present at every high school basketball game I played. I think they were proud of me. In retrospect, I am aware that the Rauch family members were not athletes. I guess I got what athletic ability I had from my mother's Wohl side of the family."

During World War I, the Army put Nathan Rauch's college education and knowledge of chemistry to good use by assigning him to study the effects of mustard gas and other chemical weapons. After the Armistice, he joined the family business, which flourished in the decade after the war. Business was so good that Nathan and his uncle Louis founded a separate women's garment company, L&N Rauch. It was not intended to compete with Rauch Brothers but to carve out a separate niche within the garment industry.

When the stock market crash of 1929 plunged the world into the Great Depression, L&N Rauch was forced to close, and Nathan rejoined Rauch Brothers as a minor partner. The Depression soon caught up with Rauch Brothers, too, but the collective efforts of the family were enough to keep it afloat until the national economy improved.

Following the Depression, Nathan Rauch worked diligently to ensure the success of Rauch Brothers. But his heart was still in the university classroom. He remained a clothier out of need rather than choice. Marshall Rauch thinks of his father whenever he makes the connection between work and the love of work. He also connects the concept with Maimonides, a twelfth century rabbi and philosopher who promulgated eight degrees of charity as a means of helping people in need. The eighth and highest degree calls for aiding a person by offering financial and personal assistance so the person can become self-supporting. Rauch said of his father:

> I think Pop should have remained a professor. He would have been happier.
>
> It's hard to learn without actually experiencing something yourself, but if you can profit from something that happened in your family, it is important to apply that lesson in your own life. The thing I learned from my father's experience is that the first and most important thing in your work or business is to enjoy what you do. No matter how much money you might make, if you're not happy, get out and find something else. I've been extremely lucky in my business because I've been excited by my work and have been financially rewarded far beyond what I ever dreamed of achieving. That's just one reason that I'm so driven by the thought of building the Rauch Foundation. I want the foundation to be a force for good and to be the instrument our family uses to give back, to give to others, and to do as Moses Maimonides teaches in his Eighth Degree of Charity.

Isaac Rauch and his brothers clearly set an example for determination and the work ethic that would influence later generations. It was Nathan Rauch, however, who ingrained—sometimes through tough love—in his son Marshall the importance of wise financial management. Nathan Rauch's heart may have been in the chemistry classroom, but in his head was a finely turned sense of business and financial priorities that contributed significantly to what became Rauch Industries and the Rauch Foundation.

"He taught me everything he could," Marshall Rauch said of his father. "The Depression greatly affected his life. It taught him the importance of saving and being conservative in financial matters. He taught me those things, and every one of those lessons has served me well. He always said to save something out of every paycheck."

People who knew Nathan Rauch describe him as a very intelligent man, but one with definite, sometimes predetermined, views that seldom changed. He also had a demanding personality that sometimes tested the patience of those who loved him most.

One example, recounted with a smile by his son, occurred three months after the elder Rauch, at age ninety-six, came to live in Gastonia because he needed family care. The father, who no longer had any family in New York, wanted to go back to the city to visit old friends. Marshall Rauch felt strongly that if his dad returned to New York, he would never come back to North Carolina where, for his own sake, he clearly needed to be.

"He got really disturbed and demanded that I take him home," Marshall Rauch recalled. The father continued to insist, and the son continued to decline.

"I knew I was doing the right thing for him, but he refused to accept it," Marshall said.

After a time, agitated and angry, the senior Rauch proclaimed in a harsh, authoritative tone, "From this day forward, you are no longer my son. You are my torturer."

Nathan Rauch and Tillie Wohl, Marshall Rauch's parents, on their first date, May 1915

Two years later, the elder Rauch privately wrote to a retiring friend in New York urging him to go live near his son, that such a move was the best thing he could do, and that there was no substitute for the closeness and love of family. By that time, of course, he had

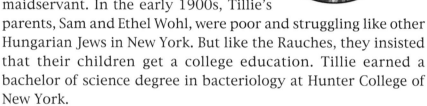

Sam and Ethel Wohl, maternal grandparents of Marshall Rauch, who were immigrants from Hungary in the 1880s

long since forgotten the "torturer" outburst.

But Nathan Rauch provided only half of Marshall Rauch's family inheritance. The other half came from Marshall's mother. Early in those years of striving in New York, Nathan Rauch met and married Tillie Wohl, the beautiful and vivacious daughter of a cigar maker and a maidservant. In the early 1900s, Tillie's parents, Sam and Ethel Wohl, were poor and struggling like other Hungarian Jews in New York. But like the Rauches, they insisted that their children get a college education. Tillie earned a bachelor of science degree in bacteriology at Hunter College of New York.

Nathan Rauch and Tillie Wohl were married in 1921 and started their family two years later when son Marshall, now eighty-one, was born on February 2, 1923. A daughter Jacqueline was born July 2, 1927.

Marshall Rauch's recollections of his Wohl grandparents are as vivid as those of the Rauch side of the family. The Rauches, he said, were better off financially because of the clothing business, but the Wohls were a happy and loving family, content with their four children and varied interests.

Marshall's remembrances were enriched by a lengthy tape recording his wife, Jeanne, made with his mother at a Passover gathering at his Gastonia home shortly before Tillie's death in 1975. That recording, one of Marshall's prized possessions, rekindled memories of growing up on Long Island and also included information he had never known about his grandparents and their early lives and challenges.

Tillie Wohl was the second of four Wohl children. Rose was the oldest, David (nicknamed Dewey) was third, and Joe was the youngest. Dewey, a graduate of New York University, became a

Nathan and Tillie Rauch, Marshall's parents, at the Atlantic Ocean in the late 1920s in Edgemere, New York

lawyer and an assistant district attorney in New York. Joe earned a law degree at Syracuse University and became head of the New York office of the FBI. With her college degree, Tillie remained at home to care for her two children until the economic distress of the Great Depression forced her to find part-time work.

During her college years, Tillie was courted heavily by a "wealthy judge" who regularly sent her chocolates and dispatched his chauffeur-driven car to pick her up from class. Tillie said on the family tape that she rejected the candy and the fine car for the man she loved, Nathan Rauch.

Both of Tillie's brothers were outstanding athletes. Dewey Wohl played basketball at NYU and also played professionally. Joe Wohl learned to swim in New York's East River and went on to captain the swim team and win All-America honors at Syracuse. In 1931, he made news by breaking world records for the 500-yard and 880-yard backstroke. The Wohl's Manhattan home had a veritable trophy room with more than 150 gold medals and silver loving cups won by Joe. The trophies, Joe once told a sportswriter, were used by his brother as ashtrays.

The eldest Wohl child, Rose, didn't earn the degrees and honors of her siblings, but she achieved a lot more in young Marshall Rauch's eyes. After her husband Jacob Marks died of pneumonia, "Aunt Rosie" devoted her life to caring for other family members, including saving money from her job as a bookkeeper to send nephew Marshall Rauch to a summer camp.

"She devoted all her time and love to the family," he remembered. "I always loved her. Obviously, I loved and was proud of my uncles, too, but I just can't say enough about Aunt Rosie. She gave all she could and, in looking back, I now realize she

28

Marshall Rauch's Uncle Joe Wohl, a champion swimmer who later became an FBI agent, with a 1931 newspaper story about his record-breaking performance during a swim meet

1931. FOUR PAGES—THREE CENTS

Joe Wohl Smashes World 500 Yard and Half-mile Backstroke Tank Records

Orange Tank Captain Pares Many Seconds From Long-standing Best Performances; Clocked At 6:48 2-5 and 12:33 5-10.

MERMAN ACE STROKES TWO RACES IN ONE

Has Won Hundreds of Awards; Starred With Kojac; Expects to Try For 500 Meters and 1000-yard Honors Before Graduation.

Propelling his lithe, tan-colored body through the green tinted, chlorinated waters of the famous old Archbold Pool yesterday afternoon, Captain Joseph "Bud" Wohl smashed to bits two world records in the 500-yard and 880-yard swimming events. Urged on by a throng of enthusiastic students who crowded the Hill swimming room to capacity, the new record holder pared over a half dozen seconds from each former time.

The Orange ace was clocked for the 500-yard backstroke in the time of 6 minutes, 48 and 2-5 seconds. The best time previous to Wohl's try was 6 minutes, 55 and 4-5 seconds made by Conrad Mils, of the Illinois Athletic Club, on July 2, 1935. The Hill captain took 7 and 2-5 seconds from this record.

In the 880-yard backstroke, Wohl cut 6 and 1-10 seconds from the former time, by swimming the distance in 12 minutes, 33 and 5-10 seconds. The old record of 12 minutes, 39 and 3-5 seconds was made on Feb. 20, 1926 by Robert Hosie.

The Orange merman, although he had previously intended to try also for the 1,000-yard backstroke record, was unable to do so because of a lack of necessary stop watches. As it was, Wohl performed the remarkable feat of swimming two races in one—the 500-yard event being the first 500 yards of the longer distance.

JOE WOHL.

probably gave much more than she ever received. Each time I saw her, she had something special to give me."

Among her gifts to Marshall was her late husband Jacob's coin collection stacked in an ancient black box. Seventy-five years later, Marshall Rauch still has that entire cache—stored in the same black box. The coins spurred his interest in collecting and he now has a large coin collection of his own. "I remember as a child playing with those coins because I was so proud of them," Rauch said. "When I was home from school, I'd get out those coins and spread them on my bed. I really developed an interest in collecting. It has always been fun. Now I have complete sets of uncirculated and mint-proof United States coins. I also have begun collecting documents and letters of United States presidents. Today, I have a large, valuable collection that I intend to leave to my family and the Rauch Family Foundation."

The Wohls made up in family togetherness what they lacked in financial resources. Father Sam was an "extremely bright" man who spoke several languages (in addition to English and Hebrew) and played flute in the New York Philharmonic Orchestra. He also left his family a collection of phonographs recorded by such artists as Enrico Caruso, Amelita Galli-Curci, Louisa Tetrazzini, Nellie Melba, and others. Rauch has donated those recordings to

Marshall Rauch's sister Jacqueline at Silver Point Beach, Long Island, N.Y. in the early 1930s

the music departments at UNC Charlotte and Gaston Community College.

Tillie Rauch's family history tape also recalled regular family gatherings in which she played the piano, her father played the flute, and her sister Rosie sang "Ave Maria." Father Sam Wohl was an opera fan and, when money would permit, took his family to the theater. "My mother said that my grandpa was often distressed that his wife Ethel would fall asleep at the opera," Marshall Rauch said. "She obviously didn't have his appreciation for that music. She worked as a maidservant and, I suspect, was tired at night, opera or not."

Sam Wohl didn't make much money as a cigar maker, but he never found or wanted another career. He was happy. He made cigars in an area enclosed by chicken wire at the rear of a tiny storefront on Manhattan's Lower East Side. He began by stuffing small tobacco leaves into a mold and wrapping them with larger leaves. "To this day," Marshall Rauch said, "when I smell a good cigar I think of Grandpa Wohl and remember how he felt and tasted when I kissed his cheek."

On numerous occasions, Ethel Wohl worked in the cigar store after her daily chores as a maid, even using her feminine attributes to marketing advantage. Marshall Rauch recalled that in the taped recollections his mother "laughed outrageously" at the thought of her mother, who had a big bosom, leaning forward over the counter to sell more cigars than anyone else did.

When Tillie Wohl was growing up in New York, her parents lived on the fifth floor of a tenement on Avenue A on the Lower East Side. In those years children wanted snacks after school just as they do now. Tillie and her mother Ethel created a simple system to speed the snacking process. Rauch's sister Jackie

30

recalls her mother telling about Tillie's getting home from school and shouting up to the fifth story tenement to let her mother Ethel know she was home. Ethel would quickly spread chicken fat and onion on a piece of matzo or rye bread, put it in a brown paper bag, and throw it out the window for her daughter.

In addition to the coin and record collections he received from his Aunt Rosie and from his grandparents, Marshall Rauch also prizes other family heirlooms: a tallis (a Jewish religious shawl) bag made by Grandmother Rauch for his grandfather in 1893; his grandfather's tallis (which has been used in great-great-grandchildren's bar and bat mitzvahs); Grandfather Wohl's pocket watch; a watch that his mother Tillie gave his father Nathan on their twenty-fifth wedding anniversary in 1943; a watch that his wife Jeanne gave to Marshall on his thirtieth birthday; and a diamond ring that Grandfather Rauch gave his father (copies of which Marshall has had given to each of his children). The stone in the ring was the stone that Grandfather Isaac gave Grandmother Esther when they were married in 1894. Those items he cherishes as tangible reminders of his heritage.

Both the Rauch and Wohl families had a strong and abiding religious faith and followed the conservative tradition in

Isaac and Esther Rauch's fiftieth wedding anniversary, November 1944, at their apartment on West End Avenue in New York City. Standing behind Isaac and Esther are their three sons with their wives, from left to right, Miriam and Elias Rauch, Tillie and Nathan Rauch, and Darcy and Al Rauch. Seated are three of their six grandchildren: Renee, Robert, and Lois. Marshall, Jacqueline, and Steven not shown.

practicing it. The Rauch side of the family was the more traditional, however. Speaking of that legacy from his ancestors, Rauch said:

> I now realize how fortunate I was to have been able to know and learn from both sets of grandparents and even from one great-grandparent. Not many people have that opportunity. When at seventeen I left home for college and then at nineteen went into the Army, it was an absolute change in my life. Until that time, my parents and grandparents had sheltered me. I now realize how important growing up with all that love and attention has been for me. Those early years have meant a lot and are still a part of what I am, the things I have done, and things I do or hope to do. My mother and father, along with their generation and the generations before them, are all gone now, but they are often in my thoughts, always in my heart, and alive in my memories wherever I may be.

His feelings about the importance of family ties were reinforced by similar sentiments expressed in a letter he received from his cousin Marvin, son of Willie Rauch, and Marshall's uncle. In the letter, Marvin said: "In other times, *tsuris* [troubles], poverty, and need kept the family together. Now we are all self-sufficient and independently successful, so family ties dwindle away. All of us are in the same boat of having succeeded because of our parents and grandparents—because of their hard work and intense drive for betterment, and, of course, because of opportunities offered by our country."

The ancestors of Marshall and Marvin Rauch put down deep roots for the generations they knew would follow. As Marshall Rauch's successful life clearly attests, he learned a great deal from those forebears. Marshall's children and grandchildren— and generations to come—may have only a limited knowledge of what their forefathers lived through in their early years in America. He hopes this book will enable his descendants also to learn and profit from their experience.

Chapter 3
The Goldbergs & Jeanne

I grew up in a matriarchal family. My mother was reserved, but always in charge. My father was more the outgoing, fun-loving type. He had a keen business sense and became quite successful in the textile industry. For my own security, he wanted to make sure I learned typing and shorthand, because if I became a secretary, I could always find work.

Jeanne Rauch, discussing her parents.

Frank Goldberg had no need to fret over his youngest daughter Jeanne's ever having to support herself by doing office work. Favorable circumstances, including the diligence of "Miss Sadie," his wife and Jeanne's mother, took care of that. If Frank Goldberg was the sail in the family, the resourceful Miss Sadie was the anchor. She buttressed the family finances and security during the lean years.

Frank Goldberg had known hard times often in his life, and he wanted to shield his family against such eventualities. In the first decade of the twentieth century, he peddled dry goods from a horse-drawn buggy in Atlanta. As a result of his hard work, things got significantly better—until the Great Depression. Then the family struggled all over again.

By the late 1930s, when Jeanne Goldberg was in her teens, her father had become a textile manufacturer whose mills were running profitably. Though the family was at that time financially secure, it certainly had not always been that way, and Frank Goldberg didn't know how long his prosperity would last.

Just in case the economy went sour again, he wanted his daughter to have a skill to fall back on. Secretarial work was among the few jobs open to women who didn't work on a farm or in a textile mill. Jeanne Goldberg didn't openly oppose her father's choice of her career, but she was anything but enthusiastic.

As she studied typing and shorthand, she also pursued interests in the theater and art. She never had to work as a secretary, but as a mother of three sons and two daughters and the organizer of a household for a successful businessman-politician husband, she found she could put her clerical skills to good use.

"My mother always kept things together in our family," Jeanne Rauch said. "She taught me that. And things worked out just fine. I try to do the same for my family and hope that the results are the same."

Her mother, Sadie Paradies Goldberg, did indeed keep things together during the years when her husband was a peddler and later during the Depression. Over several decades, she quietly squirreled away money that, when times were tough, put food on the table for her family and helped to keep her husband's mills running.

"Somehow she was able to save," Jeanne Rauch said. "My father never could do that. She's the one who made sure we got through the Depression."

Jeanne Rauch was too young to remember those economic trials firsthand. But like so many others of her generation, she remembers well the stories her parents told of the hard times they endured before and during the Depression.

Like Marshall Rauch's grandparents who fled Austria-Hungary in the late nineteenth century, the Goldbergs had come to America in search of a better life. Frank Goldberg was born in Latvia, a small nation—about the size of West Virginia—on the southern shore of the Baltic Sea.

Sandwiched between Estonia and Lithuania, Latvia is covered by snow three to four months of the year. But the country's greater menace has been the aggression of its neighbors. With Finland and Sweden to the north, Poland to the south, Germany to the west, and Russia to the east, Latvia has been a political and military doormat for much of its existence. Over the centuries, Germans, Poles, Russians, and Swedes have conquered it.

At the time of Frank Goldberg's birth in 1879, the country was occupied by Czarist Russians, whose generals were actively seeking Latvian recruits for their army. The young and ambitious Frank Goldberg decided that life in the Russian army was not for him. Though he was deeply in love with a young Latvian woman named Sadie Paradies, he was determined to seek a better life somewhere else.

At age twenty, he fled his homeland with I.J. Paradies, the brother of his beloved Sadie, and went to South Africa, where for several years they worked as sheepherders. Then they sailed for America, landing in New York in 1902.

Goldberg and I.J. initially settled in New Brunswick, New Jersey, where they worked in a retail store. There Goldberg was cited for violating New Jersey's "blue laws," which banned the sale of goods on the Sabbath. Because he had been brought up as a Jew, Goldberg didn't consider Sunday the Sabbath and was unaware of these laws.

After a short stay in New Jersey, Goldberg moved to Atlanta, where he became an itinerant peddler, selling dry goods from the bed of a horse-drawn buggy. Over time his brothers Robert, Max, and Ben, and his sisters, Helen and Jenny, followed from Latvia. Helen was the oldest of the Goldberg children. Frank was the oldest of the sons. Following in age were Max, Ben, and Robert. Jenny was the youngest member of the family.

Shortly after the Goldbergs migrated to America, Sadie Paradies left her home in the Latvian province of Kurland and began making her way to the United States.

"I remember my mother telling how she and her friends walked for several days across much of Latvia as they made their way to the boat for America," Jeanne Rauch recalled. "She said they slept in barns along the way. She told of waking up and feeling rats running across her face. But they didn't give up. They were determined to get to this country."

Sadie moved directly to Atlanta where she lived briefly with cousins who had arrived earlier from Latvia. The cousins' parents hired tutors to teach their sons English. Education was not considered important for girls, and Sadie was not allowed to participate in the lessons. Later Sadie told her children that she

Frank and Sadie Paradies Goldberg, parents of Jeanne Rauch, who immigrated from Courland, Latvia about 1896

tried to learn by eavesdropping outside the door, picking up English words.

Frank Goldberg and Sadie Paradies were married in Atlanta in 1907 and began working to build successful lives. It was not easy because Jewish families were perceived by their Southern neighbors as alien and different. Members of the Jewish community were often looked on with disdain.

"Those were very tough times," Jeanne Rauch said, recalling her parents' stories of life in those years. "There was virtually no money, but there was always hope—and children." In Atlanta, three sons and one daughter were born to Frank and Sadie Goldberg: Ethel in 1907, Sam in 1908, Cy in 1911, and Herbert in 1918.

After several years in Atlanta, Frank Goldberg decided there were greater opportunities in textile-rich Columbia, South Carolina. He moved his growing family there and began selling textile plant wastes and remnants. His brothers Robert and Max joined him.

In the decade from 1910 to 1920, sales increased, as did limited profits. The Goldberg brothers began looking beyond the peddling trade. With the help of his textile contacts, Frank Goldberg learned of a fledgling textile plant for sale in Bessemer City, North Carolina, a small town west of Charlotte.

Despite his inexperience in running a textile mill, Goldberg was courageous enough to try. "He somehow finagled a loan with the help of contacts from his previous business," Jeanne Rauch said. His brother Robert joined him in the enterprise.

Goldberg had never been to Bessemer City until that day in 1919 when he arrived with the loan in hand. He bought the plant, ran it successfully, and later secured another loan to start a second mill. He named the mills American Mill No. 1 and No. 2.

On September 15, 1923, a fifth child and second daughter joined the Goldberg family. Jeanne, now eighty-one, who would grow up to become Mrs. Marshall Rauch, was the only child in the family born in a hospital, the old Gastonia hospital situated on what is now Main Street in Gastonia.

When Frank and Robert Goldberg entered textile manufacturing in Bessemer City, their brother Max continued to sell textile wastes, and another brother, Ben, became a grocer on the grounds of one of the textile plants. Later, the Goldbergs would add three more textile plants to the family network, all in neighboring Gastonia.

That was after his eldest son Sam graduated from college with a degree in Spanish and came home to recommend a new name for the mills. At Sam's urging, Goldberg chose the name *Algodon*, a Spanish word meaning *cotton*.

Throughout those early years, Sadie Goldberg maintained a

Sadie Goldberg (center) with her five children:
from left to right, Cy, Ethel, Sam, Jeanne, and Herbert

steadying influence on the family. Though lacking a formal education herself, she insisted that her children do better. All five attended college and three earned degrees. Sam was graduated from Georgia Tech, Herbert from UNC at Chapel Hill, and Jeanne from Syracuse University after first studying at Duke. Cy attended Georgia Tech, and the eldest daughter, Ethel, attended the University of Miami.

In addition to economic distress, the lack of formal education was one of several hardships the Goldberg parents endured. Sadie Goldberg never really learned to write English beyond signing her name. With help from her children, she did learn to read the language.

With sons Cy and Herbert involved in management and son Sam working as a sales representative in New York, Algodon Mills began to flourish in the late 1930s, thanks to major fabric contracts with companies such as Goodyear. That's when Frank Goldberg bought his first automobile, a Packard. The first sure sign of Goldberg prosperity, however, didn't come until the early part of World War II when the mill secured a huge government contract to provide material for the military.

"That contract was for yarn that the Navy used to make mops," Jeanne Rauch recalled. "My father told me that was the most profit the mills ever made."

The additional income allowed Goldberg to purchase land for a vacation home at nearby Crowder's Mountain. He liked to entertain friends there and called the place his "farm" although he grew no crops.

"My father always loved to have a lot of people around. That made him happy," Jeanne Rauch said. But all the "farming" in the family was done at the Goldberg home in Bessemer City, where Sadie raised horses and kept a cow, a goat, and chickens. She also made wine from homegrown grapes and hatched chickens from eggs her hens had laid.

As the Goldberg mills continued to expand, differences in management philosophy arose between brothers Frank and Robert. They split their holdings in the early 1940s, with Robert taking over three plants and Frank and sons Cy and Herbert retaining two—the original Algodon and another named Stevdan.

Stevdan was named for Cy's sons, Steve and Danny. That name had special meaning: at age two Danny had drowned in a family lily pond.

While World War II brought prosperity to the family textile business, it also brought personal anguish. Intense anti-Semitic feelings arose across the United States and helped to create divisions within the Goldberg family.

Sam Goldberg wanted to join the United States Navy but feared ridicule if he entered the military with the Goldberg name. The family had always been proud of its Jewish heritage and never tried to hide its religious commitment, either at home or in business. But Sam feared the military would be different.

"He really wanted to join the Navy," Jeanne Rauch said. "But people in the Navy weren't fond of Jews, so he decided to pick another name before volunteering for military duty. He felt the Goldberg name would immediately put a spotlight on him. He didn't want that, and neither did we."

Sam Goldberg's wife, Mimi, liked French names, so at her suggestion Samuel Goldberg legally changed his last name to Girard. Following their older brother's lead, Herbert and Cy Goldberg also changed their names to Girard. Jeanne Goldberg, then a student at Syracuse University, studying drama and radio, joined her brothers in the name change, primarily because name changes were common among Jewish actors.

"My reason for the name change was the theater, which I loved," Jeanne Rauch said. "There weren't many Jewish names in the theater in those days."

Other family members also took new names. Jeanne's uncle Robert Goldberg, later a well-known entrepreneur and philanthropist in North Carolina, chose the name Gurney. When he signed his name *Goldberg,* it looked like the word *Gurney,* he said. Two other uncles, Max and Ben Goldberg, reverted to using the last name Planer, the original Latvian name the family had used generations before.

Frank and Sadie Goldberg declined to join the name-change trend. "They were willing to accept what we had done," Jeanne Rauch said, "but they didn't think it was right or necessary for them. They chose to remain Goldbergs." Their name, the parents decided, would not create any more problems than they had encountered on their arrival in America or in the early days of getting their business started in the South.

In his declining years, Frank Goldberg gradually lost his eyesight to glaucoma and was blind during his final fifteen years. He used a cane and a seeing-eye dog to maneuver through his mills. After someone fatally poisoned his faithful dog, Goldberg relied on his cane and the assistance of company employees to make his way through his plants. He died on November 20, 1945.

Anti-Semitism had not been a major problem in Gaston County as the Goldberg children were growing up, although the Goldbergs were among only four Jewish families in Bessemer City, and Jeanne was one of only four Jews at Gastonia High School. Prejudice was present, but not pervasive.

However, when the celebrated labor strike hit Gastonia's Loray Mill in 1929 and spilled over to her father's mills in Bessemer City, Jeanne Goldberg was at times ridiculed by other students who labeled her a "dirty Jew" and hurled rocks at her after she left the school grounds. But those were isolated incidents.

"During the strike was the only time that happened to me," she said. "Those who threw the stones were children of striking parents who worked in my father's mills."

Aside from that example of religious discrimination in grammar school, Jeanne Rauch enjoyed what she recalled as an extraordinarily happy childhood, crowned by attending Duke University where she met Marshall Rauch (before transferring to Syracuse), and later marrying him.

On returning to the United States after serving with the Army in Europe during World War II, Marshall Rauch had planned to return to Duke University, resume basketball, and complete his education. But marrying Jeanne Girard and supporting her became a higher priority.

In the spring of 1946, Cy and Herbert Girard offered Marshall a job at $60 a week in the family business at Algodon Mills. The offer came on the day Marshall married their sister Jeanne. He put a hold on his formal education, gave up basketball as a player, accepted their offer, and began his own economic struggles.

Recalling those first years of her marriage, Jeanne Rauch said, "My brothers didn't throw money around. Marshall got a raise only when we had another child. It was hard with two children. We didn't live as well as my brothers, who owned the mills. But that didn't bother me. I always had total faith that Marshall would be successful and make a fine living for his own family."

The decades have since proven her more right than she could have ever imagined.

The business of Cy and Herbert Girard continued to flourish throughout the late 1940s and 1950s. Marshall Rauch worked at Algodon for most of the last half of the 1940s before starting his own textile business with help from the Girard brothers and another in-law, Clarence "Clanky" Ross, who was married to Jeanne's sister Ethel.

In the early 1960s, however, Cy and Herbert Girard began to disagree on business philosophy and dissolved their joint operations—just as their father and his brother had done decades before. They had become quite prosperous by that time. Cy sold his share of the mills to Herbert, and Cy and his wife Dorothy moved to Europe.

Herbert and his wife, Phyllis, later moved to Florida. Tranquility lasted for three decades. In 1994 and 1995, Phyllis and then Herbert each died at comparatively early ages.

By the summer of 2004, sister Ethel was ninety-five and living in New York City. Brother Sam also lived there until his death in September 2001. In his later years, Sam had developed an avid interest in art. After completing his career as a sales representative for the family mills, Sam Girard painted and sold impressionist art. Among the owners of his works was former New York Mayor John Lindsey.

Sam's wife Miriam (Mimi) Eaton became well known in New York for her work with the Republican Party. She was one of few Republicans in the Goldberg or Rauch families. Sam and Mimi had two daughters, Andrea and Constance.

Herbert was the financial whiz in the family. He was what Jeanne Rauch and other family members call "very bright." After moving to Florida, Herbert and his wife lived lavishly. Phyllis pursued her interests in singing and acting until her health failed. Herbert and Phyllis had four children: Frank, Meg, Kenny, and Suzy.

Cy was the handsome, gregarious sibling. He enjoyed entertaining friends after he and Dorothy moved to Europe. Cy and Dorothy had three children: Stephen, Danny (the drowning victim), and Maxine. Cy died on May 10, 1982. In the fall of 1997, Dorothy sold her home in France and moved to New York City.

Ethel Goldberg married Clarence Ross, who also worked with the Goldberg family mills before opening his own plant in Taylorsville in Alexander County, NC. They had one daughter, Barbara. After selling his mill, Ross moved to New York City. Ethel Ross had many of the same attributes as her mother and is credited with helping her husband become a business success.

Jeanne Rauch spoke as warmly of her parents as of her siblings. It was obvious that the Goldbergs held firmly to what today would be called family values.

"My mother was a very adventurous lady," Jeanne Rauch proudly said. "She loved entertaining and was very kind to people. But she was also concerned that her children receive a good education. She insisted on that. She was also energetic and supervised the building of our home in Bessemer City when we lived on Airline Avenue in Gastonia. The Bessemer City home was originally intended to be a summer place, but it turned out to be so beautiful that the family moved there when I was a year old."

Sadie Goldberg loved the land and took advantage of the Bessemer City home to pursue that passion. "She had such an interest in farming that she was always doing things with the land, maybe because she was raised on a farm in Latvia," Jeanne Rauch said. "The house had pecan trees and fruit trees surrounding it. We had goats. She gave me goats as pets, and I was terrified of them. We had a barn and a second house for the lady who helped us. Her name was Mary Pressley. She was like my second mother, and she helped raise me. Mother also had horses and loved to ride. She raised chickens and made homemade wine."

Sadie Goldberg with seven of her grand-children: from lower left (clockwise), Kenneth Girard, Marc Rauch, Frank Girard, Maxine Girard, Ingrid Rauch, Meg Girard, Peter Rauch

Jeanne's mother also had what some might call quirky ideas about health. "She allowed herself to gain a lot of weight," Jeanne remembered, "and when my sister Ethel announced she was going to get married, my mother dieted for almost a year. She basically existed off of grape juice and cigarettes. That, of course, destroyed her health. She went from 200 pounds to 118 pounds in time for the wedding."

Jeanne Rauch admiringly recalled her father. "He was a tough employer," she said. "But he was fair. And he was very generous and active in his community once he was in a financial position to do that."

Frank and Sadie Goldberg also were dedicated to their religion. Frank Goldberg helped start the synagogue in Gastonia and worked to see that the temple debts were paid off, as did his wife whose religious beliefs were even stronger than her husband's. One of their debt-reduction contributions in the early days of the synagogue involved the *aliyah* (ah-lee-ah), a blessing said before and after the reading from the Torah.

"My brothers always got to do that," Jeanne Rauch explained, "because my mother would always make extra temple donations that would earn them the privilege of doing the blessing. That was one way the temple debts were paid."

The Goldberg parents insisted that their sons learn about Judaism and become fluent in Hebrew. When the family lived in Gastonia, Sadie hired a rabbi to live in the Goldberg home to serve as a tutor for her sons.

In later years, Sadie Goldberg prepared kosher meals for her adult children and delivered food to each family on the Jewish Sabbath. "She would get up at 5 a.m. to bake *challah* (Jewish bread) to take to her children along with other Sabbath foods," Jeanne Rauch said. "In earlier years when kosher food was hard to find in Bessemer City, she would go to Charlotte to buy groceries. She was very dedicated to her faith and to her family."

In addition to caring for her own, Sadie Goldberg became known in Bessemer City as the woman with a big heart and a helping hand for others. "She never turned anyone away," Jeanne Rauch said. "She routinely fed hobos during the Depression. I think they all knew where we lived. And she was the one person people would always come to when they needed something."

Sadie Goldberg died on New Year's Eve, 1961, a victim of emphysema induced by smoking cigarettes. Jeanne Rauch, also a smoker at the time, quit the habit shortly after her mother's death.

After finishing college and starting a family, Jeanne Goldberg Girard Rauch gave up her ambitions to be an actress but not her love of the theater. She also never gave up her art and continues to paint. Many of her finished pieces hang in her home. She has sold some of her work, but has never painted full-time.

"Instead of becoming an artist, I became an organizer," she says of her adult life. For many years, she was also a full-time mom. In both jobs, she was more than a little successful.

Jeanne Rauch was instrumental in organizing the Gastonia Little Theater, the Art Guild, the Art and Science Council, and the Gaston County Museum of Art and History. She served for twenty years as a board member for the North Carolina Museum of Art, resigning in the fall of 1997, and is now a director emeritus. She started a North Carolina Artist Collection of paintings, which includes more than one hundred pieces, most of them displayed at Rauch Industries when her husband owned the company.

She was the driving force behind the restoration of the Francis Speight canvas at the Gastonia Post Office and was the first person to make a purchase award for the benefit of the Gaston Art Guild. Through her influence in the North Carolina Senate, the Gaston County Museum of Art and History, as well as the Schiele Museum, receive yearly grants in state funds. Marshall and Jeanne Rauch personally donated $10,000 for a room at the Gaston Art and History Museum.

Through her love of the arts and her ability to get things done, Jeanne Rauch is leaving her own mark on North Carolina. In November 1997, the Gaston County Art Council honored her and husband Marshall for outstanding service and leadership.

Those generous actions on behalf of their community have become traditions that Marshall and Jeanne Rauch hope and expect their children and grandchildren to continue. Surely, Mr. Frank and Miss Sadie would be proud.

Chapter 4 - Pigeons &
Basketball: The Early Years

*I don't remember the stock market crash of 1929, and I don't
remember anyone actually saying we were poor. I just know
we moved to a smaller house shortly before I was ten years old.
No one at the time said why. I know now we moved to save money.
That's when I first learned about values and
the importance of right and wrong.*

Marshall A. Rauch, reminiscing on his
childhood in Woodmere, New York.

Reflections on childhood conjure mixed emotions in most of us.
That is certainly true for Marshall Arthur Rauch. For him, the
memories are mostly upbeat, but in those early years there was
always an unspoken concern, an uneasiness implanted by
stories of his grandparents' hardships in coming to New York as
impoverished Hungarian immigrants determined to make a
better life for themselves and future generations.

It was that kind of concern, a blend of fear and uncertainty,
that in 1933 caused his parents Nathan and Tillie Rauch to move
to a smaller house from their comfortable home in the upscale
Woodmere neighborhood on Long Island. The economic crash
had wiped out most of their assets. They remembered what their
earlier lives had been without resources, and they didn't want
to suffer that indignity again. If it took cutting costs to avoid
such a downfall, they were willing to sacrifice for the sake of
their young family. Moving to a smaller home was one way to do
it.

Rauch's parents were prepared for hard times. Their own
immigrant parents had ingrained in their children an appreciation for the hard work and frugal management that had earned
them limited success. Prosperity, the parents taught, was not an
entitlement; it was the fruit of constant effort. They never forgot

their early trials and instilled in their children the importance of honesty and frugality—lessons their children later passed on to their children. The stories of past hardships were not lost on Nathan and Tillie Rauch, or on their son Marshall and daughter Jacqueline.

Nathan Rauch certainly never forgot the strain of his early years. Though he went on to earn a master's degree from City College of New York and become a chemistry professor at Columbia University, he was forever mindful of his parents' experience.

So was his wife Tillie. She also had earned a college degree, but hoped she wouldn't have to work outside the home during her son and daughter's childhood. Out of financial need, however, Tillie took part-time work, selling the Book of Knowledge and subscriptions to *Reader's Digest*.

Before the stock market crash, their son Marshall had been attending Woodmere Academy, a private tutorial school known for excellence in teaching and building character. The change in family finances required that he begin attending public schools for the first time. As he explained:

> No reasons were ever given. It was just done. I didn't understand why, but it didn't really matter at the time. Now I know why and both understand and appreciate what my parents were willing to do for my sister and me. I had wonderful parents, and I know how important personal sacrifice can be to young people. I think they instilled this trait in me. My father was stern and strict, but he always wanted to do the right thing. And because of those early struggles of his parents, he was always frugal. He taught me that, too. My mother was protective but also extremely affectionate. I was fortunate to have two caring parents.

> Life, of course, was much simpler then. There were no malls, and really there was not much money to go shopping. In fact, I can't ever remember going shopping except to go with my mother to buy shoes. We always played in the streets, playing football, basketball, and kick the can. That's about all we had to do for a pastime.

Marshall and Jeanne Rauch at Atlantic Beach, New York, following their honeymoon in Bermuda in the summer of 1946

Nobody rode to school in cars. Few people had cars. Sometimes we rode bikes to school, but most of the time we just walked the two or three miles. There was no thought of driving because there was nothing to drive.

Throughout that difficult time, the Rauch parents still kept their religious faith at the forefront of family life. Temple attendance and Jewish teachings were mandatory, and at the end of his regular school day young Marshall attended Hebrew school, initially to learn the language and later for more detailed training in preparation for his bar mitzvah.

In Marshall's early years, the family home on Harold Road in the Woodmere neighborhood was an area of ethnic diversity, but Jews were in a minority. None of that was a concern to Marshall because his parents taught him to accept people as individuals rather than to judge them on some preconceived notion.

While faithful to their Jewish heritage, the Rauch household turned away from some of the Orthodox beliefs of earlier generations. They accepted with openness others' views and beliefs but remained Reformed Jews.

Young Marshall's honesty about their openness once got him in trouble when his family put up a Christmas tree for purely pleasurable, rather than religious, purposes. When Grandfather Isaac came to visit, knowing he wouldn't approve of such a symbol, the family removed the tree and hid it in a corner of the garage, only to have a happy and talkative young Marshall proudly pull his grandpa into the garage to show him their decorated tree.

"I don't exactly remember the results," Rauch recalled. "But

Nathan and Marshall Rauch,
wearing matching shirts, 1928,
at Edgemere Beach, New York

it is safe to say my parents weren't real pleased." Neither, of course, was his Orthodox grandfather. After Isaac Rauch left, the tree was restored to its previous place in the family circle and remained for the rest of the holidays. But after that, the only trees given tender loving care in the Rauch household were those planted and nourished in the yard.

By New York standards, Woodmere was relatively rural. The Rauch home had yard space for flowers, a vegetable garden, and chickens. That's where Marshall's love for plants took root. It was a passion implanted by his father. To this day, the grounds of the Rauch home in Gastonia are adorned with flowers, and Marshall's spring enthusiasm for growing tomatoes and sharing the harvest with neighbors has become something of a legend.

Nathan Rauch's flower and vegetable garden on Long Island, a plot that young Marshall often raked and weeded, was also in part a laboratory for his scientific interests. He conducted a number of experiments in growing ivy for various nurseries. Marshall's gardens in Gastonia also contain experimental plants, following his father's earlier teachings.

The roominess of that first Woodmere house and yard gave way to a less spacious home when the Rauches moved to 1078 Quinton Place in 1933. But it was Marshall's transfer from a private academy to public schools that caused the greatest wrench, more for Rauch's parents than for him.

The move turned out to be a blessing because it introduced Marshall to many of life's diversities and values, the importance of establishing friendships, and the rewards of working to achieve success. The private academy likely would have done the same thing, but young Marshall wasn't old enough to understand what it all meant until he started public school in the fifth grade.

Even after the move to the smaller house, things continued to be financially tight for several years. Though Nathan Rauch's heart was still in the chemistry classroom, he had bowed to his father Isaac's wishes after World War I and joined his brother Al and his uncle Willie Rauch in their Manhattan clothing company, Rauch Brothers.

Nathan Rauch put in long hours and long days, leaving home before dawn and returning after dark, riding the train into the city to work. But that allowed Tillie Rauch to remain at home with her son and daughter and sell book and magazine subscriptions during the hours the children were in school. The children thrived among new schoolmates, and their father continued his labors and savings.

The long hours paid off. After several years in a cramped house, the family was able to move to a larger home in the same neighborhood, this time to 998 Allen Lane. That home had a yard big enough for children's play and for Nathan Rauch to resume his gardening.

Things were definitely looking up financially when Nathan Rauch purchased the family's first automobile. "I remember when my father brought home that automobile. I bragged to my friends that we had a new car," Rauch said. It was not until sixty years later, in recalling that first purchase that Marshall learned from his father that the auto was not new, but was a ten-year-old well-used car. That was all the family could afford.

About the time the family's first car came home, young Marshall launched what would be the first of his many business enterprises. He began raising pigeons. One aspect of that venture got him into trouble. He needed a coop in which to cage the birds, but lacked the money to buy lumber. He looked around and found some boards in the basement and used them in constructing his coop. He was pleased with the results—until he learned from his angry father that one of the boards he sawed for the coop was, in fact, the extension leaf to the family's mahogany dining room table. That ended Marshall's career in carpentry and woodworking.

Even so, Marshall continued his pigeon enterprise, once entering a favorite bird in a contest for the best-looking pigeon—and winning first place. The choice of prizes was either twenty-five cents worth of bird feed or a blue ribbon. He chose the decoration, figuring he could always scratch up pigeon feed but might never get another chance at a blue ribbon.

Unable to buy more pigeons, he sought other means of acquiring them. He rigged an upside-down cardboard box with a stick attached to a string that held up one end of the box. On the ground under the box, he scattered kernels of corn to lure pigeons. When the birds took the bait, he jerked the string, causing the box to fall and trapping the pigeons. That ploy expanded his brood of pigeons, some of which he traded with friends in an effort to acquire better or stronger birds.

The trapped pigeons also gave rise to a brisk commerce in pigeon eggs. Unable to afford mature birds of top quality, Marshall found he could acquire them by buying eggs. After trapping wild pigeons, called "rats" by Woodmere youngsters, Marshall bought eggs from owners of better birds and nested them under his "rats." As the eggs were hatched, he raised the animals to maturity and sold them as better fliers than he could have gotten from his own pigeons. That was one of his first lessons in marketing.

Marshall also got his first unwanted lesson in violence when a raccoon tore into his pigeon coop and killed a dozen birds in a bloody battle that he still remembers with anguish. "At the time, it was a real disaster in my life, the first one," Rauch recalled. The slaughter convinced him it was time to close up the pigeon shop.

Tillie Rauch, feeding four-month-old Marshall, June 1923

At the same time his teenage interests in athletics and team sports were becoming more important, even if academic pursuits were not. "I wish now I had paid more attention in school," Rauch said. "I wasn't a bad student, and I never got into any serious trouble. But like so many young people, my interests were more with sports than books in those days."

In addition to loving parents, there often are other guiding influences in a young person's life. For Marshall Rauch that influence was exerted by two people, both teachers. One taught about life; the other about self-reliance.

The first was Louis (Brud) Gamp, an architect specializing in school construction. He also was a coach with a big heart and a commitment to honesty and integrity. The second was Arloeen Griswold, a strict yet caring geometry instructor who taught the importance of giving your best effort in every classroom endeavor.

"Brud Gamp was a great influence on me," Rauch said. "By my teen years, our neighborhood had become more mixed with additional Jewish, Irish Catholic, African-American and other residents. Brud taught me that people are people, and they all should be treated fairly. He taught me about right and wrong and about having values and about caring. He was the coach of a kid's team I played on, and he taught us about life, about what is important. He also taught me about things other than sports, to love music, especially opera and symphonies. We would just sit and listen to music at his house."

Gamp and young Marshall also spent time talking about religion. Gamp was a Presbyterian. The two discussed their personal beliefs about faith, accepting each other's views. They kept in touch after Marshall left home for college, and even visited after Marshall moved to North Carolina. Gamp died in 1972 in New York while Rauch was on vacation with his family in Florida.

"I still regret not going to his funeral," Rauch said. "In life, we all make mistakes that we continue to regret. This is one of them for me."

Rauch took some solace, however, in a later act of kindness. It was the kind of thing Gamp might have interpreted as evidence that his teachings about the need to help others had paid off. Following Gamp's death, Rauch donated $10,000 in his memory to the First Presbyterian Church retirement complex, Covenant Village, in Gastonia. One of Rauch's prized possessions today is a set of small vases that belonged to Gamp. They were gifts to Rauch from Gamp's mother.

Like so many high school students, Rauch had no particular affinity for geometry—or for what at the time he thought was a tough and dour Miss Griswold. But his appreciation for her improved as a result of what he first thought was a snub.

"I thought I was a pretty good math student," Rauch said. "I certainly was better at math than at languages. But when Miss Griswold picked her best students to solve a particular problem, she didn't pick me. I was upset. I was determined to show her I was as good as the kids she chose."

Marshall and Jeanne Rauch with their families on their wedding day, May 18, 1946 at Gaston Country Club: from left to right, Marshall's grandmother Ethel Wohl, Marshall's mother and father Tillie and Nathan, Jeanne, Marshall, Jeanne's mother Sadie Goldberg, and Marshall's grandmother and grandfather Esther and Isaac Rauch

Rauch asked his buddy Bill Immershiem to help him work out the solution to a Griswold assignment. They succeeded. "I realize now what Miss Griswold was doing to us," he said. "She was challenging us to do things on our own. I learned that I could solve problems myself. Each person needs to learn that. That classroom exercise made a big impression on me. She was testing me, and it worked."

Rauch lost track of Miss Griswold for almost a half century, but learned in 1991 that she was living in Florida. He located her and made phone contact shortly before her death.

"I was able to tell her what a positive influence she had on me," he said. "I am glad I did that and feel good about it. I wish I had taken the opportunity to do that with Brud Gamp. I now know that those things are important. We should all do it more. When we give roses, the best time to give them is when the recipient can smell them."

The early training in basketball with his friend Brud Gamp put Marshall on the road to early success in athletics. He stuck with basketball because his parents wouldn't allow him to participate in organized football—out of fear he might get injured. From the early coaching by Gamp, Rauch and neighborhood friends shot hoops day and night, burning scrap wood in garbage pails to provide light for after-dark practices.

His first efforts at organized sports came in the ninth grade at Woodmere High School. In his first game as a freshman, he scored fourteen points. In the next game Rauch was lethargic and scored only two. It turned out there was a reason. His coach and parents agreed something was wrong. They sought medical advice and learned that Rauch had scarlet fever. Time needed for recovery prevented his playing any more that year.

By the next season, he was healthy again. Coach Daniel J. McSweeney chose him for the varsity team. His first varsity game, however, included an embarrassing moment. When Rauch was called off the bench to enter the game, he was too nervous to unbutton his uniform jacket. The coach had to help. "Unfortunately, I remember that all too well," Rauch recalled. "I was so scared that I wasn't worth a damn."

By his junior year, he still wasn't a star but played regularly and was considered a positive influence on the team and was an instrumental part of the team that won the South Shore Championship. He still has the miniature basketball those team members received as a reward.

"I remember one game at Woodmere when I scored near the end and put us ahead by one point," Rauch reflected. "I was running down the court thinking of a newspaper headline that would give me credit for the win. Suddenly the other team scored and won at the buzzer. I've always wondered if I had concentrated more on the game and less on that imaginary headline whether we might have won. There was a lesson in that."

Those Woodmere basketball games more than sixty-five years ago reflect how much basketball has changed over the years. During timeouts, Coach McSweeney fed his players chocolate bars for quick energy. At halftime, Rauch skipped the coach's pep talk and strategy session to remain on the playing floor where he coached a small kids' team in short games. That obviously doesn't happen today.

In his school days, basketball was played more deliberately. There was a center jump after every basket, all shots were made with two hands, and free throws were shot with a two-hand, underhand motion. Final scores of games were low, often in the teens or twenties.

Sports, however, didn't consume all of Rauch's high school time. That's when he got his first taste of politics. He was elected treasurer of his junior class and president of the senior class. "I really don't remember campaigning for those jobs," he said, "but I obviously did to some degree because I won."

His 1940 yearbook hints that his popularity among classmates meant he didn't need to do much campaigning. He was what today would be called a BMOC (Big Man On Campus). The yearbook also offers a prophecy: "Look for Marshall in tomorrow's headlines." The text beside his senior picture reads: "The yearbook heaps high praise on his many strengths, but laments his shortcomings in solid geometry. A quiet chap, but under those broad shoulders he carries a heart that is as sympathetic and genial as the voice of your favorite master of ceremonies. Masked in modesty, he displays his athletic prowess only in the field of competition. His leadership ability reveals itself, but solid geometry shows him in an altogether different light. He has never yet been able to find which line goes where, or if it is the square root of two or three that gives you the diameter of the area."

Rauch chuckles at that assessment of his math skills, but he doesn't dispute it. "I always considered myself a fair student, not an outstanding one," he said. He has obviously lived up to the prediction of being a future leader who wouldn't be denied his share of headlines.

During his high school days, Rauch also picked up the nickname "Mush." The Hebrew name for Marshall is Mosher, which accounts for the moniker that other Jewish boys in his neighborhood hung on him.

In addition to classrooms and gymnasiums, high school also provided Marshall his first sweetheart. Theirs was a typical teenage crush but was not destined to last. Her Catholicism and his Judaism were impediments to both sets of parents. "Totally unhappy," is the way Rauch recalled the family attitudes. That didn't keep him from walking five miles to her house on weekends. He had no car, so walking was the only option.

Marshall Rauch (standing third from right) with his Woodmere High School Southshore Atlantic League Championship 1940 basketball team

As enjoyable as his childhood was, and despite several moves to different houses, Marshall Rauch never seriously considered going to college near his home. His father's choice of a university for him was Columbia, of course, and his father's choice of a profession was medicine. Rauch didn't show much interest in either.

Several of Rauch's high school friends were heading south to college, and he decided to follow their lead. He applied and was accepted at both Duke and the University of North Carolina at Chapel Hill, where some of his buddies had enrolled. He chose Duke where he played freshman basketball and then played varsity basketball before entering World War II.

In the spring of 1940, Rauch received his diploma from Woodmere High School. That fall he headed to exciting new surroundings at Duke University in Durham, North Carolina. When he unpacked his bags as a scared freshman, he had no idea what lay ahead. What he found was a mixture of happiness and anxiety.

Chapter 5
The Years at Duke

*I have no doubt that many good things came from my
attending Duke. I'm proud to say I went there. It has a great
and deserved academic reputation. I've watched its continued
rise in stature and have been proud when its athletic teams have
done well. It's just that many of my experiences during my years
at Duke won't go down in my mind as positive.*

Marshall Rauch, on his years as a student at Duke University.

It is easy to see how seventeen-year-old Marshall Rauch, an ambitious student and aspiring basketball player, was attracted to Duke University. By the fall of 1940 Duke had become one of the most exciting higher education venues in the country, one widely associated with excellence in academics as well as athletics and drawing students from across the country.

In only sixteen years, the university's then president, Dr. William P. Few, had transformed Trinity College from a small Methodist liberal arts school into what was at the time North Carolina's largest university. The rest of the nation had watched in fascination—and occasional scorn—as tobacco baron James B. Duke poured millions into creating what he envisioned as "the most beautiful educational plant in America."

The result was a spectacular new campus of Tudor Gothic architecture on the edge of Durham, a city that literally reeked of ripening tobacco. Using Johns Hopkins University as a model, Dr. Few and James B. Duke intended for the new school to become a major research university that would attract students from around the world and bring light and learning to a backward and benighted South.

That ambitious plan not only made Duke University an academic powerhouse, but also won the admiration of the renowned football coach Wallace Wade, who had been taking

Alabama teams to the Rose Bowl. Asked to name a coach capable of leading Duke to the top ranks of college football, Coach Wade offered to take the post himself.

In only a few years, Coach Wade had built a juggernaut at Duke, whose football teams were routinely ranked among the four or five best in the country and had gone to the 1939 Rose Bowl, unbeaten, untied, and unscored-on.

The profit from that appearance in the granddaddy of all post-season bowl games—in which Southern California beat Duke, 7 to 3, on a last-second pass completion—enabled Duke to build a 9,500-seat basketball arena that was said at the time to be the grandest of its kind south of the Palestra in Philadelphia. Formally dedicated in January 1940, the new arena was needed to house a basketball program that then young coach Eddie Cameron had led to the Southern Conference Championship in 1939 and was on its way to winning similar championships in 1941 and 1942.

Many years later, in another era of basketball glory at Duke, that arena, initially named Duke Indoor Stadium, would be renamed in honor of Coach Cameron and would win fame around the world by accommodating thousands of student fans known as "the Cameron Crazies."

By 1940 Duke also had made a name for itself as a school with a glamorous social life. Student-led dance bands organized by Johnny Long and Les Brown had overcome Methodist objections to dancing on campus and gone on to achieve national fame for their smooth performance of popular music. The bands of Benny Goodman and Tommy Dorsey played for dances on the Duke campus. In short, Duke was widely perceived as a swinging institution, by standards of that day.

Though Duke was in the South, it was not a "southern" school. Its student body represented diverse geographies, nationalities, cultures, and religions. Though supported by the Methodist Church, it prided itself in being open to all people without regard to faiths or social classifications. Total enrollment was 3,716, making it slightly larger than the University of North Carolina at nearby Chapel Hill. Duke's enrollment included 2,674 undergraduates, 1,799 men, and 875 women. Among the men, only 451 came from North Carolina.

In enrolling at Duke, Marshall Rauch was among 306 students from New York State. Also enrolling at Duke was Jeanne Goldberg, one of 223 women from North Carolina. The two met at Duke in the second semester of their freshman year.

On entering Duke, Marshall Rauch understood that classroom work was important, but it wasn't on his short list. While not always the first priority with him, it certainly was to his parents, who were sacrificing to pay his tuition, room, and board. What Marshall really looked forward to was making the basketball team and enjoying an active social life away from home. He was a handsome, engaging fellow whose open, outgoing manner allowed him to make friends easily. He would also play on the Duke lacrosse team and become a regular participant in intramural wrestling and handball. In all three endeavors—academics, athletics, and social life—he expected to be judged on his own merits.

Marshall's father Nathan Rauch, the former chemistry professor, was disappointed that his son did not take his advice and attend Columbia University close to home in New York. In exchange for allowing his son to go to Duke, he insisted that Marshall pursue a pre-med course with an eye toward going to medical school and becoming a doctor. Marshall consented, and in his first semester pulled down four B's and a C, a grade-point average that not only qualified him for basketball but also made him eligible to join a fraternity.

Like most other players of that time, Rauch did not receive an athletic scholarship but the tall, lean New Yorker was determined to make the basketball team. In those years, freshmen could not play varsity basketball, but they practiced regularly with the varsity and displayed their talents to the coaching staff, which included Gerry Gerard as coach of the freshmen and Eddie Cameron as varsity coach.

The stars of the freshman basketball team in 1940–41 were three young men from Durham: Bob Gantt, and the Loftis brothers, Cedric and Garland. Their local popularity assured that Duke had large and vocal crowds for its games, not only in the freshman year but in the three years following, when Duke

Marshall Rauch,
Duke University
varsity player, 1941

romped to conference championships.

It was during a freshman game that one of the spectators in the crowd began to make a lasting impact on Marshall Rauch's life. "My buddy Cedric Loftis and I had just come out of the game and were sitting on the bench when he pointed out this very pretty girl sitting in the stands," Rauch said. "He told me she was someone I ought to meet and someone he thought I would be interested in. He was absolutely right, too, especially after I learned she was Jewish."

Rauch hadn't dated much in his first semester, but when he spotted the beautiful Jeanne Goldberg sitting in the stands, he knew he was interested. The feelings, however, were not immediately mutual, according to Jeanne.

"I had seen him earlier at a dance on campus," Jeanne recalled, "but I wasn't particularly impressed. I thought he was so different from me. He was from New York and seemed so sophisticated. I was from a very disciplined family in the South. He just didn't seem like my type."

Jeanne said that when she noticed Marshall looking up at her from the players' bench, she was sitting between two other students, each holding one of her hands. "I felt good that he was looking at me with two other guys paying me such attention, but I didn't know if I would hear from him.

"Several days later his roommate, Murray Brandt, called and asked me for a date. Marshall then called and asked me out for the next night. But instead of Brandt showing up for the first date, Marshall came. Apparently they had planned it that way. I still wasn't overly impressed when Marshall called, but female freshmen just didn't turn down dates. We went to dinner, talked for a while, and he took me back to my dorm. We kissed good night, and that did it."

That indeed did it. They didn't date anyone else the rest of their freshman year but dated each other often and became a regular couple on campus. That's the reason, Rauch said, his grades suffered during his second semester, when he pulled down four D's and a C. The combinations of playing basketball and spending time with Jeanne were higher priorities for him than academics.

Another thing happened in that freshman year to chill Marshall Rauch's academic interests. Having made the freshman basketball team and qualified to join a fraternity, he considered pledging Sigma Chi, as the rest of the basketball players had done. Then came a rude awakening. If Rauch wanted to join a fraternity, his only choice would be Zeta Beta Tau, the campus fraternity reserved for Jews. Similar discrimination restricted Jewish women at Duke to Alpha Epsilon Phi sorority. Jeanne Goldberg could only be a member of A.E.Phi.

It was Marshall Rauch's first personal encounter with institutional religious prejudice. He also was led to believe that Duke routinely limited its enrollment of Jews to 3 percent of the student body, though the university never acknowledged having any such quota system.

"When I was growing up on Long Island," he recalled, "certainly there was some discrimination, but basically it was name calling. You could immediately handle that in your own way and it would be over with. But when I got to Duke, it was different. There was a subtle discrimination with invisible guidelines. It was frustrating because there was no opportunity to equalize things."

At the time, Rauch didn't complain, publicly or privately. He didn't express his feelings to his family, friends, or university officials. With Hitler raving about Jews in Europe, exploiting them, rounding them up, and sending them to labor and concentration camps without a protest from the rest of the world, it was not an opportune time to mount a campaign for Jewish rights. But Marshall said he felt demeaned and believed the policies at Duke were unfair. "Looking back," he said, "I just felt the university wasn't what it should have been."

In the years since, and especially after long conversations with his friend Jim Woodward, the chancellor at UNC Charlotte, Marshall Rauch learned that such discriminatory policies were not limited to Duke, that many colleges and universities in the 1940s imposed similar or even more stringent restrictions on Jews. In fact, he says, Duke may have been more open than most.

He was pleased, he said, when former North Carolina Governor Terry Sanford became president of Duke in 1970. "One of the first things he did was change those guidelines."

Though Rauch's feelings about his experience have been tempered over the years, he said he couldn't "change the distress I felt then and have continued to feel over the years, any more than I can change what happened to me back then. I've thought a lot about it, and now, at least intellectually, I understand what the world was like then. I know it is a better world today."

Despite his deep feelings about institutional prejudice, Rauch recalled that most of his experiences at Duke were positive. He had won his numerals for freshman basketball and made the varsity basketball squad the next season, playing for Coach Cameron in the old Southern Conference. He remembers his first varsity game — against Davidson College, then a basketball power. As he came up court dribbling the ball and crossed the centerline, people in the crowd began shouting for him to shoot. He looked at the defense, decided the fans were offering good advice and arched a long two-handed set shot from about half court. He watched it swish through the net. It was his first shot as a varsity player and a great thrill.

He was not a starter, but he did get to play and competed against some great players. One of them was a tall, skinny kid from Durham with a mischievous grin. His name was Horace McKinney, better known as "Bones," who later became a basketball legend. Though he grew up in Durham with the Loftis brothers, McKinney played college basketball for North Carolina State before World War II, for UNC Chapel Hill after World War II, played professionally for the Washington Capitals of the National Basketball Association, and later coached at Wake Forest after a career in the Baptist ministry. Rauch and McKinney renewed their long friendship when Marshall's son, John White, played freshman basketball at Wake Forest.

Many of the friends Marshall made at Duke a half century ago are still his friends. "I had a lot of good times during my Duke years," he recalls. "I can remember some poker games with penny and nickel bets with a limit of three raises. There were some good frat parties. During those moments, I was having a good time."

Among the many friends he made at Duke was Lou Bello, a funny kid with crew-cut hair and a showman's instinct. He was too small to play on the basketball team, but went on to become a schoolteacher and made a name for himself along the East Coast as a basketball referee. Bello loved the officiating role, chatted incessantly with players, and displayed a flair for humor. He didn't just blow his whistle to call an infraction; he would point to the offending player and, anticipating protest, sing out in a loud voice, "Oh, yes, you did. I saw you do it." Often even the offending player laughed.

Once when refereeing a game, in which Bones McKinney was one of the coaches, Bello thought he had heard enough complaint from McKinney about Bello's calls. When the ball went out of bounds and landed in McKinney's lap, rather than return it to the court, he tossed it straight up in the air. Bello raced to the coach and said, "If that ball comes down, I'm charging you with a technical foul." Everybody within earshot laughed, even the mischievous McKinney.

Another of Marshall's friends at Duke was basketball team-mate Bob Gross, now a semi-retired veneer company owner in High Point, North Carolina. Gross remembers Rauch as "the first Jew I had ever met who could laugh at himself about his religious faith. He had a wonderful sense of humor, and we kidded around a lot. At some point, I good-naturedly started calling him 'Irish' because I thought that fit his personality and appearance. The nickname stuck with the team members. He was just an all-around good guy. We liked him then and still do."

Gross recalls the time that Marshall won a sport jacket in a poker game on the Duke campus. Proud of his new coat, Rauch showed it off on a trip home to New York. "His father told him if he had known Marshall needed a sport coat, he could have bought him one. Marshall never told him he had won the jacket in a poker game."

Marshall readily concedes that he was not what you would call a top academic student, the kind he insists that his grandchildren should be. He has been known to lay heavy words on his grandchildren who slacked off in their college classroom work, just as his father did to him when he failed to meet expectations.

After the disastrous academic record in the second semester of his freshman year, Rauch attended summer school at his father's insistence. The goal was to improve his grades. On the advice of some fellow athletes, he signed up for a course in Greek mythology. He made friends with the professor, and they became partners in frequent games of handball. Rauch aced that

Duke University Southern Conference Basketball Champions 1942;
Marshall Rauch third from left in back row (photo from Duke archives)

course, making both himself and his father happy, though his father never knew that the handball relationship might have been a factor in the good grade.

Rauch also abandoned his plans to pursue a pre-med course. He found that, though he was the son of a chemistry professor, he couldn't learn enough chemistry to pass the course. So he changed his major to math.

As a math major, he enrolled in a physics course and worked hard to earn an A. At the end of the term, he had a grade-point average of 94.1. But the professor, who was not a handball enthusiast, gave him a B. When Marshall asked why, the professor said he graded on the curve and the cutoff for an A was a tenth of a point above Marshall's average.

"I didn't know about grading on the curve until then, but I realized that I could do a lot less work and still get a B, so that's what I did after that. I just took the easy way out. I really don't want my grandchildren following my example, but those are the facts. I am afraid my sons inherited some of my academic bad habits, because they had a lot of trouble with some courses in college."

As his career at Duke continued, Marshall's grades got better, but not much. "My life tended to revolve around athletics and not academics," he acknowledged. "My grades were not as good as my father wanted them to be. I did enough to get by, but I was no great student."

Complicating matters was his romance with Jeanne. By the end of her freshman year, Jeanne and her parents agreed that she would leave Duke for Syracuse University, where the academic programs were more suited to her interests in drama and the theater. While Duke's discriminatory rules were not a primary factor in her decision to transfer, they were clearly no incentive for her to stay.

"I left Duke primarily because I was interested in the theater," Jeanne Rauch said. "But one of the campus rules at Duke was that women students couldn't be outside their dorms after 7:30 p.m. That meant that I could not participate in theater productions. Because of those rules, I had already decided to transfer from Duke before I met Marshall. My roommate, Yetta Sawilosky, and I both transferred." Sawilosky later married Murray Brandt, Marshall's Duke roommate.

Marshall Rauch likes to joke that "when her parents learned she was dating me they took her out of Duke and shipped her to a school out of state." But the distance between Durham and Syracuse did not end the relationship. Regular contact was by mail, telephone, and train during the next year and a half of Marshall's career at Duke.

Throughout 1940 and 1941, news of the war that was raging in Europe created great concern among university students. Most males feared that sooner or later the conflict might involve the United States and affect their education. The Duke student newspaper, *The Duke Chronicle*, cautioned men against making hasty judgments and urged them to stay in school as long as possible, pointing out that the military and the nation were going to need educated leaders during and after the war. In his sophomore year, Marshall Rauch joined an Army Air Corps reserve unit and stayed in school. That didn't last.

In February 1943, in the middle of his junior year, his unit was called to active duty. Three years later, after having survived months of combat in Europe, Marshall Rauch was discharged. He and Jeanne were married in May of 1946, a month after Rauch returned from his Army duty. They celebrated their fiftieth wedding anniversary in May 1996 with a gala at the Gaston Country Club, filled with family, friends, and great memories.

Their initial post-war plan called for Marshall and Jeanne to return to Duke for his undergraduate degree and her master's degree. "We both initially decided that I should get my degree," Rauch said. "We went back to Duke, and I saw my old coach Eddie Cameron, who welcomed me back to the team." The couple rented an apartment upstairs over a garage in Durham and prepared to return to classes.

But before the fall semester began, Jeanne's brothers (on her wedding day) offered their new brother-in-law a job in their Bessemer City textile plant at a salary of $60 a week. "And that's when I decided to go for the $60 rather than the college education," Rauch said. "I have always regretted that decision because not getting that degree is one of the few things I've started and never finished. It would also have really been fun to go back and play basketball when I was more mature."

At the time he wasn't thinking of basketball or academics. He was a married man, and he felt he ought to go to work and support his wife and what would soon become a family. Still, Marshall wanted the Duke degree. After he went to work, he asked Duke if he might pursue his degree by taking correspondence courses while working for his brothers-in-law in Bessemer City, 150 miles away. Duke rejected his request, saying that it didn't offer off-campus studies.

More than twenty-five years after his military service, Marshall enrolled at Belmont Abbey College, a small Catholic institution near Gastonia, but found he was unable to attend classes regularly because of his heavy work and travel schedule. Belmont Abbey awarded him an honorary doctorate in 1987 in recognition of his years of community service. Pfeiffer University in Stanly County did the same thing in 1993.

As Rauch discusses his college experience, he speaks longingly, even at age eighty-one, of one day getting an earned degree. "If I could get credit for some of my life's experiences, I would qualify. I would still love to get a degree," he said in the spring of 2004.

As an adult and a successful businessman and public official, Rauch has taken an active role in the governance of other higher education institutions in North Carolina, where his power and influence have been significant. In addition to serving in the North Carolina Senate for twenty-four years, he has been a trustee of the University of North Carolina at Chapel Hill and chairman of the Budget and Finance Committee of the Board of Governors that oversees the University at Chapel Hill and fifteen other public universities across the state.

Closer to home, Rauch has been an active participant in numerous educational causes in and around Gastonia. He has donated large sums of money to various higher education institutions as well as to individuals attending those schools. He hasn't kept track of all his financial contributions, but the total is easily in the millions.

In 1996 Rauch and his wife Jeanne pledged $700,000 to Gaston Community College for a new campus science and fine arts building. Construction began in 1998. He has endowed a professorship in political science at UNC Charlotte and created a scholarship at UNC Chapel Hill. His daughters Ingrid and Stephanie have contributed $50,000 for a tennis facility at UNC Chapel Hill where both were members of the varsity tennis team as undergraduates. Rauch has privately paid tuition for numerous students to attend the public university system and has financed nursing and law school costs for others.

His generosity to public institutions, he said, was not intended to slight Duke, but rather reflected his involvement in politics and service on appointed boards overseeing public institutions.

In the long run, Marshall Rauch's feelings about his experience at Duke may have had a positive result. "Perhaps," he said, "everything does happen for the best. One reason I have been willing to help others, especially minorities, is that I have personally felt the hurt that prejudice can cause. What happened to me at Duke has helped motivate me in my efforts at helping people reach their potential. It has also caused me to work against all forms of prejudice."

After rethinking his Duke experience and putting it into historical perspective, Marshall Rauch did something in the spring of 1998 he had never done. He sent $1,000 to the Duke Alumni Association, securing lifetime memberships for himself and his wife Jeanne. He explained his decision this way:

"After thinking about the whole situation again more openly, I think that's only fair and the right thing to do. The past is still there, but this is a different time. I want to look to the future and try to make things better. Also, I had a wonderful experience at Duke during the 1997 basketball season when my daughter, Stephanie, and I went to Cameron Indoor Stadium to see a Duke-UCLA game at the invitation of my good friend Michael Holton, former assistant coach at UCLA.

"As we were walking through the Hall of Champions

inside Cameron Indoor Stadium, Stephanie saw a picture on the wall that stopped both of us. It was a photograph of the 1942 Southern Conference champions with a record of 22 and 2. I was a member of that team. I was in that picture. I really cannot describe how I felt at that moment. It was something I am extremely proud to have been a part."

Chapter 6
World War II

The last thing I wanted from the military was a career as a combat infantryman. So as a college sophomore, I volunteered for the Army Air Corps reserves, hoping for a glamorous assignment. But when my unit was called to active duty, the Army tried to make me a fighter pilot. I flew fourteen times, and fourteen times turned green with air sickness. So much for a career as a military pilot. I wound up in muddy France with an M-1 strapped on my back and German soldiers as adversaries.

Marshall Rauch, describing his entry into World War II.

The entire time Marshall Rauch was at Duke University, the shadow of World War II hung ominously over him and young people like him across the country and around the world. War had been raging in Asia since 1937 and in Europe since 1939. Japanese bombs were killing American missionaries in China, and German submarines were menacing American ships off the Atlantic coast. Hitler had annexed Austria and Czechoslovakia, blitzed Poland, and in rapid succession had conquered Belgium, Holland, Norway, and France. Only England was left, and it was under constant bombardment. Americans sensed that it was only a matter of time before the United States would be drawn into the conflict.

As Marshall Rauch was settling into his Duke dormitory in September 1940, Congress enacted the first peacetime draft in American history. A month later, in a somber speech to male students at Duke, the University's thin, soft-spoken president, Dr. William P. Few, warned that the United States "was being pushed into a war" that it was unprepared to fight. He challenged the Duke students to do their best. "This generation is to be tested as by fire," he said. "I earnestly hope that everyone of you tested by fire may prove to be of true gold."

Though isolationist and pacifist sentiments were being strongly expressed across the country and on the Duke campus, Marshall Rauch never gave a thought to avoiding military conscription. Neither did most of his classmates. In a campus poll, 66 percent of the Duke freshmen indicated their willingness to fight in foreign wars to preserve freedom. Among upper classmen and graduate students, the percentage in favor of fighting was much lower.

Marshall Rauch knew he would serve his country when the need arose. But only twenty-one-year-olds were required to register for the draft, which suggested that he and his freshmen friends still had time to pursue an education. In hopes of staying in school as long as possible, he joined the Air Corps Reserves in the fall of his sophomore year. Three months later, the Japanese bombed Pearl Harbor, plunging the United States into the war.

"I admit I didn't relish the thought of becoming an infantryman," Rauch said of his Air Corps enlistment. "I thought signing up might increase my chances of getting a degree before being called to active duty and would give me more choices of assignments once I was called."

But that wasn't to be. Becoming a reservist allowed Rauch to finish his sophomore year at Duke and to complete the first semester of his junior year. But on February 10, 1943, his reserve unit was ordered to active duty. Two weeks later, he was a full-time soldier. His college career was put on what he thought was a temporary hold.

His first reaction was hardly surprising. "First, I wanted to go home to see my parents, then go on to Syracuse to see Jeanne," he said. His parents were living on Long Island, and girlfriend Jeanne Girard was at Syracuse University, having transferred from Duke at the end of her freshman year. His second reaction was more humorous. "I realized I wouldn't have to turn in my term paper—which I hadn't finished anyway," he said.

An anxious Rauch left Duke on February 13, 1943, but not before he and some college buddies who also had been called into the armed services went into Durham for far more merriment than he had ever experienced. "That was the first time I drank alcohol and even though it was just beer, I got pretty sick," he remembered. The next day—with a bad headache and a sad heart—he said good-bye to his Duke friends and headed home to New York.

Memories of that final night of partying have stuck with him for more than half a century. Since then, he has always been about as close to a teetotaler as one can get. His alcohol consumption now is limited to an occasional glass of wine with dinner or as part of Jewish holiday rituals. He has attended hundreds of political or business cocktail parties through the years without consuming alcohol.

Once home in New York, he spent a week with his parents and girlfriend Jeanne before boarding a train to Miami, where his initial Air Corps training was scheduled. "Jeanne was at our house in Woodmere (about twenty miles east of New York City). On my last night there we both fell asleep on the living room floor and woke up at 4:30 a.m. I remember thinking 'What a way to say good-bye, asleep on the floor,'" Rauch said.

The next morning, Rauch's parents and Jeanne hugged him at New York City's Pennsylvania Station as he began a thirty-eight-month stint in the military, including combat in France and more brushes with death than he prefers to remember. At the time, he looked upon military duty as just another adventure, but maturity and experience have taught him it was a lot more. He now understands his parents' anguish over his departure.

"Looking back, of course, I have different feelings," he said. "I now realize what sending children into a shooting war does to the hearts of parents; they try to act bravely, though they know they may be seeing their children for the last time."

Rauch arrived in Miami on February 27, 1943, for Air Corps cadet training and got a quick lesson in military foot-dragging. He had taken only the clothes he was wearing. Five days passed before the Army issued him military clothing. That was just the first of many examples of waste and inefficiency he would come to accept as military routine.

From the spring of 1943 until late fall of 1944, when Rauch was assigned to combat in Europe, he was shipped back and

Before Marshall was sent overseas in October 1944, his mother and father and aunts and uncles took him and two of his Army buddies to dinner in New York City. From left to right are Ellie and Miriam Rauch, Nathan Rauch, Marshall, John McDonnell, John Calvert, Tillie Rauch, Al and Darcy Rauch, and Mae and Joe Wohl.

forth across the country and up and down the East Coast in moves that made little sense to him. "I had been in college paying my own way; then the Army put me on active duty and sent me to college at government expense for more than a year.

"It was expensive to do that, and I still don't understand it. I turned twenty-one in the Army, and I now think about what a waste it was to spend those years like I did. And I was just one of hundreds of thousands of young men in the same circumstance. We gave part of our lives that we can never have back."

In the Air Corps, his base pay was $37.50 a month, plus another $25 a month for flight pay. He frequently supplemented those earnings with winnings from poker games.

He never really wanted to be a fighter pilot. He joined the Air Corps hoping for other kinds of assignments. "I asked for something related to meteorology because of my college major in math," he said. "They told me they didn't need any meteorologists. They needed pilots, and I was told I would become a pilot. But they didn't know what they were asking for when they told me to fly an airplane."

Both Rauch and the Air Corps soon learned. Throughout his years in the Army, he recorded his impressions of military life in a weathered diary. That diary details both happy and sorrowful events—friendships developed, buddies who came and went, and many that died.

It also chronicles his growing frustration with military waste. Although Rauch cherishes that diary as especially meaningful, he did not have the heart to sit down and read through it until more than fifty years had passed. Then he did so only in preparation for reviewing recollections for this book.

For the young soldier, the first months in the Air Corps were more frustrating than sad. Rauch still cannot understand why the Air Corps was transforming him and so many others into nomads. In the first thirty days as a soldier, he and his unit were housed in three different Miami hotels. "I have no idea why they moved us so much. That first month was just a game. We played basketball but did little of anything else," he recalled.

The one special treat during those first days was when Rauch's Uncle Joe Wohl, an FBI agent from New York, came to Miami. He treated the young soldier to dinner and good conversation about family and home. Rauch recalled with a chuckle that when his uncle—who identified himself only as a federal agent and not as a relative—came to the hotel and asked for him, his Air Corps buddies thought he was in big trouble. Only later did he tell them of the family connection.

After a month of basic idleness in Miami, Rauch and his fellow cadets were moved from Miami to a junior college in Williamsport, Pennsylvania, for pre-cadet training. "I became captain of our basketball team there," he said. "It was more a college life than a military life. The classes were easy, and all the officers were nice to us."

When the flight training began, it was not a pleasant experience. Rauch's diary entries of April and May reveal the nauseous details:

April 22, 1943: Made my first flight. Got sick.

April 23: Made second flight. Got sick as Hell.

May 3: Made a lousy turn. Got sick again. This might be fun except for the throwing up.

May 4: Made first tail spin. Really got sick.

May 14: Flying is for birds, not for people. Still got sick, but not as sick as earlier.

May 15: Made my first landing. Instructor told me if I kept flying I would never have to worry about getting shot down because the way I fly I would kill myself.

May 16: As a pilot, I'm still lousy. I made my last test flight today. I might like flying if I didn't get sick so much.

Ultimately, the young soldier asked to withdraw from pilot training. "I was not just sick in the plane, but I was sick for hours afterwards," he said. He quickly learned that in the military a person just can't quit because he wants to, sick or not. The Air Corps ordered him to see a military psychiatrist. When Rauch described his airsickness in vivid detail, the Army doctor quickly signed the documents that declared him unfit for flight assignments.

So what did the Air Corps do? It ordered Rauch to report for aerial gunner training. Sometimes military rules defy common sense. The fact that he was declared too tall to fit in the small space where gunners sat was all that saved him from more flying.

After two months in Williamsport, Rauch was transferred to Nashville, Tennessee. On his first day there he came down with measles.

After learning that Rauch was unable to fly, the Air Corps gave him other duties, but none related

Marshall Rauch (right) and his Duke ZBT fraternity brother Bob Backer of Greensboro while in flight training. Backer was killed in 1944 when his plane was shot down.

to his desire for meteorology. So he and others in his unit learned the art of goldbricking, although he listed such practices in his diary under other, less wholesome titles.

For example, his diary detailed the escapades of fifteen cadets who needed one entire day to mow the grass around a barracks' plot that was about seventy-five yards by twenty-five yards. Another described an assignment in which the cadets took a whole day to paint one rock, which was about thirty-six inches in diameter. "It was all such a waste, but special details like that sure beat marching and getting yelled at by officers who were mostly boorish and bullish," Rauch explained. "Most of them were career men with little formal education. They loved to yell at college boys."

After six weeks in Nashville, Rauch was moved again. In July 1943, his unit was shipped by train to Jefferson City, Missouri, where the military brass decided—belatedly—that Rauch was not Air Corps material. He was issued an infantry uniform, assigned to a new group called the Army Specialized Training Project, and ordered to train ninety miles away from the military base. "It seemed stupid to send us to one base to live and to another ninety miles away to train," Rauch said. "But that's just the Army."

On July 22, five months after entering the Army, Rauch fired a submachine gun for the first time. He also learned even better how to beat the system. "The officers were looking for troop entertainment and needed boxers," Rauch said. "I told them I could box. I never had, of course, but boxers received special consideration and got to practice in the gym a lot instead of marching and drilling."

Most of the men who volunteered for boxing did so for the same reasons Rauch did—to avoid manual labor and extensive drilling. "It was unwritten but understood that nobody would get hurt," Rauch said of the boxing matches. "Occasionally, we'd get some jerk who was really serious about it. We tried to avoid guys like that."

Thirty days after going to Missouri, Rauch's new infantry unit was moved again to Grinnell, Iowa—or two weeks. In early August it was moved again, this time to Lincoln, Nebraska, for what he recalls as more silly waste by military brass. The Army gave him a written test to determine if he could qualify as a truck driver. He passed and was assigned to drive a 1936 Chevrolet. After two weeks, he recorded in his diary:

> I must have been pretty good in that old Chevy truck. Got a new Ford truck to drive.

During his many travels, Rauch was often homesick as well as frustrated with what he felt was Army inefficiency. He stayed in contact with his family and girlfriend Jeanne by mail and phone. His September 15 diary entry read:

> It was Jeanne's birthday. Called her, but was broke and had to call collect. Vowed never to be broke again on such an important occasion, especially since her brother Cy, who accepted the collect call, teased her so much about it.

After a month in Lincoln, the unit was on the road again, this time to Northern State Teachers' College at Aberdeen, South Dakota, where more classroom assignments awaited. "The Army just kept sending me to college after taking me out of college," he said with a tone of disgust. "I still don't understand that."

Just as he kept up with family, Rauch also celebrated Jewish holidays when he could. His diary entry on September 29 for Rosh Hashanah showed he was invited to dinner with a Jewish family in Aberdeen after attending services at the local synagogue. That gave him some semblance of home.

Rauch's unit stayed in South Dakota for the rest of 1943, where the toughest duties were attending college classes, most of which Rauch had already taken at Duke. He befriended young people in the town and played basketball with many of them.

Among the young boys he taught basketball fundamentals that fall were teenagers Paul Hayes and Jack Pred.

Almost half a century later, Hayes still fondly remembered those days. In the late 1990s, he visited Rauch in North Carolina to renew his friendship and again say thanks for happy times back in Aberdeen. Hayes became a dentist; Pred was successful in a chain of retail stores.

Rauch's diary entry of January 1, 1944 records his first furlough, eleven months after entering the military. The furlough was for nine days, but he spent four of them on trains from South Dakota to New York and back. His diary entry for January 9 notes that upon his return to the barracks he felt that even for such a short trip home, the visit was well worth the long journey. He got to see Jeanne and his parents for the first time in almost a year.

Rauch had a lot of free time that winter and spring in Aberdeen. He became a friend with the family of Al Selle because Mrs. Selle was an excellent cook and the couple had a pretty daughter named Pat. Rauch went pheasant hunting with Selle and appreciated the friendship and home cooking. But hunting proved to be less than a pleasant pastime for Rauch. "I've never hunted as a sport," he said. "Killing animals bothers me."

In February 1944, seven months after creating the specialized training project to which Rauch was assigned, the Army unceremoniously decided to disband it. "I was disappointed because we had a good deal going," Rauch said. "But we also had a lot of manpower in that unit that was needed in Europe. More soldiers were needed there than in some college classroom in South Dakota."

In April, Rauch's unit was transferred from Aberdeen to Camp Robinson, Arkansas, where he was assigned to the infantry's 66th Black Panther Division. "We were told we'd all be privates because they didn't have room for any other ranks," Rauch recalled. "I was classified as a rifleman. I don't know of anything that could have been worse. I was a very poor shot." Facetiously, he chalked that up to more military wisdom.

Two weeks later, the unit was moved again, this time to Camp Rucker, Alabama. It was there, more than a year after Rauch had entered the military, that he finally began serious, grueling combat training. Some diary entries from that early Rucker experience tell the story:

April 12: Morale of most soldiers is piss poor. Mine worse.

April 13: Some soldiers were threatening to shoot themselves in the leg, and others were talking of pretending to be homosexuals, just hoping that would get them out.

April 15: Practiced with M-1. We lay in mud and rain for four days.

April 24: Up at 3:30 a.m. to hike 5.5 miles to the firing range. Shoot all day and hike back after dark. We do this day after day, rain or heat. Twenty-five mile hikes also frequent.

April 27: Several of us went into Ozark (the nearest town) and rented a hotel room just to sleep. We slept the entire day.

Despite the doom and gloom of that spring in Alabama, there was one bright spot. Jeanne Girard came to visit in early May. The diary entry is specific.

May 12: Jeanne got in on train at 3:40 a.m. On bench outside Mills Hotel, Ozark, at 4:40 a.m., I gave her the ring.

It took only one hour from the time his sweetheart arrived until he had asked her to marry him. Apparently, she was as anxious as he was because she accepted on the spot. Jeanne stayed at a hotel in Ozark for ten days. Those were unquestionably the best ten days of his Camp Rucker experience.

The war effort was growing. On June 6, 1944,

Marshall Rauch on maneuvers in Europe, 1943

One of the 40 & 8 troop trains moving through Europe in 1944 (Rauch standing at left)

while standing guard duty at Camp Rucker, Rauch learned over a radio news report that the Allies had invaded Europe on D-Day. In the next few months, Rauch was taught to fire bazookas and read military maps. He also learned, to his surprise, that he'd been assigned to the Camp Rucker football team. No matter that he had not played organized football since the sandlot days in Woodmere. Some officer, who had seen on Rauch's record that he had played basketball and boxed, decreed that he could also play football.

In October, Rauch's unit was declared ready for war and was transported from Camp Rucker to Camp Shanks, New York, to prepare for overseas duty. The route of Rauch's troop train carried it through Bessemer City, North Carolina, Jeanne's hometown. The train stopped momentarily within sight of her family home. Military officers, however, would not let any soldiers step off the train.

At Camp Shanks, after a brief furlough with his parents, Rauch was given specialized training in war survival, including ways to escape enemy prison camps. That training lasted two weeks. Besides learning serious military maneuvers, Rauch also became skilled in printing fake passes to visit his nearby family.

His unit was shipped into the war zone in mid-November. His diary describes the dreary mood of those first days as the large convoy of troop ships and destroyers crossed the Atlantic. He remembers being impressed with the huge guns on the ships—until he realized they were just for show. They were fake wooden guns mounted on the decks. "Not much of a sense of comfort," his diary says. Here are other entries, starting with the day he set sail:

Nov. 14: Boarded the ship USS *George Washington* for Europe. Lousy conditions. Got seasick. About as bad as being air sick. Two meals a day served, but ship so crowded soldiers had to eat standing up. But I couldn't eat anyway because I was so seasick.

Nov. 18: Still sick, but ate meal today for first time since sailing (four days).

Nov. 23: Thanksgiving dinner at sea. Had turkey and cranberries, but clearly something missing.

Nov. 25: Ship is basically one big gambling casino.

Nov. 26: Docked at South Hampton, England.

Nov. 27: Lousy barracks at Dorchester.

Nov. 28: One man in our unit clearly unstable at best. We heard him scream for help, saying he had been shot in the foot. Then we heard the gun fire. He wanted out real bad.

In England, Rauch witnessed racial disharmony among the troops because of skin color. The military was still segregated, but black troops were arriving in England and beginning to mingle in the pubs with white soldiers and English women. Trouble lay ahead. "Black soldiers who were seen with the white British women caused quite a stir," Rauch wrote in his diary. "White soldiers, especially the Southern fellows, resented the fact that the women were talking with black troops. That caused some problems."

Rauch volunteered for kitchen duty in the officers' quarters during his brief stay in South Hampton. The food was better there. He also arranged passes, some forged, to go to the Red Cross headquarters for hot showers and higher quality meals.

On December 23, 1944, the Red Cross provided coffee and doughnuts as Rauch's unit boarded the SS *Cheshire* and headed for combat in France. There were two ships loading to cross the English Channel together. Luckily, Rauch was assigned to the *Cheshire*. The other ship was the *Leopoldville*.

He got his first taste of the real hell of war on that trip across the Channel. It happened just as the ships sailed within sight of the lights of Cherbourg. It was a sight he will never forget.

The *Leopoldville* was no more than 100 yards ahead of the *Cheshire*, when a German torpedo exploded in the lead ship. Rauch and the other 2,000 troops on his ship didn't learn the severity of the attack for several days, but they knew at the instant of the blast that they were in a fighting zone and that death could come at any moment.

As the *Cheshire* moved around the *Leopoldville*, surveying the damage before moving on into port, fear and anxiety mounted among the troops. Not only had their sister ship with their fellow soldiers been hit, but also they wondered when or if they would be next.

The Army later listed 800 casualties in that single *Leopoldville* attack. "It was terrible and a very chaotic time," Rauch wrote in his diary for Christmas Eve, 1944. A soldier on the *Cheshire* with Rauch, Jacquin Sanders, wrote a book, *A Night Before Christmas* (1944), which details that fatal torpedo attack on the *Leopoldville* and the aftermath. The loss of lives on the *Leopoldville* was one of the worst naval disasters of World War II.

On Christmas Day, as soon as the troops landed at Cherbourg, south of the Normandy invasion site, each man was ordered to immediately write letters home. "I later realized that the military wanted to fly those letters directly to the United States so families of survivors of the ship attack would know their sons and husbands were not hurt or killed."

The week between Christmas and New Year's was spent in combat near St. Nazaire on the Brittany peninsula, a finger of land on the northwest coast of France, jutting into the Atlantic Ocean, as opposed to the English Channel, which was farther north and which the troops had crossed to get to Cherbourg.

It was cold, rainy, and muddy as the troops dug foxholes and set up field tents. "We thought at the time it was pretty bad, but we were probably lucky," Rauch recalled. "The Battle of the Bulge was underway on the northeastern front, and certainly we were fortunate not to be there." The Battle of the Bulge had begun just days before Rauch's unit landed in France.

Rauch had always felt that his religious faith was reasonably strong, but the exposure to combat caused him to take that faith much more seriously. "You might say I matured religiously that first night on the line with an M-1 rifle in my hands and artillery shells going off all around me," he said.

Rauch's unit spent the first months of 1945 in the killing fields of France, rotating in and out of front-line combat. One of his duties during the fighting was dismantling booby traps set by retreating German troops. One diary entry explains:

It is pretty dangerous. Some of our men were hurt pretty bad by explosives and spikes set in the traps.

Danger was all around, but Rauch said one of his closest encounters with being shot—so far as he knows—was when one of his buddies, Alberto Esqueda, accidentally fired his weapon as he was cleaning it when they were behind the enemy lines. The bullet whizzed only inches from Rauch's head.

During the fighting, Rauch found three things that helped him maintain his composure. One was the relief provided by trips off the front line. Another was the regular care packages he received from his parents and Jeanne back home. The third was basketball.

In their idle moments away from combat, soldiers occasionally spent their time playing basketball. They created a crude dirt court by blasting stumps from the ground. They used a wire hoop from a wine barrel as a basket and a machine-gun belt as a net. Somehow, they secured a basketball.

"As I think back on those days," Rauch said, "I realize just how much my mother and father cared for me. My dad was never very demonstrative in saying how he felt, but those regular packages of nonperishable food and gifts showed me he was thinking of me and caring constantly. That meant a lot then and still does." He regularly shared his gift packages with fellow soldiers, many of whom got little or nothing from home.

He also shared his letters from home and from Jeanne. "I

think I might have been the only unmarried guy who didn't get a 'Dear John' letter during those months. Some of the married ones got them, too. So it was important for me to share Jeanne's letters. The guys needed something. If you weren't there, you just can't understand it."

His diary shows that on February 7, 1945, Rauch was offered a nine-day pass to England but turned it down because the trip would have meant crossing the English Channel twice. He didn't want to get seasick again.

Among the many sad notes in his diary was one dated February 27, 1945. That day, while fighting on the front lines, he learned that his good friend and Duke fraternity brother Bob Backer of Greensboro was missing in action.

Backer and Rauch had entered the Air Corps on the same day and had begun air cadet training together. They had been separated for more than a year; Backer had remained in the air unit after Rauch was transferred to the infantry. Backer had been killed the previous fall, in September 1944, but it took more than four months for the mail to reach Rauch in France.

The journal entry for that day reads:

Feb. 27: Got word that Bob Backer was reported missing in action.

Rauch later would learn that Backer had been flying over German marshland when his engine failed. He and four other soldiers parachuted out. The other four were rescued, and Backer's chute and helmet were located, but his body was never found.

In Backer's memory, his mother in Greensboro commissioned Winston-Salem artist Joe King to paint a portrait of Backer, which she cherished and hung in her home until her death. The portrait later was donated to Elon College by Backer's younger brother, Dick.

When Rauch wasn't in combat, he spent time searching for food through either barter or theft. He swapped government-provided soap and the cigarettes his father sent (even though he was a non-smoker) to French civilians for eggs, guns, and fur jackets. "It's hard to believe, but those guys were giving up guns and heavy coats for cigarettes," Rauch remembered. "They seemed addicted, even then." Other diary entries detailed the life and the fighting:

March 9: Heavy artillery. Spent half the day on my stomach and face in the mud crawling in ditches and fox-holes.

March 16: Off front lines again.

March 20: Got big meal. Ate three steaks, two bowls of soup, eight eggs, and two eclairs.

March 28: Went to Blaine. Got first hot shower since December 1944. That felt real good.

April 7: Went to a rest area where we found real eggs, not the powdered ones. I ate 17 fried eggs for breakfast, a company record. Found stray dog. Named him Gene (in honor of Jeanne).

April 15: Got word of death of FDR. Paused for a few minutes of silence in his memory. Hoped war would soon be over.

April 18: Fighting heavy. Helped carry wounded off lines. Asked for extra artillery and was told it was too expensive. Enemy cannon fire was 50 yards behind our advancing troops.

April 27: Germans within 40 yards. We were hit with heavy fire. I was lying in mud, very nervous. I made a deal with God that if he would let me live and get me out of there I would wear my mezuzah [a Jewish symbol signifying one God] around my neck the rest of my life. [Rauch still wears a mezuzah today. So do each of his sons, and each time he learns one of them needs a new one, he gives them his and gets another.]

May 2: Got more packages from home and from Jeanne. Alberto Esqueda (Army buddy) up for Silver and Bronze Stars for combat. Rocky Pyle (another buddy) up for being out of uniform. I was up for refusing to get out of my sack.

When the Germans formally surrendered at 1600 hours on

May 10, 1945, Rauch was at Lorient, a seaport on the southern coast of Brittany. He wrote in his diary: "Left front lines of combat for last time. What a wonderful feeling."

Rauch still possesses photographic essays of what his Black Panther unit of the 66th Division endured in that dreadful winter of 1945. The pictures are heartwarming, but what they don't show are the long, cold, arduous days of battle. Personal discomfort, pain, and danger can't be easily photographed.

But May 10, 1945, was clearly an eventful day for Rauch and all Allied troops. Good had triumphed over evil. As the pictorial essay of the Black Panthers shows, the German attempt to hold onto the empire the Nazis had carved out of a peaceful world had failed. The victory had been costly in terms of human lives lost and property destroyed, but at last peace was at hand, at least in Europe.

The killing was over, but Rauch's military service was not. Although he had accumulated enough points to be sent home— based on time in the military, time in combat, and medals earned —it would be another ten months before he would see his beloved family. Another reminder of the way the Army worked.

When they left Lorient and St. Nazaire, the Black Panthers were herded like cattle onto a train of freight cars, thirty men to a car. The manure encrusted on inside walls was evidence that cattle had recently been in the cars. Each carload of soldiers was given a five-gallon can of water. Food was Army K-rations and C-rations. The wood floor was the soldiers' bed.

"I remember the train stopping several times along the way," Rauch recalled. "Each time 500 or more men would hop off and relieve themselves. That was better than having to urinate one or two at a time through the open doors as the train moved."

The troop train passed through France en route to Belgium where, Rauch recalled, the first sights were "complete devastation" as the trip continued on to Boppard, Germany, on the west bank of the Rhine River, south of Koblenz.

"The people of Boppard seemed well fed and clothed," Rauch said. "But there were no men, just women and children. The men had all been at war, and everywhere there were graves with crosses and helmets hanging on top." It was one more vivid reminder of the reality of war.

On May 28, Rauch ate his first hot meal in weeks, but he was anxiously awaiting mail from home. None had arrived since before he had left the front lines.

From Western Germany, the Black Panthers were moved south to the splendid city of Marseille, France, on the Mediterranean Sea — heaven compared to the war zones. The troops realized, however, that they were about to be sent to the Pacific Theater for combat against Japan.

Among Rauch's duties in Marseille was to help guard German war prisoners. He took a leadership role in ensuring discipline when the war prisoners were refusing to follow orders. "They were sullen and wouldn't do what they were assigned," Rauch said. "I guess my Jewish presence put some anxiety in them. This group kept insisting they were not Nazis, but all German prisoners said that under those circumstances. However, they followed orders quickly when I pretended to be upset."

On August 16, 1945, word came that the war had ended in the Pacific—Japan had surrendered. "But there was little immediate celebration. Most of us didn't believe it was true," Rauch said. "Later, when we did realize it was over, you couldn't imagine what went on. All our ammo was supposed to have been turned in, but everyone had hidden cases of it. That night the sky was lit up by tracers like I had never seen before."

He was ready and eligible to go home, but the Army had other ideas. There were too many troops preparing to leave. The Army couldn't handle them all at once, and, according to the military, there was still work to be done in Europe.

For Rauch, there was something to be done, all right, but at the time he didn't consider it work. He was again assigned to a military football team and volunteered for an Army swimming team, which had a meet scheduled in Paris. His swimming coach was Bill McDonald. Rauch thought at the time McDonald was just another soldier looking for post-war relaxation in France. He soon learned differently. McDonald was, in fact, an All-American diver from Iowa State University.

"But we didn't know that about him," Rauch said. "We thought he was just one of the guys. He was always willing to help any of us. He never mentioned he was such a great diver. He never bragged like the rest of us did. The thing is, we bragged but weren't worth a damn as swimmers. He never said anything and turned out to be great."

McDonald won the Paris swim meet. Rauch and his other military buddies, not surprisingly, didn't place. "But I had a great time. It was a good trip," Rauch said. The adventure lasted more than two weeks in July. He spent the remainder of the summer and fall playing team sports and entertaining himself with trips to scenic sights in France and Italy.

His diary shows he made a trip to Spain for a basketball game,

The 222nd Infantry basketball team in Vienna, Austria in January 1946.
(Rauch is wearing jersey number 10.)

but it was a trip that the Army didn't sanction. When he returned to Marseille, he was given a choice: thirty days confinement or possible court martial for being AWOL. Rauch opted for confinement, figuring it wouldn't make much difference in what he was able to do. He was right.

In September, Rauch had a surprise meeting with a neighborhood friend from Woodmere, New York. The friend,

Charles Marquessee, was in the Navy. His unit was stationed nearby. Rauch visited Marquessee on his ship and ate a turkey dinner, the first turkey he had tasted since leaving the United States the previous year. Rauch also accepted a gift of several of Marquessee's white T-shirts. It had been months since he had seen or worn a white T-shirt.

"That visit convinced me of the tremendous difference between life on a big ship and in the infantry. Certainly there were dangers in both places," Rauch said, "but the Navy guys had good food and sheets and laundry. The Navy had life a lot more civilized than foot soldiers."

Rauch actively practiced his religion during those dull days. His diary entries showed he celebrated both Rosh Hashanah and Yom Kippur during September.

Rauch saw little chance of getting home in the fall of 1945, so he accepted assignment to yet another Army football team. The games were played in Vienna, where he met another Woodmere friend, Arthur Rittmaster Jr., who was there with his Army unit. Rittmaster and Rauch had been pals growing up on Long Island. Rittmaster later became a successful stockbroker and, since retiring, moved to the coastal section of North Carolina. He and Marshall are still friends.

Marshall Rauch and his dog "G.I." in Vienna, Austria in late 1945. G.I. came home with him from World War II.

"It was great," Rauch said of his Vienna experience. "All we did was play football. There were no officers over us, just coaches. The head coach was named Gaskins, a former halfback at the University of Georgia. The only thing we had to do was get up, practice, and be there for the games. We got regular rations and actually lived in real homes with hot showers. We didn't have sheets on the beds, but we had blankets. There was no bed check and no curfew. It was real luxury compared to what we had been having."

The first game was on October 7. Rauch's team won 14-0. Rauch scored a touchdown on a twenty-yard run. Their defense did not allow the opposition a single first down. Victory on the football field was far easier than in the battlefield. Rauch's teams usually won handily, and, not infrequently, he and his buddies would bet on the outcome.

"We never shaved points, but we did play harder at times than at other times depending on what we needed in a score to win our bets. Generally, everybody on the team bet everything they had on the games."

Rauch kept his dog Gene, a stray he had adopted, with him on the football excursion, just as he would later. The sports activity lasted through the remainder of the year, but Rauch's diary entries stopped for awhile. He doesn't recall why, but suspected it was because life was not presenting any obstacles or anything unusual.

Football was over in early February 1946, and the Army promised Rauch and the other players they'd be sent home when the games ended. It didn't happen. More broken Army promises. After another month, mostly spent playing basketball, the military brass relented. By the end of February, Rauch began processing to go home.

Even that wasn't easy. The day he was scheduled to leave Austria, February 29, 1946, he was ill with flu, too sick even to walk. His football buddies wouldn't leave him behind. They packed his gear and literally carried him to the Army truck that would take them to the next town. They brought Gene along, too. Rauch resumed his diary notes at this point.

The troops were scheduled to leave Austria on March 8 and sail for the United States on March 18. Then, unexpected and unexplained, a decision was made to delay their departure until March 11. "There was much bitching and moaning," Rauch wrote in his diary, "but that's the way the Army works."

Rauch left for Reid, Austria, on March 11 and was thrown in with a new batch of soldiers, most of whom he didn't know. The first day was memorable. While he was taking a shower, a few of his buddies from the Black Panther unit insisted he quickly come, buck naked, to the cot where he had left his clothes.

There he found his dog, whose name Rauch had changed to G.I. when he left Vienna, teeth showing amid fierce growling, holding several strange soldiers at bay in the corner of the room. The soldiers had attempted to go through Rauch's pants pockets. G.I. had protected his belongings, just as Rauch knew he would.

On March 18, Rauch sailed for America and spent the next ten days on a Liberty ship headed for New York City and a joyous reunion with his family. The Army wouldn't allow the dog G.I. on the ship, so Rauch arranged to have the dog sent home on a different ship. The rough seas got to Rauch on the trip home, just as they had on the trip over. He was seasick most of the way and ate only three meals in ten days. He has avoided ships ever since.

"I will never forget seeing the Statue of Liberty as we arrived at New York," Rauch said. "What a wonderful thing to see as we came in. It was a very emotional moment, and the memory of it still is. My mother and father were there to meet me as were Jeanne and my grandparents and my sister."

Tears came to Rauch's eyes and his voice choked as he recalled that reunion. "To me that moment was pure joy," he said, "but at age eighty-one, I now realize what it must have been like for parents and grandparents like mine to have sent a boy off to war, the love they must have felt after all the anguish and worry and sleepless nights to see him come back in one piece.

"I get very emotional just thinking about it. My sister told me one of the reasons my mother worked as a volunteer every day in the hospital was to increase the chances that I would come home safely."

When he felt the embrace of his family, he stepped into a new phase of life. It was at that very moment, in fact, that Jeanne suggested the date for their wedding, which he readily accepted. The wedding took place a month later, on May 18, 1946.

A week later, G.I. arrived in a shipping crate. He became part of the family, too. G.I. lived with Marshall and Jeanne Rauch for another ten years.

From these experiences in the war, Rauch maintained warm and lasting friendships. In 1996, he invited three of his Army buddies who shared his combat experience in France for a long weekend reunion at his summer home at the Elk River Country Club in Banner Elk in the mountains of western North Carolina.

"We had a wonderful time and did a lot of reminiscing," Rauch recalled. Present were Rocky Pyle of Chicago, John McDonnell of Detroit, and John Calvert

Marshall Rauch (right) with two of his World War II army buddies, Rocky Pyle and John McDonnell

World War II Army buddies (from left) John Calvert, Marshall Rauch, Rocky Pyle, and John McDonnell at a reunion in 1997 at Elk River Club, Banner Elk, North Carolina, fifty-one years after their infantry service together

of Morehead, Kentucky, and their wives Norma, Jeanne, and Joyce. "It was great to see them and visit after all these years," Rauch said. "They're all great guys, but the four of us had not been together since the war in France. It was great to reminisce, sitting up until 3 a.m. talking and just being thankful."

As a practical joke, Rauch also arranged for the chef at the country club to prepare a special meal for his Army buddies. The meal was creamed chipped beef on toast, a delicacy commonly known among soldiers as S.O.S. (short for S—t on a Shingle) "I arranged for the chef to serve that meal formally on dinner plates with silver covers," Rauch said. "Everyone got a real kick out of that dinner, because in the Army we ate that meal many, many times. A piece of dry toast was thrown onto the mess kit, and some cook would slap a ladle full of creamed chipped beef on top of it. The Elk River Country Club had never before and probably never will again serve S.O.S. But that one night, it was great."

When the trio left for home after that weekend, McDonnell and Pyle wrote in Rauch's copy of the book detailing the torpedo attack on the *Leopoldville* their expression of appreciation for the reunion. "It has been a fantastic reunion. We love you," said the message signed by the pair. Calvert didn't write a message, but he made his feelings of appreciation known. "He told me no one had ever treated him like I did," Rauch said. "That made it more than worthwhile."

War may be hell, but it also produces lasting friendships, as the reunion of those four old soldiers verified.

Chapter 7
First Lessons in Business

In those first years of the business, Marshall would leave home at 5 a.m. in order to build a fire to heat the building before the weavers showed up for work. Later, although he was happy working for my brothers, he was determined to start his own business and make it successful. He has done that through hard work and perseverance.

Jeanne Rauch, describing her husband's early business years.

When Marshall Rauch was returning from Europe and service in the Army in 1946, he had every intention of returning to Duke and resuming his basketball and academic career. But when he saw Jeanne Girard standing with his parents, sister, and grandparents at the dock in New York City, he knew that marriage would be the first item on his agenda.

Jeanne, his first real love, was just as pretty as she was the first day he saw her sitting in the stands at a Duke basketball game. They agreed within moments of his stepping off the troop ship and onto American soil that they would be married a month later. The wedding, attended by a large gathering of Rauch and Girard family members, was held at Gaston Country Club. With money his parents provided, he took his bride on a honeymoon to Bermuda.

Still, they intended to return to Duke, where Marshall would get his undergraduate degree and Jeanne would pursue a master's degree. They rented an apartment in Durham near the Duke campus. Former Coach Eddie Cameron had promised that Rauch would be welcomed back to the basketball team. Coach Gerry Gerard had moved up to become varsity coach, and a new era of basketball glory was beginning at Duke.

But marriage brought a new perspective to the newly wed Rauches. Jeanne's brothers, Cy and Herbert Girard, ran a textile mill in Bessemer City, southwest of Charlotte. They felt their new brother-in-law ought to join the world of work rather than score points for a university basketball team.

Their offer to their new relative of a job in their mill at a starting salary of $60 a week was what Rauch considered too good to turn down. An annual salary of $3,120 was irresistible to a young man who was ready to settle down with a new bride and start a family. At the time, a college degree didn't seem as important.

Thus began a long and rewarding lifetime of business experience. Despite Rauch's strong work ethic, success didn't come without disappointments and failures along the way. Further, Rauch still regrets not having earned the Duke degree. However, for the young veteran and his bride, joining the world of work seemed the best decision at the time.

Although a salary of $60 a week (more than triple his Army pay, not counting the frequent poker winnings) seemed like big money to Rauch and his new bride, they agreed they couldn't afford a home on that income. When Jeanne's mother, the widow of the founder of the textile plant now run by her sons, invited them to live in her home, they also decided they would not waste money on rent.

"Jeanne's mother, Sadie Goldberg, was a truly wonderful woman," Rauch said. "She wanted us to save money, so we lived with her for a year, along with Jeanne's brother, Herbert, and his new wife, Phyllis. The four of us had a fantastic year with Sadie, who provided all kinds of food and care. She was the greatest cook and devoted herself to making us all comfortable."

As Rauch was about to begin work with his brothers-in-law, a new opportunity presented itself. He met Dick McPhail, who was looking for someone to help him start a small weaving company. McPhail had a textile degree but needed a partner. He and Rauch each invested $2,500 to start production. Rauch, who borrowed money for his share of the investment, wanted the chance to learn, and his brothers-in-law agreed to delay his starting to work with them. Each drawing salaries of $60 a week, Rauch and McPhail launched their fledging business, Finer Fabrics.

The beginning was something less than auspicious. Rauch

and Mcphail purchased four used C&K looms to weave upholstery fabric, and the two partners—with two employees— opened their weaving operation in an aged, 2,000-square-foot building. "I had no knowledge of what the upholstery business was all about, but I just jumped in and started to work," Rauch explained.

His investment in the company amounted to both money and sweat. Among his early duties at Finer Fabrics was to arrive early on the winter mornings, build a fire in the pot-bellied stove to heat the building before the two workers and McPhail arrived. The four men struggled to keep the business going.

Soon Rauch and McPhail realized that they wouldn't be able to succeed at producing fabric. They switched to become fabric distributors, first sending out sample books and, after getting an order from an upholsterer whose customer wanted a specific material, shipping small quantities of material for a single chair or couch. The business grew slowly, but also slowly became profitable.

Success aside, however, both Rauch and McPhail agreed this was not the business they wanted to stay in full time, but neither did they want to close it down. Instead, they agreed to keep the business going, but hired one person, George Fraser, to handle the entire sampling, receiving, and shipping of merchandise.

"We came to realize that the financial rewards were not commensurate with the efforts we were expending," Rauch said. For several, Rauch and McPhail continued to run Finer Fabrics as a sideline. They changed its name to Luxury Fabrics before McPhail bought Rauch's interest. Luxury Fabrics remains in the McPhail family and still operates in Gastonia as a successful supplier of upholstery materials to manufacturers and retail customers.

With the Finer Fabrics experience behind him, Rauch then joined his in-laws' business. He worked the 6 a.m. shift at the same $60 a week he had been promised the year before. The early hours didn't bother him, but that schedule was just the beginning of some very long days, weeks, and years of hard work. Rauch worked in the mill from 6 a.m. until 2 p.m. and then drove to the nearby Belmont Textile School to attend classes from

3 p.m. until early evening.

His wife's brothers treated him fairly, but they didn't cut him any slack simply because he was married to their sister or because he was devoting extra hours to classes. They insisted he learn all aspects of the business, go to school after regular working hours, and gain practical experience in different sections of the production process at their Algodon Manufacturing Company, Inc. Algodon also operated another company, Central Yarn and Dying Company, in nearby Gastonia.

Rauch proved to his in-laws that he could learn and was capable of accepting additional responsibilities. Cy and Herbert Girard agreed to make Rauch their purchasing agent and also let him handle sales to two major customers, Hickory Fabrics, in nearby Catawba County, makers of upholstery material, and Hooker & Sanders, in New York, which marketed crochet thread. One of the major products Algodon turned out was crochet yarn, an item that later would precipitate a major change in Rauch's life.

In the first year after joining Algodon, the Rauches welcomed their first child into the world. Ingrid Rauch was born December 18, 1947. That's when Marshall received his first $20 a week pay increase, up to $80 a week. "I got the raise not because I was worth any more, but because I had a new daughter," Rauch said. Also at that time Rauch was playing semi-pro basketball for a team called the Charlotte Clippers, which provided additional income for expenses incurred by the expanding family.

With his new salary and a new daughter, Marshall and Jeanne Rauch decided it was time to become homeowners. They purchased their first home at 110 North Belvedere Drive in Gastonia. That first home had two bedrooms and only slightly more than 1,000 square feet of living space. Rauch bought that home in early 1948 for $9,500 with a G.I. loan and a $500 down payment. The loan rate was 4 percent and mortgage payments were $54.54 a month.

"It was a brick house without a central heating system and no air conditioning, but it was our home," Rauch said with obvious pride. That amount of money going to a mortgage was scary at the time, but Rauch decided the risk of such a debt was worth it because he felt that a working man with a family ought to own a home. That mortgage was the first debt Marshall Rauch incurred. Little did he know how many more debts would come or how large some of them might become.

After securing his mortgage, Rauch worked to secure more business for his in-laws' textile plant in hopes of increasing his own earnings. That was when he got his first lesson in business negotiations, an experience that was traumatic at the time but that later paid handsome dividends.

Each week Algodon shipped crochet manufacturer Hooker & Sanders thousands of pounds of heavy, four-ply, dyed crochet yarn. Hooker & Sanders, in turn, rewound the thread on balls and sold it through variety stores to women who crocheted bedspreads and other things. Because they were such large buyers, officials at Hooker & Sanders asked Rauch to cut Algodon's price a penny a pound, from 60 cents to 59 cents. Without the price reduction, Rauch was warned, he might lose the next contract. Rauch explained his conflict at the time:

> I thought they were bluffing. I knew that every inch of crochet thread went through the fingers of women everywhere in the country, and I didn't think Hooker & Sanders would risk not having our same quality thread available. The women who used our thread were accustomed to it, and I just didn't believe Hooker & Sanders would risk giving up what their customers wanted. They told me they could get thread for a penny a pound less and wanted me to meet that price. I refused. I went to [brother-in-law] Cy, who was our sales manager, and told him about the problem. He told me to handle it, but not to lose the account. Hooker & Sanders kept insisting on a lower price. Cy and Herbert both told me to do what I thought was best, but not to lose the account.

Deciding he could be as hard-nosed as his large customer about a contract price that he badly needed but felt was safe, Rauch held firm. Hooker & Sanders officials showed they were serious and refused to pay the 60 cents a pound. "And we lost the account," Rauch recalled. "I was absolutely devastated."

He didn't feel sorry for himself for long. "I thought it over and decided I ought to try to take a bad situation and turn it into something good," he said. He did just that. "As it turned out, losing that contract was one of the best things that ever happened to me."

Rauch had seen the Hooker & Sanders plant in New York and knew it was small. "Basically all they did was take our different color-dyed yarns, wind them on balls, and package and label them for sale to stores," he explained. "I decided I could do that and I could make a lot more money by selling the yarn myself than selling it through them. There was more profit in it for me if I did it myself."

At about the same time, Rauch decided he had worked for his brothers-in-law long enough. He was itching to try his own business again. He had learned a great deal from Cy and Herbert, whom he credits with teaching him the essentials of business. He was certainly more knowledgeable than he had been six years earlier when he and McPhail had struggled with their upholstery fabric operation.

"I told Cy and Herbert that I would like to start out on my own," Rauch said. He and Jeanne were still in that tiny $9,500 home but had a second child on the way. A son, Marc, was born May 28, 1949. They needed more space. By then Marshall was making a salary of $15,000 a year at Algodon and thought he could risk starting over in business again.

The family purchased its second home on the same street, at 1111 South Belvedere Drive. That house had more than twice the space of the first home. Their children had separate bedrooms, but the greatest convenience was a central heating system. The second house cost $21,000, more than double the purchase price of the first.

In the spring of 1952, Rauch founded Pyramid Mills, the forerunner to Rauch Industries, and became a private business owner. Small and under-capitalized, to call its beginning a struggle would be an understatement. But over time it would change and grow. With hard work and a lot of help from friends, Rauch made Pyramid Mills successful beyond even his most optimistic expectations. He and thousands of others have been the beneficiaries.

102

Chapter 8
Pyramid Mills

There is no such thing as a self-made man. Anybody who is successful has gotten a lot of help. That's certainly true in my case.

Marshall Rauch, on starting his own businesses.

Marshall Rauch's decision to start his own business was, in a sense, forced on him. He had to find a market and a means to make up for the loss of the Hooker & Sanders contract for crochet yarn. But his timing was poor and his financial resources were thin. Even starting small, Rauch knew he had a struggle ahead.

Further, he had just moved into a larger house, doubled his mortgage payments, and now had three children to feed on a $15,000 annual salary. His third child and second son, Peter, was born September 30, 1952.

"I was determined but cautious," Rauch said. Seeking a safety net, he asked his in-laws if he could keep his job at Algodon Mills and start his own business at night in his spare time. They said yes. Even so, he was short on capital and had no equipment. Call it determination or call it stubbornness: he wouldn't give up the dream of having his own business.

To get capital, he arranged for a second mortgage of $3,500 on his home, using the money to buy labels, boxes, yarn cores, and other supplies. The Girard brothers-in-law rented him a 5,000-square-foot building and extended him credit for dyed yarn. They also told him about their friend Jake Gray who owned some well worn, but workable, ball-winding machines.

"My brothers-in-law wanted me to succeed and extended me far more credit than I deserved," Rauch said. "They supplied yarn on extended terms until I could get the money to pay for it. I will forever be indebted to them for what they taught me and how they helped me get started."

Jake Gray also was willing to help without immediate compensation. "He just let me borrow three ball winders, because I explained to him I didn't have any way to pay. He said I could pay him when I made some money. That's how it all began."

Rauch started with three borrowed machines, working at night in his in-laws' Bessemer City building, which they leased to him for $50 a month. He hired three employees, the most important of whom was Robert Stroup, who was experienced in crochet-yarn manufacturing.

His brothers-in-law gave him time off from Algodon to travel around looking for customers. "I had never even seen any of the customers I wanted to sell to," Rauch said. "I really didn't know the industry at that point." He didn't let his potential customers know how small his business was or how few resources he had.

The selection of the name Pyramid Mills is an example of Rauch's ingenuity. "We had so little going that I didn't want anyone outside to know how tiny we were," he explained. "I picked the name Pyramid because it sounded impressive—big, old, and established. I thought that might help me make some sales if customers thought Pyramid was something really substantial. It worked. The business began to take off. We made a few sales right away."

Rauch was able to pay his three employees, but at the beginning he didn't take any salary for himself because he still was working at Algodon. Pyramid ran on a shoestring for two years, barely making ends meet with token sales volumes. Rauch himself comprised the entire Pyramid management, sales, and janitorial staff. As sales gradually increased, Rauch was convinced he could make a go of a full-time business.

In 1956, Rauch left Algodon and began full-time work at Pyramid, paying himself an annual salary of $10,400. That was 33 percent less than his in-laws had been paying him, but he was on his own and was convinced things would get better. He was right, but he had a cushion then, too.

"The person who really gave me the courage to try it on my own by leaving Algodon was another brother-in-law, Clarence Ross," Rauch said. Ross was married to Jeanne's sister, Ethel. He also had worked for Algodon before starting his own business. "He told me I'd have a job with him at $15,000 a year any time I wanted it if my business didn't succeed," Rauch said.

"He strongly advised me to just get out there and get started. I'm sure my in-laws at Algodon would have said the same thing if I had asked them. So, at that point, there was no reason not to proceed. I owe a great debt to my wife's family who taught me the textile business, extended their kindness, and gave me the opportunity to make a go of my own business. I couldn't have done it without them."

As it turned out, Rauch didn't need the safety net his relatives offered. In fact, it never occurred to him that he actually might fail. He was too determined. Also he had some special assistance.

When Rauch left Algodon, he arranged through his in-laws to take two key people with him. One was Wade Fowler, the company's night supervisor and self-taught engineer who would

The first home of Marshall and Jeanne Rauch in December 1947 in Gastonia, 110 N. Belvedere Avenue, as he began his business of manufacturing crochet thread and kite string

become a major reason Pyramid was able to expand and become so successful. Fowler was a valued friend and adviser until his death in early 1967.

The other key player was Louise Fortenbery Beane, Rauch's secretary at Algodon. She still works with Rauch in 2004 as a part-time secretary and capable right hand for the entire family. Rauch says Beane can do anything he can do, and likely do it better.

When Rauch started at Algodon in 1946, he went to the local high school principal and asked for the name of the smartest student who had graduated the previous year. That student was Louise Fortenbery, who at the time was working up to fifty-seven hours a week at Smith's Variety Store in Bessemer City at a salary of $30 a week. Rauch promised her fewer hours and a raise of $7.50 a week to $37.50. She accepted.

By the end of the first year of full-time operation, gross sales at Pyramid Mills shocked Rauch by climbing to more than $250,000. The company showed a net profit its first year of $9,040. Those profits meant that Rauch could pay Jake Gray $3,000 for the winding machines he had borrowed more than a year earlier.

By the end of 1957, Pyramid sales had almost doubled to $464,000 and Rauch moved quickly to branch out. He wanted to open a dye plant so he could produce his own colored crochet yarn.

He was later forced to relocate the dyeing outside Bessemer City because that city's sewage facilities couldn't handle the volume of wastewater that Rauch anticipated his plant would generate. That turned out to be Rauch's first of several problems with waste-treatment plants and environmental issues. Later problems in that area would be far worse and more costly to solve.

When Rauch started his dyeing operation in 1957, he needed a boiler. He didn't have enough capital for a new one, so again he went shopping for used equipment. Two friends, Bonnie Norris and Bud Gray, had a well-worn boiler that would serve his needs.

"I told them I couldn't pay them immediately," Rauch recalled, "but they said not to worry. They'd talk with me before they billed me. I didn't hear from Norris and Gray for more than two years. Then they asked if I thought I could begin paying them. By that time, I could. That's the way we got the boiler and were able to get the dye plant up and running. It wasn't easy and it wasn't efficient at first, but it worked."

Rauch and Fowler also found and dismantled a used dryer they needed to start the dyeing operation. They painted the parts with matching numbers and colors so they would be able to put it back together at the Pyramid dye plant.

The price of getting that phase of the business going was pocket change by 1990s standards, but at the time it was big money for Rauch. The total cost was a little more than $2,500. That included the 40-horsepower, high-pressure boiler and lines for water, steam, and gas.

The new business continued to increase as more retail chains were accepting the jumbo packages of crochet thread that Pyramid specialized in producing. The process for winding and packaging crochet thread also was used to develop twine products for wrapping packages. Rauch's wife Jeanne came up with the idea of selling wrapping cord in a large plastic vial with a metal cutter cap, like dental floss, to make it easier for customers to use.

Rauch also entered the men and boys' market by selling kite cord, but not just any kite cord. Primarily with the engineering genius of Fowler, they designed a spool for the kite cord that made handling the string easier and more popular.

"Kids didn't have to wrap their cord around a stick any more," Rauch said. His kite string spool was large enough to hold in both hands while flying kites. Sales of kite cord climbed along with the volume of crochet thread.

The dyeing plant also was flourishing, but Rauch saw a niche for waste material from hosiery mills. He bought leftover loopers (the name for a hosiery waste), dyed them bright colors, and marketed them for use on small, simple looms on which potholders could be hand woven. Those looms and loopers became extremely popular among children and helped to increase Pyramid's profits.

Crochet thread was still the big seller as Rauch continued to work hard to make sales, often putting in as many as eighteen hours a day handling sales, bookkeeping, and manufacturing. He also continued to sweep floors. He steadily added to the production staff and by 1958 had fourteen workers on the Pyramid payroll.

By 1959, Rauch had bought out a small crochet-thread competitor in Philadelphia for $4,000 and a looper competitor in Brooklyn for $6,000. Basically all he bought in each instance was a list of customers, inventory, and the hope that he would get the additional sales volume for himself.

Rauch drove to Philadelphia in a rented truck to pick up the inventory and machinery of the competitor he purchased. All the machines wouldn't fit on the truck, but he didn't want to make another trip because the leftover equipment was of little value. To make sure no one would be able to salvage any parts he didn't haul away, Rauch personally used a sledgehammer to smash the leftover winders into small pieces of scrap iron.

Business boomed. By the close of the 1950s, Rauch's company had grown to thirty employees and made a profit of $24,000 after paying himself a salary of $25,000. Brighter days still lay ahead. Word of Rauch's business acumen spread as his sales volumes grew, and people came to him asking for his help in their own business.

Jim Hamrick, a Charlotte electrician, asked Rauch to develop a special nylon line that could be blown with air pressure through a conduit for electrical work. Again, with Fowler's ability, they did it. Hamrick patented the process and founded Jet Line Products, a company that marketed the nylon line.

Again seeing potential for profits, Rauch reinvested the money Hamrick had paid him for the nylon in Jet Line stock, which quickly rose in value. "I made a lot of money out of that," Rauch recalled. "So did Hamrick."

Rauch and Hamrick are still friends, although neither has any remaining ties to Jet Line. Hamrick sold the company and opened a golf course in Kings Mountain. In 1990, Hamrick helped Rauch design and develop a Moravian Star as part of the line of Christmas merchandise produced by Rauch Industries.

By the end of the 1950s, Rauch felt comfortable financially

and contracted to build a new home. In addition to his three children, the family had welcomed a fourth child. John White, a Gastonia teenager, was taken into the Rauch home in the middle of the 1950s and became a member of the family. White is not Jewish, but his religious faith has never been a problem in the Rauch household.

One more child would be born later, but the Rauch household had already become too large for the Belvedere Avenue house. In 1960, the family built a new, brick, two-story house containing 5,500-square-feet at a cost of $70,000. The contractor was Roy Barnes, who would later build the Rauch Industries plant. The home and manufacturing plant were built with no written contract, only a handshake and verbal agreement between Rauch and Barnes.

The new home at 1121 Scotch Drive was luxurious compared to the family's earlier residences. "It was wonderful," Rauch said.

Pyramid Mills (predecessor of Rauch Industries) Christmas Party at Helen's Restaurant in Bessemer City in 1960. Wade Fowler, plant manager and developer of the satin Christmas ornament, is first person on left. Louise Beane, who is still Marshall Rauch's administrative assistant, is in the far back right-hand corner. Marshall Rauch is to her right.

"It had all kinds of room for the children and it was air conditioned—the first house we had ever had with central air conditioning."

Rauch later built his present home and sold the Scotch Drive residence to his son Peter and his family, who still live there.

Throughout those successful early years, Rauch was primitive in his recordkeeping. He still smiles now when he pulls out some of his early financial files consisting of plain yellow legal paper on which he drew penciled lines for keeping up with salaries, inventories, and accounts receivable.

"I did it that way for a long time, because it's the only way I knew how and it worked," he said. As business continued to expand, however, he hired accountants to handle the records. The success of the early 1960s was just the beginning of the rewards that would follow in the ensuing twenty years.

"I've really been lucky," Rauch said. "That's why I say there is no such thing as a self-made man. Everybody has a lot of help. Teamwork is essential. I certainly had that. I had my father and mother, brothers-in-law, and the generous and timely help from friends and suppliers. They all helped me prosper. Without them, I couldn't have succeeded the way I have."

Some of Rauch's best luck started in the spring of 1963, with some help he never could have predicted. During one otherwise routine day, Rauch received an unexpected phone call from a stranger. That day turned into anything but routine.

The caller initially identified himself only as "Bill"—with no last name. His call became a major turning point in the life of Pyramid Mills and its successor, Rauch Industries. Sometimes in business—as in life—events take unexpected turns. That stranger's telephone call was one of those twists for Marshall Rauch.

Chapter 9
From Crochet to Christmas

Plan your work and work your plan.

Henson Barnes, former president pro-tem
of the North Carolina Senate.

When he was founding Pyramid Mills and Rauch Industries in the 1950s and 1960s, Marshall Rauch didn't know Henson Barnes. Their friendship came later, after both men had achieved positions of power and influence in the North Carolina legislature. But as Rauch thought back over the success of his business ventures, he was struck by how closely his practices in the early years of his manufacturing operations had foreshadowed the advice he would later get from Barnes in the state legislature.

Rauch planned his work well and worked his plan effectively. He also had the wisdom and pluck to take advantage of opportunities that came his way. He had an abundance of common sense, some old-fashioned good luck, and a lot of help from friends.

Luck is said to be the point at which good preparation coincides with opportunity. The dictionary defines *opportunity* as "a favorable juncture of events leading to a good chance for advancement or progress." In his early years in business, Rauch enjoyed both good luck and inviting opportunities. His careful preparation and the circumstances he created for himself fell into place in such a way that he was able to make progress beyond even his fondest dreams.

By the 1960s, after more than a dozen years in a yarn business focused on crochet thread and kite cord, Marshall and Jeanne Rauch thought things were going quite well. Both the family and the business were growing. On December 2, 1961, a

111

fifth child and second daughter, Stephanie, was born to join sons John, Marc, and Peter and daughter Ingrid.

With a family that size, the new home on Scotch Drive was certainly an added benefit for comfortable living and ample space for the children to play. Rauch and his family were happy with that home, having built it to fit their needs.

But its location wasn't their first choice. The lot they really wanted was for sale, but the owner made it clear he did not want to sell to Rauch, who feels the reason was because he was a Jew. Such religious discrimination was distasteful, but rather than protest the family chose an alternative site on Scotch Drive.

As the family grew, so did Rauch's duties and responsibilities with his businesses. Pyramid Mills was successful in large part because Rauch worked hard to make it so. He traveled one week out of every month as the company's entire sales force. When he was at the mill, he served as bookkeeper, chief executive, and floor sweeper. As business continued to expand, Rauch added staff. He couldn't do it all.

Part of his time crunch was self-imposed, however, because in those early days he never used airplanes. Flying still made him airsick, just as it did in his pilot-training days in the military. Thus, on his marketing travels, Rauch traveled by train. That meant his trips were long, but at least he stayed healthy and comfortable.

To accommodate his preferred method of travel, Rauch worked out a routine. He was on the train four consecutive nights and worked three full days in the Northeast. He took the train from Gastonia to New York City on Monday night, made a half dozen calls on customers on Tuesday and was on the night train to either Pittsburgh or Chicago by Tuesday night. On Wednesday, he worked one of those cities, and Wednesday night he was back on the train to New York City. There he called on another five customers before taking the Thursday night train back to Gastonia. He was back in his Gastonia plant each Friday morning.

After three years on that schedule, he was on a first-name basis with virtually every conductor and porter on the railroad along his routes. His major retail customers were the major five-and-dime store chains: F.W. Woolworth, S.H. Kress, W.T. Grant, McLellan, S.S. Kresge, McCrory, Ben Franklin, Silvers, H.L. Green, J.J. Newberry, G.C. Murphy, Eagle, and Roses stores. Once giants in American retailing, all were virtually out of business by the late 1990s, replaced by Kmart, Wal-Mart, and Target stores, which also became customers of Rauch Industries.

The beginning of the end of crochet thread and kite string as Pyramid Mills' principal products came in May 1963, with that phone call from the stranger named "Bill."

"Hey, Marsh, this is Bill. How you doing?" the caller said. He sounded like an old friend, but Rauch searched his memory, without success, for a clue that would identify that voice.

"Fine," Rauch responded, buying time but still not recognizing the voice. He was convinced it was someone he didn't know. Rauch was good about remembering names and voices. And even though forty years have passed, he still has no trouble remembering that fateful conversation:

Nobody I know ever called me Marsh, but I just let the fellow talk because he was very friendly. He asked how my family was, and I just said fine. He asked how my golf game was, and I said it was passable. He asked if I had been playing much gin rummy, and I said, 'Well, some.' It just went on like that. We were just talking like we were old friends although I had absolutely no idea who I was talking with. Then he said, 'Marsh, can you wind a ball?' I thought he was talking about the balls of crochet thread and balls of kite cord. So I said, 'Sure. I wind balls every day.' He said, 'Yeah, that's what I heard and I'm going to send you a sample of a ball, and if you can wind this ball, we are going to do a lot of business.' Well, I liked the sound of that. And he said he would get the sample ball right out to me. I said, 'Wait, wait, before you hang up, Bill, because you have me at a disadvantage. Which Bill is this?' He said that we had never met, and his name was Bill Spiegel from Chicago. Well, I immediately recognized that name and realized he was with the large Chicago mail-order house. Needless to say, I was excited about the chance of doing business with the Spiegel Catalog Company.

Bill Spiegel was William Spiegel Jr., son of the founder of the huge mail-order firm. The junior Spiegel owned a company operating under the name of Aldeck, which produced holiday decorations that were sold through department stores and out of the giant Spiegel catalog. Young Spiegel sent a sample satin ball to Gastonia, and Rauch knew immediately he had a problem.

Rauch had been winding crochet thread on cylindrical paper cores that fit on machines designed specifically for that purpose. Spiegel sent a hollow, round papier-mâché ball that needed a different holder as well as a different winding traverse. Rauch's machines couldn't wind the round balls.

Rauch and his plant engineer and trusted friend Wade Fowler faced the challenge together. "I showed the Spiegel ball to Mr. Fowler and told him there was a great deal of business involved if we could figure out a way to wind it," Rauch said. "Mr. Fowler just looked at it and said, 'If someone else can do it, I can do it.' At about that same moment, the phone rang and it was Spiegel." Rauch recalled:

He asked if we had seen the ball and if we could wind a ball to look like the sample he had sent. My answer was the same as Mr. Fowler's, that if someone else could do it, we could do it. We started to work on winding the fine rayon thread over a Styrofoam ball without knowing how it might work. What we didn't learn until later was that the Japanese, who had been making those ornaments, were using a one-spindle machine and traversed the thread by hand so it had a shiny parallel, satin-finished appearance.

Our machines were semi-automatic, had never done anything like that, and were not built to do anything like that. But we wanted to do it, and with Mr. Fowler's determination and ability, we eventually began to figure it out. But before that was accomplished, Spiegel kept calling me every few days asking where we were. I kept putting him off, saying we just about had it. Actually we had nothing.

In the beginning, I didn't realize the magnitude of the potential sales because I thought what we had was a piece of artificial fruit. I didn't know it was a Christmas ornament. To me, the papier-mâché ball wrapped with a shiny, red rayon thread and a velvet leaf on the top looked exactly like an artificial apple. I wasn't that experienced in the Christmas world and had no idea that what I thought was a red apple would become a large holiday industry in its own right.

As we continued trying to figure out how to manufacture what I thought was an apple, Spiegel was getting more anxious, putting pressure on me. I asked Mr. Fowler every day if he was making progress because I sure didn't want to lose that business. Every day, when Spiegel called, I put him off with promises.

After about two weeks, Mr. Fowler came to me and said he had it figured out. The idea, he said, had come to him while he was home taking his nap after lunch. He went home, ate lunch, and slept for a little while every day. He said that while he was lying down and resting, he figured out how he could change the head end of one of our machines in a way we hadn't tried before so that we would be able to wind the ball Spiegel wanted.

I said great, but then Mr. Fowler told me it would take some money to make the changes in the machines, maybe as much as $700. Well, let me tell you, in those days $700 was a lot of money. But Spiegel was pushing hard, and I had made so many promises that I had to take the chance. I told Mr. Fowler to just go ahead and spend the money if he felt it would work. That was the best $700 investment I ever made. It turned into multimillions.

It took Mr. Fowler a couple days to modify the machine by putting in some new gears and changing the ratios. But the first time he tried to run the ball it worked almost perfectly. We made three or four. I was excited. I called Spiegel and told him we had it and I would send him a sample. He said not to send him anything, because he wanted to come down and see for himself.

I should have realized at the time how important this was to him, but I didn't. But he did come down and liked what he saw. That's how we got started with what turned out to be Christmas tree ornaments, although I thought we were making artificial fruit.

Once Spiegel saw what Rauch could do, his question was no longer whether, but how many and how soon. "He wanted to know how many of those balls we could make, wrap, and send him by October. He wanted 300,000 dozen—about 3.5 million balls—for a production schedule of 30,000 a day. That sounds like a lot, and it was at the time because we were starting from zero. But I told Spiegel we could do it. I sure hoped we could."

That was sweet music to Spiegel's ears because he had been accustomed to the handmade balls from Japan, where the volume was a mere fraction of what Rauch promised to produce. Spiegel knew he had a gold mine on his hands. Rauch didn't know it at the time, but he later learned the same thing.

By comparison, it is significant that the 30,000 ornaments a day produced in 1963 climbed to more than one million a day by the time Rauch sold his company in 1996. When Rauch sold his company, he was running plants in two states and making glass and satin Christmas balls along with other holiday decorations. The goods were marketed all across the country through the nation's largest retailers.

For a while Rauch Industries also manufactured and marketed ornaments for Easter, Halloween, and Hanukkah, but those products didn't sell as well so production was halted.

Being Jewish and manufacturing ornaments for a Christian holiday has never bothered Rauch. Although friends sometimes kidded him about it, he always took such comments in stride. "Through the years when my friends questioned why I made decorations for a religious holiday I was not involved in, I just told them I felt right at home because a Jewish fellow started it all," Rauch said with a grin.

Although Rauch didn't know in the early days of collaboration with Spiegel that he was making Christmas ornaments, he did know that what he was doing was far more profitable than spinning crochet thread and kite cord. In the first year, however, he still didn't know the potential for volume or profit.

Given the volume Spiegel wanted and the profit margin, Rauch thought he had struck gold. He had been turning a profit of ten cents a dozen for rolls of kite twine. Spiegel was willing to pay considerably more, but he was a hard sell.

"He was tough," Rauch said of the early negotiations. "We went back and forth and wrangled over price. We finally reached a figure that we could both agree on. I thought I had made a really good deal."

The price they agreed on was 50 cents a dozen. Rauch had calculated his cost at 30 cents to produce each dozen balls. "I wanted 52 cents a dozen, but he wouldn't do it. But at 50 cents a dozen, the 20-cent profit was twice what we were making on crochet thread. So I agreed to that."

Soon Rauch was in for more surprises. He was still turning out crochet thread and kite cord in addition to satin decorations for Spiegel, but word had spread that Rauch was the manufacturer of Christmas ornaments that Spiegel was selling. Various retail chains came to Rauch and asked to buy the products directly from his company.

"I honestly don't know how people found out I was making the balls for Spiegel," Rauch said, "but they wanted to buy from me and they were willing to pay $2.10 a dozen because I believe that's what Spiegel was charging them. And I thought I was making money selling them to Spiegel for fifty cents a dozen when he was charging $2.10. Only then did I realize what a bargain he was getting from me. He was the one really making money. I wasn't even close."

Rauch had committed to Spiegel for a production of 3.5 million balls for the 1963 holiday season, and he never considered breaking his word. Spiegel wanted another exclusive contract from Rauch for the next season, but Rauch declined because he knew he could sell directly to retail chains and generate far more revenue for himself and his employees.

Rauch promised Spiegel the same volume, and no price increase, for the year 1964 because he realized Spiegel had put him into a great new opportunity. Rauch was gearing up to expand his production, but all additional ornaments he could produce would be sold independently. Spiegel wasn't happy with that, but he agreed because he still wanted and needed the Rauch product, on which, by that time, Rauch had applied for a patent.

Rauch was able to turn out more satin ornaments, but he couldn't market large volumes independently because he didn't have a sales staff. Then another piece of luck came his way. When Rauch and his wife Jeanne were attending a general-merchandise trade show in Chicago in the spring of 1964, a fellow he had never met stopped at his booth and introduced himself as Kurt Shindler. "He asked where I got those satin balls I had on display. I told him I made them. He then asked if I really knew what I had or what the potential was. I guess at the time I didn't really know. Then he asked if he could be a sales representative for me."

Thus began a long and profitable friendship that still exists. With his partner, Ronnie Dudwick, Shindler maintained a general merchandise sales office in the Toy Building at 200 Fifth Avenue in New York City and had contacts across the country. Rauch and Dudwick-Shindler have made handsome profits as a result of that first Chicago encounter.

Reflecting on his long association with Shindler, Rauch said that one of the smartest things he ever did in business was to take those satin ball samples to the Chicago trade show, and one of the luckiest things he ever did was meeting Shindler who in 2004 lived in retirement in Florida. Clearly, the Shindler connection ranks right up there with the phone call from Bill Spiegel in its importance to the success of Rauch's businesses. Those two Chicago connections have meant multimillions for Rauch Industries.

"Things just took off like gangbusters after I hooked up with Dudwick-Shindler," Rauch said. "Sales were outstanding." Rauch increased production of the balls, eventually completely automating the process. As a result, Rauch Industries grew into the largest Christmas ornament manufacturer in the world, and Dudwick-Shindler became the largest Christmas sales representatives. After that initial Chicago meeting, Shindler recommended hiring sales representatives to operate out of Dallas, Chicago, Minneapolis, Los Angeles, and Greensboro, North Carolina.

One indication of the trust Rauch and Shindler had in each

other from the start is that they never had a written contract. They worked together for more than thirty years with a verbal understanding between them to do the right thing in their business dealings.

"I just knew there would be a wide market for that ornament," Shindler said from his retirement home in Palm Beach Springs, Florida. "And I wanted to be a part of it. Marshall has been and remains a true friend. I am fortunate to have had that friendship and business association."

Despite the popularity of the Christmas decorations, Rauch didn't give up his other business ventures, at least not immediately. In fact, he expanded into several additional enterprises. He kept Pyramid Mills and Pyramid Dye Corporation going, but gradually turned away from crochet thread and kite cord. "You didn't have to be very smart to realize that there was a bigger profit in Christmas ornaments than there was in crochet thread," he said.

With the rising demand for Christmas ornaments, however, Rauch found he couldn't continue serving the dwindling crochet-thread market and still keep up with customer orders. He began working on new production methods to increase volume. He explained:

Once satin balls became a real product for us, we began selling about a million dozen a year. During the first eighteen months in this production, we were using Styrofoam balls, which we were purchasing from Spiegel's company Aldeck. Then we began buying expandable polystyrene balls from a company called Plasteel in Inkster, Michigan. But they were not producing enough balls to meet our needs. I went to Michigan to discuss higher volumes, but the company wasn't interested in going into overtime to provide what we needed. The only way I could get them to do it was to pay them a premium. This, of course, is just the opposite of what I thought ought to be the case. The more you buy the lower the price should be per unit, not higher. But that's the only way they would agree to increase volume. I paid the premium because we had to have the production increase immediately.

Feeling that he had to keep costs as low as possible, Rauch decided to design a system for making the expandable polystyrene balls himself, cutting out the other company. "I came home from that trip in 1965 and arranged a loan of $10,000 from my father so we could start our own small molding company. Once we could get in production, I knew that would save us money."

Given the source of the money to launch the new production process, Rauch thought it appropriate to name his new polystyrene division Narco Molding Company, in honor of his father Nathan A. Rauch, and to set up ownership in the names of his children.

Rauch could afford only one press, a Miller Van Winkle, which went off the market shortly after he purchased it. He soon learned why the Miller Van Winkle brand didn't last. "Their original mold was not properly conceived," Rauch explained, "because we ran two-inch, two-and-a-half-inch, and three-inch balls in the same mold. The inefficiency caused the cycle time to be overly long.

"That was costly, but it was still a lot less than what we had been paying for the balls we were buying from Plasteel. As soon as we could afford it, we replaced that original mold [called a 'family' mold because it ran different size balls]."

Rauch switched to Springfield H-10 presses, and production continued to increase. By 1985, Rauch had sixteen presses operating. Each press ran three shifts, twenty-four hours a day, six days a week.

Even with the giant strides in production and cost reductions, Rauch wasn't satisfied. He kept working to create further efficiencies. By 1993, the company had improved its manufacturing methods so dramatically that it was making a higher quality ball core in larger amounts with only ten presses running eight hours a day, five days a week.

"Our own staff," Rauch said proudly, "developed those increased efficiencies. That is one of the reasons why by 1995 we were by far the largest manufacturer of satin ornaments in the United States. Even low-wage foreign manufacturers could not compete with us because of our effective production techniques and the freight involved in bringing their products to this country. It was probably that process of molding and automatically winding satin ornaments, more than any single phase of our business, that earned us the 1995 North Carolina Entrepreneur of the Year Award."

With all his successes with satin balls, Rauch correctly concluded, that if satin holiday decorations were so popular, glass ornaments with bright colors would be even better sellers. He explained:

> We were very anxious to go into the glass ornament business, because we had the satin business and it was a natural for us to add glass. But we couldn't get the product because Corning was the only company in the nation making glass ornaments at that time, and they wouldn't sell to us. I asked Corning if our company could become a distributor of their glass ornaments. We had learned how to market our product and were efficient at it. Corning officials told us they felt it would not be in their best interest to sell their glass ornaments through our company. They never explained why they felt that way, but I thought I knew.

In later years, Rauch would have the last laugh. Shortly after rebuffing Rauch's offer, Corning sold its glass-ornament equipment to Colby Manufacturing of Woonsocket, Rhode Island. Colby subsequently went bankrupt and was put on the auction block. The high bidder for Colby was Essex-Franke, a division of Essex Chemical Company of Summit, New Jersey. Essex-Franke is a name that would ultimately become important to profits at Rauch Industries.

Rauch had not given up his desire to market glass Christmas ornaments and decided if he couldn't sell Corning glass products, he'd try to make his own. When Corning sold its glass-manufacturing division to Colby, some worn parts and machines had been discarded.

"We heard that Corning had thrown out some of its old machinery and that a man named Allen Fields had picked up those used parts from a junkyard and was attempting to put them back together. I tracked him down in Montreal, Canada. He was very cordial on the phone when I told him we might want to do business with him. He invited me to Canada to see what he had."

Rauch and his son Peter made the trip, hoping for the best, but expecting the worst. After all, this man was working, literally, with throwaway parts taken out of a junk pile.

"Fields had taken Corning's junkyard parts and put together one machine that would take clear glass blanks from light-bulb manufacturing machines and turn them into Christmas ornaments." Fields' process was complicated and highly inefficient, but he had the concept to do what Rauch had in mind.

Fields' machine injected silver nitrate inside the glass ball and jiggled it to form a mirror, dipped the ball in lacquer paint, and fed the balls on a conveyor through an oven to dry and harden the lacquer before packaging. "That one machine was running poorly, but it was running," Rauch remembered.

He had a pile of what looked like junk over in the corner that he said were the parts for another machine that we could buy and put together ourselves. Actually, that pile of parts didn't just look like junk, it *was* junk because Fields had gone to a dump and bought parts for so much per ton. He wasn't buying machines. He was buying cast iron waste. Fields suggested that we just buy the parts lying there in the corner. I might have settled for that but Pete wouldn't think of it. Pete pulled me aside and said we ought to ask to buy the machine that was running. Of course, he was absolutely right, but I had no idea Fields would sell us the machine that was working. Well, I starting to talk with Fields again and told him what a great engineer he was for putting together that machine and getting it working. I told him he was so good that I felt sure that he could do the same again and asked if he'd consider selling us the machine he had put together. I figured he'd just say no. He surprised me by asking what I'd give for it.

Rauch began some immediate calculating in his head. The machine itself wasn't worth much, he realized, but the engineering that he could duplicate back in Gastonia, he felt, would be worth several hundred thousand dollars. "Now, as I look back on it," Rauch says today, "I realize how wrong I was. That engineering has been worth millions to our company."

Fields again asked Rauch for a purchase price. "I figured he didn't have much invested in all those parts," Rauch said, "because he had bought it all as scrap. I offered him $15,000 and was absolutely amazed when he accepted the offer on the spot."

Included in the purchase was a promise that Fields would send a mechanic to Gastonia to help set up the machine if Rauch would cover his expenses. "But I'll never forget what happened when that mechanic came down," Rauch said.

The mechanic brought only one tool—a hammer. I didn't know what we had gotten into, but he figured it all out and got that machine working. It was not efficient. It was not profitable, but it made glass balls. The concepts were there. We improved over time and it wasn't too many years before we had five efficient silver and lacquer machines running. Each machine was making 120,000 glass balls every eight hours. Our production exceeded one million glass ornaments a day on an annual basis. We became what I feel is the most efficient glass ornament ball manufacturer in the world. We finally threw out that original $15,000 machine, but I assure you we took sledge hammers and broke up every single part into tiny pieces so nobody else would be able to do what we had done in order to compete against us.

As Rauch was getting started with glass-ornament manufacturing, Colby, which had bought Corning's glass division, went bankrupt. Rauch hired the defunct company's chief engineer, Charlie Morton, to come and assist in the start-up process. Between the Canadian with the single hammer and Morton's engineering expertise, Rauch launched his glass-manufacturing enterprise in a big way. Production and sales began to soar.

There was yet another chapter to be written in the saga of Corning's 1966 rejection of Rauch as a distributor. In 1984, approximately ten years after Corning sold its glass-ornament business to Colby Manufacturing, which was sold to Essex-Franke at a bankruptcy auction, Rauch bought Essex-Franke for $4.7 million. With that purchase came several production plants in different states, the largest in New Madrid, Missouri. That gave Rauch control of the majority of glass-ornament manufacturing around the world. It was another stroke of sharp business acumen.

"Pretty soon we had the lion's share of the satin production business and the majority of the glass business," Rauch said. One can only guess what might have been different if Corning hadn't turned a deaf ear to Rauch when he offered to help increase the company's glass ornament sales as a distributor.

As the volume of sales of satin balls increased, Rauch opened his own printing company, under the name of E.P. Press, for printing brochures and other marketing products to help increase sales.

By 1968, Rauch's companies had outgrown the space available in Bessemer City. Because he had earlier decided to make Gastonia his family home, Rauch decided it was time to relocate his businesses there, too. The plant site was in the country then, some five miles from the center of the city on Highway 321 South at Forbes Road, just a few miles from the South Carolina line. Rauch purchased ten acres, more than he thought he'd ever need, for $2,500 an acre.

At the new site, purchased from his banker friend Tete Pearson, Rauch built a new brick, sprinkler-equipped 20,000-square-foot manufacturing plant for $3.78 a square foot. The contractor was Roy Barnes, the same man who had built Rauch's home years before.

As with the house, Rauch had nothing in writing with the contractor. They made their deal on a handshake. Pearson's bank approved the construction loan under that same arrangement.

Little did Rauch know that his ten acres would become inadequate so soon. He purchased ten more acres in short order and then added another five acres for a total of twenty-five. "And we could have used more," Rauch said. In fact, by the early 1990s Rauch considered buying a vacant building on adjacent property, but backed away when he learned there might be environmental problems stemming from earlier manufacturing.

Two years after he finished construction on his first 20,000-square-foot manufacturing plant at Highway 321 and Forbes Road, Rauch added another 20,000 square feet—and two years later he added another 20,000. That additional construction showed the incredible trust Rauch and his banker Pearson had for each other. After buying the original Forbes Road site, Rauch wanted to buy adjacent, Pearson-owned land for the later expansions. "He [Pearson] told me to go ahead and build on whatever land I needed and let him know how much land I had taken. I could pay him after we determined how much we needed. And that's what we did."

Of that arrangement, Pearson said he felt it was the right thing to do because he had no reason to doubt Rauch would be honest with him. "I knew I could trust him to do the right thing," Pearson said. "I wasn't worried that he would use land he wouldn't pay for."

Because his businesses were growing rapidly and were so widespread, Rauch combined the five companies under the single corporate name of Rauch Industries in 1973. Rauch took preferred stock in the merged company and divided the common stock among his children.

Throughout most that decade, Rauch continued to expand his manufacturing operations. That stopped for a while in the mid-1970s when he was saddled with millions in bad debts from separate real estate ventures with two partners that he later wished he had never joined.

In 1980, he bought a 65,000-square-foot building in Gastonia, a structure that formerly housed Burlington Industries' Modena Plant to house a specialty division that his daughter Ingrid created and made successful.

"Ingrid started the specialty division from New York City, where she was living at the time, but because it became so successful, she decided to move back to Gastonia to run it full time. I knew she could do it. She really knew the advertising business and was a natural in our new division which she built from scratch to a multimillion-dollar a year segment of our operation."

Ingrid had moved to New York City fifteen years earlier to

launch a successful career in advertising. Beginning as an administrative assistant at Ketchum, MacLeod & Grove Advertising, she had worked her way up the corporate ladder to become an assistant account executive with Grey Advertising and finally an account executive at Martin Landey Arlow Advertising.

Rauch's sons Marc and Peter were already part of the company management with responsibility for sales and production. His other son John had become a successful stockbroker, also in Gastonia.

By 1983, Rauch wanted to expand even further. To increase resources, he took his company public on April 12, 1983, selling 550,000 shares of stock at an initial offering of $11.50 a share. That raised approximately $6 million, half of which was put into the business for expansion. The other half went to the Rauch family.

In the twelve years the company was public before Rauch sold it in 1996, there were three stock splits and each original share had become two-and-a-half shares, with a market price of $13 a share, or

Noel Hall of Fame: Kurt Schindler (left), forty-year friend and business associate, as president of the National Ornament and Electric Lights Christmas Association, inducts Marshall Rauch into the Noel Hall of Fame at the March 1990 Toy Show, 200 Fifth Avenue, New York City

$32.50 for each original $11.50 share, plus quarterly cash dividends. Clearly, shareholders came out ahead. Rauch and his family, of course, held the majority of the shares, but all investors profited.

By the time Rauch Industries went public, the original core business of crochet thread and kite cord was virtually a thing of the past. Christmas ornaments were the centerpiece of the manufacturing and sales operations. As Rauch wound down his original businesses, he entered an arrangement with National Spinning Company of Washington, North Carolina, to take over the hand-knitting yarn, crochet thread, and dyeing work.

"I don't regret that," Rauch said. "From our perspective, Christmas ornaments were a lot more glamorous and profitable." By 1990, Rauch Industries was totally out of its original business and into holiday decoration manufacturing and sales.

The fire that destroyed a warehouse full of inventory in October 1994 was a major setback, but only a temporary one. Insurance covered the loss, but a lot of retailers were left with greatly reduced inventory that Christmas season. In rebuilding after the fire, Rauch had no plans to slow his own work schedule or to see his sons and daughter leave the family business. But in late 1995, he received an unexpected offer from Boston-based Syratech Corporation to buy Rauch Industries.

Rauch first said he wasn't interested, but Syratech made enhanced bids, eventually offering a premium of more than 40 percent over what the stock was selling for on the American Stock Exchange. After extended discussions with his family and with Syratech, and only after obtaining Syratech commitments to protect his employees, did Rauch agree to sell. The transaction was finalized in February 1996.

The successful and profitable sale is a tribute to the combined efforts of the Rauch family working together, their fair treatment of employees, their determination to produce quality products, and the respect they earned from their customers. All these factors resulted in a manufacturing and distributing facility with a reputation that was appealing to Syratech.

Leonard Florence, chairman of Syratech Corporation, and his

board of directors clearly saw Rauch Industries as a company they wanted to be part of their organization. For the high quality and reputation the Rauches had built, Syratech was willing to pay a premium.

The sale, however, was the beginning of the end of a thriving Rauch family enterprise that, over a forty-year period, grew from a few workers using mostly cast-off equipment into the world's largest Christmas-ornament production and distribution facility with state-of-the-art machines.

At the time of the sale, Rauch Industries produced and distributed approximately 50 percent of the glass and satin Christmas ornaments for Kmart and the majority of glass and satin ornaments for both Wal-Mart and Target stores. When the sale was being negotiated, Rauch, his two sons, and two daughters were all actively involved in the company management and daily operations. In the following eighteen months, all of that changed.

The youngest daughter, Stephanie, was working at Rauch Industries part-time while studying for her master's degree in counseling at the University of North Carolina at Charlotte. She resigned her company job shortly before the sale was completed.

Daughter Ingrid Rauch Sturm was a senior vice president and ran the Signature Specialty Sales Division, handling both manufacturing and distribution. She resigned when the sale was finalized.

Son Marc was president of the sales division and son Peter was president of the manufacturing division. Marc and Peter remained with Syratech for approximately one year after the sale before both resigned.

Company founder and chairman Marshall Rauch, with a three-year contract from Syratech, chose to remain with the new owners when his sons left in frustration, hoping to help maintain the steady course of expansion and customer satisfaction he had built up over the years. Unfortunately, that was not to be. Rauch explains:

> When we sold the company, I accepted the thirty-six-month contract that gave me a great deal of freedom and few duties even though I was paid $300,000 a year. That

certainly was a lot of money, because I was not working full-time on company responsibilities. But that was the agreement we had. When my lawyer looked at my arrangement, he called it a 'hell or high water contract' that I thought meant getting paid regardless. However, at the end of the second year the Syratech chairman, Lenny Florence, called and basically said they had had about all this good stuff they could handle. Specifically, he indicated he had been very good to me for two years, not calling on me for much. I certainly had to agree with that. But now he said it was a different ball game. He said that they were losing money, and they needed to cut all the extra expenses they could. He also suggested that if I chose to stay the third year, I could not continue with my long-time secretary, Louise Beane, even though I had been paying her out of my own salary and not out of company money. He added that Syratech directors were going to see to it that I had something to do for the company for at least forty hours a week. Then he suggested that he might be interested in buying up my remaining contract for a reasonable fee.

Rauch wanted no part of the new arrangement, but he made a counteroffer in May 1998. "I told (Florence) I would agree to letting them buy out the last year of my contract [worth $300,000] for one dollar if they would agree to end the non-compete clause for my sons and me on January 1, 1999." Rauch said. "Lenny thought about it and came back and said no, he wouldn't do that. He said he'd rather pay me two-thirds of my last year's salary and let me leave without changing the non-compete clause. So that's what we did, and I left."

Rauch's leaving was obviously emotional. The personal relationship he had with most of his employees didn't exist with the new owners. "Unfortunately, the corporation is still not doing as well as it once did," he said years after his termination. "The top executives keep turning over, and it is extremely difficult for me to see so many of the community and civic groups that our company once supported not being supported by the new owners. If I had a way of taking the Rauch name off the water tower, off the stationery, and off the minds of everyone involved, I would do it."

Despite the fact that his successful enterprise turned a profit of more than $4.5 million the last year he and his family ran it, Rauch was given some warnings of what might lie ahead when he agreed to remain with the new owners. Shortly after the sale to Syratech, Rauch got a phone call from his long-time friend John Medlin of Winston-Salem, retired chairman of Wachovia Bank. Medlin called to congratulate Rauch on the successful sale, but issued some words of caution based on his own experiences. "He warned me that change always comes with a sale," Rauch said. "He said in talking with other entrepreneurs who had sold their own companies and remained on the job, each one had said that the faster they left, the better off they were. An entrepreneur perceives the new owners are destroying what he built." That's a feeling Rauch now understands.

Despite his frustration over the outcome, Rauch still looks back with pride at the company he and his family built. He knows it was solid when he was in charge. He can only wonder what might happen next.

Regardless of the future of the company, however, the solid foundation that Rauch and his family built when they owned and ran the business allowed him to pursue another set of important priorities. Civic responsibilities have been one of his lasting avocations. First he built his company. Then he built a reputation as a dedicated civic and political leader.

Chapter 10
Civil Rights & City Council

*When it came to civil rights and fairness, Marshall had the vision
and the courage to act, to do something positive rather than just
sit back and wait for something negative to happen.
This community should be thankful for his leadership.*

Former Gaston District Judge Donald E. Ramseur, Sr., commenting
on Marshall Rauch's public service achievements in Gastonia.

When the United States Supreme Court ruled in 1954 that
segregated schools were legally wrong and morally unaccept-
able, public officials across the South and throughout much of
the country reacted with dismay and defensiveness. Sometimes
they reacted with resistance, encouraged by prejudiced local
government and law enforcement officials.

That display of bigotry wasn't limited to the South, but was
most pronounced below the Mason-Dixon Line where governors
Orval Faubus of Arkansas, Ross Barnett of Mississippi, and George
Wallace of Alabama fanned the fires of racial hatred with their
rhetoric and bigoted actions. While the South initially fought to
impede court rulings on school desegregation, other areas of
the country soon adopted similar patterns of discrimination.
Ultimately, public demonstrations against desegregation
stretched as far north as Boston, a perceived hotbed of liberal-
ism.

As cities and states wrestled with issues rising out of school
desegregation, similar issues arose to challenge traditions in other
aspects of life, particularly access to public accommodations such
as restaurants and theaters. Again, the South won the distinction of being more adamantly opposed to racial equality than
other parts of the nation, but problems arose in other sections
of the country as well.

Of course, enforcement of civil rights could not be limited to public schools. It wasn't long before racial restrictions were being tested in all arenas of human relations—and in most instances provoking emotional reactions. In Southern towns and cities, especially those like Gastonia, North Carolina, civil rights and human relations were considered synonymous.

In fact, during the first half of the twentieth century, Gastonia had earned an international notoriety for discrimination, not only in race but also in labor relations. A violent strike in 1929 over union efforts to organize workers at Gastonia's huge Loray Mill is still a topic of frequent discussion and has been the subject of numerous books and films. That strike took the lives of Gastonia Police Chief Orville Aderholt and of a labor organizer, Ella Mae Wiggins.

The Loray Mill factory survived that bloodshed, but bitterness over the discrimination exposed by that strike lingered in Gastonia and environs for decades. When the Supreme Court handed down its school desegregation decision in 1954, the old anxieties over human relations again rose to the surface.

Given that history, Gastonia leaders were understandably concerned about court rulings on pupil assignments to schools and equal access to public accommodations and public housing. Officials began searching for ways to keep disturbances down and civic progress up.

One of the strongest proponents of keeping the peace in the city was Marshall Rauch, by then a well-known and respected businessman. He already had shown his interest in municipal affairs by completing three terms on the City Council and serving as mayor pro-tem. As Rauch was finishing his last term on the City Council, the idea of forming a civil rights leadership group moved to the forefront of community consideration.

Rauch was looking ahead at other political and public service opportunities. The state legislature was the logical next step. His friends as well as his political detractors were aware of his plans. He made no secret of his ambitions.

But when the City Council decided to establish Gastonia's first Human Relations Committee to promote racial accord, Rauch's colleagues turned to him. He was aware of the need and was willing to help, though many of his friends advised him against it. Heading a committee on human relations and civil rights inevitably would mean integrating public facilities, hardly an opportunity to enhance a political career. The job would be controversial and would create opposition among people whose future political support he might need.

Rauch also was warned by friends in other parts of the state that he shouldn't accept the appointment. Jews, he was told, shouldn't "rock the boat" because such action might provoke negative economic and social consequences.

Rauch listened to all that advice. Then he ignored it and did what he thought was right. In January 1964, he accepted the chairmanship of a twenty-three-member Gastonia Human Relations Committee.

The group was comprised of thirteen whites and twelve blacks, all with differing political loyalties and social philosophies. Rauch felt that they would contribute to a broad base of local thinking.

One of the members was Donald Ramseur, a lawyer who would later become the first African-American to serve as a district court judge in the county. Two other racial minority members were Thebaud "T" Jeffers, a local school principal known for his quiet approach and fairness on issues of public concern, and N.A. "Doc" Smith, the town's black druggist, a man of strong will who was determined to right past wrongs. Ten years later "T" Jeffers was elected Gastonia's first black mayor. He is now deceased.

Another school principal chosen among the minority members was Ralph C. Gingles Sr. Forty years later that name would become a part of history in an historic court case involving civil rights. Gingles' son, Ralph Jr., became a lawyer and a district court judge and was the plaintiff in a federal lawsuit that overturned North Carolina's method of electing state legislators. Ralph Gingles Jr. brought his suit on grounds that state legislative districts were drawn to make it harder for minority candidates to win elections. That case, like so many other civil rights cases, slogged through the courts for years. It was finally settled in 1990 in favor of Gingles and against the state. The younger Gingles credited his father with instilling in him a hunger for justice and fairness in public life.

The vice chairman of the Human Relations Committee was James Atkins, a conservative Republican lawyer who at the time was also publisher of the family-owned *Gastonia Gazette*, the city's daily newspaper. Other committee members were:

J.B. Adams, a barber; Nathaniel Barber, head of the Excelsior Credit Union; Glendell N. Brooks, a teacher at Highland High School and head of the local chapter of the National Association for the Advancement of Colored People (NAACP); Bynum Carter, president of the Gastonia Chamber of Commerce; Dr. Cleveland Floyd, a dentist; J.Q. Falls, a former City Council member; J. Mack Holland, the city attorney (and Rauch's personal attorney); Franz Holsher, personnel manager for Homelite Chain Saw Company; the Reverend Moses Javis, a Baptist minister; Dr. Gary Levinson, an optometrist; H.S. Mackie, chairman of the Gastonia school board; Dr. Harry Moffett, pastor of First Presbyterian Church; Dr. Charles Morgan, an orthopedic surgeon; Pat McSwain, a member of the Gastonia school board and owner of a radio station; Craig Watson, president of Watson Insurance Company; R.B. Wilson, president of the Gastonia Merchants Association and manager of Akers Hardware Store; Albert Myers Jr., a textile manufacturer; the Rev. Doug Aldridge, of First Baptist Church; J.P. Chambers; and Dr. Gene Woody, a dentist and former mayor of Gastonia.

The committee went to work immediately, but not in a public way. Members met privately, something that mass media practices of the 1990s and beyond would not have permitted. But in the 1960s, when race was an incendiary issue for most communities, the committee was given wide latitude.

"We were able to get things done quietly without any public display or opportunity for opponents to know what we were doing until after we had things worked out," Rauch explained. Rauch used his political connections to help get some things accomplished.

As a City Council member, Rauch had been effective, and he

used that experience and an earned reputation for fairness as committee chairman. While on the council, he had been out front in making sure the city paved more streets in the minority neighborhoods where dirt roads had been common before his election. That won him the trust of many black residents and committee members from those neighborhoods. With connections among many of the city's top private businesses, Rauch was known as a friend who had the city's best interest at heart.

"Certain things were happening anyway," Rauch said, "but our way of quietly bringing on equality was the best way. I can't think of anything we could have done that would have made it any easier."

Judge Ramseur agreed. "Marshall was and still is what I would call color blind; that is, he just looks at the facts and does what is right without regard to skin color," Ramseur said at the turn of the century in discussing Rauch. Until his death, Ramseur lived in the section of town where Rauch helped get streets paved long before the Human Relations Committee was ever conceived. Ramseur named Rauch as the strongest leader in the city during the early days of civil rights work:

Marshall was picked to head the committee, because he was so respected by the entire community. As a businessman, he knew the people with influence. As a council member, he was known for helping the black community. And as the principal benefactor of the Gaston Boys Club for young people, he was the natural choice. The need for his kind of leadership was obvious. Marshall looked at the conditions and wanted to be a part of making them better. He was the cog behind the scene to get so much done with so little disturbance. He had the vision to do something positive rather than just sit back and wait for something negative to happen.

James Atkins played a critical role with Rauch in keeping the Human Relations Committee work quiet and continuing. He was the local newspaper publisher but he put aside that hat during committee work and helped ensure that progress was made with little public disclosure. When his family sold the newspaper to an out-of-state chain, he gave up the publisher's post and returned to the practice of law.

"Marshall was the liaison between the white establishment and the black community," Atkins said. "His Jewish heritage probably helped in this area. He was the single harmonizing force among the diverse groups."

Despite his connection with the hometown newspaper—or, perhaps more accurately, because of it—Atkins helped keep the lid on what the committee was doing. "I could control (as publisher and part owner) what went in our newspaper. But we also went to Claudia Howe (then the Gaston bureau chief for *The Charlotte Observer*) and explained to her what we were doing, with the understanding that nothing would be in the newspaper until the action was taken," Atkins recalled.

Rauch and Atkins worked with specific members of the black community to arrange integration steps with business owners, specifically restaurant owners. At the Holiday Inn, for example, they arranged, through an agreement with the restaurant operator, for "T." Jeffers to be the first black patron to be served dinner in that restaurant. They picked Jeffers because he was well known and respected as a school principal.

That strategy proved successful. Similar activities quietly took place at various other restaurants across the city. Once integration was accomplished, few people complained. No one protested with the kind of demonstrations that were common in many other cities.

There were a series of quiet meetings of restaurant owners to discuss the strategy. Significantly, only one restaurant owner refused to participate. He told Rauch he didn't want any additional customers. Explaining the importance of racial equality and fairness, Rauch counseled with the man, who ran a small eatery named John's Grill on Main Street.

"But you don't understand," Rauch later quoted the restaurateur as saying. "I don't want any more customers of any color. I've got all I can handle. Furthermore, I've been serving blacks in my restaurant for years. The same customers, black and white, come every day, and I just don't want any more."

That interview provided an important lesson for Rauch. It

suggested that things are not always as they seem. That restaurant had been desegregated long before there were any court orders or Human Relations Committees, and no one had complained.

Integrating the theaters of Gastonia was not as simple. By the 1960s, the town's only black theater had closed, and neither of the existing movie houses, the Web or the Temple, allowed black customers. Rauch tried without success to persuade the theater manager, Sonny Baker, to open his doors to minorities. Atkins also attempted to get the change made, to no avail.

According to Atkins, Baker steadfastly said no to integration, but offered to buy the defunct black theater and operate it with upgraded movies for blacks. The committee wouldn't agree to that. The only public demonstrations in Gastonia were over the refusal of Baker, now deceased, to open his theater to black customers. The theaters were not integrated until Congress enacted the Civil Rights Act of 1964, outlawing racial discrimination in public accommodations.

Despite the dispute over theater integration, public-accommodation rules were changed in most other businesses, thanks to the activity of the Human Relations Committee headed by Rauch. Druggist "Doc" Smith, said to be the most outspoken and direct member of that committee, agreed with Atkins on the importance of Rauch's role.

"He showed tremendous courage and fortitude," Smith said. "He was respected because of his status in the business community and because, with his strong religious faith, he shared a common bond with the black community. He was the most dynamic force we had to accomplish our goals. He showed excellent leadership both in what he did and how he chose people to work with him. I'd hate to think what those years might have been like without him here."

Under Rauch's leadership, other achievements also were realized. The Gastonia Young Men's Christian Association, where Rauch was an early leader, was the second YMCA in the state to accept black members. Gastonia was named an All-America City in 1963, based in large part on the peaceful way the town had handled its racial and civil rights decisions.

His fellow committee members agreed that Rauch deserved and received much of the credit for that award. "I probably get credit that I don't deserve," Rauch said of his early 1960s civil rights work. "We had excellent members on the committee, and things really got started by the City Council. What I did is just what I thought ought to be done and needed to be done. It was the right thing to do."

Others noticed Rauch's civil rights leadership, too. After serving as chairman of Gastonia's civil rights commission, Rauch was named a member of the North Carolina Good Neighbor Council by Governor Dan Moore. That council was created to promote civil rights on a state level in the same way that Rauch had helped promote civil rights in his own community. But at the state level, it never worked as well.

"The real work was done at the local level," Rauch said. "The state group added prestige to the local efforts, but the real work was done at home."

The dire warnings given to Rauch by skeptical friends and associates turned out to be wrong. Rather than hurting his future political career, that committee work helped him in later legislative campaigns because word of his fairness and leadership skills spread from the committee's good works.

The deserved reputation for Rauch's human relations efforts still exists. Many plaques and awards were displayed in the lobby of his company offices until he severed ties with the new owners in May 1998. One plaque, from the 1992 North Carolina Human Relations Commission, reads: "To Rauch Industries for its commitment to excellence in human, economic, and educational development for its employees and the community."

Even more significant, perhaps, was the plaque on Rauch's office wall, dated 1966. That was the year Rauch was chosen Man of the Year by the Gastonia chapter of Omega Psi Phi, a black fraternity. He was the first white person to win that award, given in appreciation for his work and successes as chairman of the Human Relations Committee.

The work of the Gastonia Human Relations Committee was extended into Gaston County in the mid 1990s. Don Flowers, a Gastonia real estate administrator and a member of the commission in the late 1990s, cited Rauch's continuing influence after the city and county efforts were merged.

"County commissioners were about to cut the civil rights commission's budget, which had never been great," Flowers recalled. "I called Marshall and almost immediately the talk of budget cuts was stopped. I don't know exactly what he did, but I'm convinced he did something. He was a wonderful chairman, and his influence has remained for more than thirty years. He has been a steadfast and worthwhile community leader, one of the strongest we've ever had."

Flowers also quoted from the official records of the commission, which give Rauch and his fellow members credit for "tirelessly working for civil order and community understanding while institutions, systems, and public accommodations were desegregating."

Rauch said he never expected awards or wanted recognition or votes on election day for what he did. "Our work should not have been needed," he said of the committee, "but because it was needed, I'm proud to have been a part of it. This may be the most important thing I've ever been involved with."

Rauch's service on the Human Relations Committee brought him to the attention of people outside Gastonia, even though his earlier efforts in this and other areas were well known back home through his terms on the City Council. Rauch had been elected to the council in 1952, when he was twenty-nine. That was remarkable when one considers his background as a New Yorker who was both Jewish and relatively new to the city.

When Rauch sought his first term, he had lived in Gastonia only four years, moving there from nearby Bessemer City, where his primary textile business was still operating. At that time no one of Jewish faith had ever been elected to the Gastonia City Council. He also was from Long Island, and the city's voters had traditionally chosen local people to serve on the council.

However, Rauch already had become involved in civic and community work in town and quickly had been dismayed by the dismal opportunities he found existed for young people. That's why he initially ran for a seat on the council. "Recreational facilities were practically nonexistent," Rauch said of Gastonia's city programs in the early 1950s. One of his City Council campaign pledges was to work to help improve recreational facilities for young people.

"People still talk about the fact that I was elected," Rauch said, "especially after living in the city for such a short time. But I think that my wife helped because Jeanne's family was so well known in the county. Her family connection definitely helped me win the first city election."

Once elected, Rauch immediately went to work on his promise to improve parks and recreational programs. That wasn't all. He also exposed the city's poor record of performance in basic human services, particularly the appalling lack of paved streets in predominately minority neighborhoods and the inefficiency of the city's garbage collection system.

With Rauch taking the lead, City Manager Jim Carter began directing city crews to pave streets in black neighborhoods instead of dousing them with used motor oil to control dust, as had been the practice until that time. Rauch also convinced city administrators to change the method of trash pickups by giving incentives for more efficiency. In short order, work that had been requiring eight hours was being done in fewer than six. Efficient practices resulted in savings of time and money.

Also among Rauch's accomplishments near the end of his first term on the council was a leadership role in convincing his fellow councilmen (there were no women members then) to approve adding fluoride to the city's water system. That wasn't an easy endeavor. The local newspaper had editorialized against fluoride, and large groups of people in the town opposed it.

"I think some people still considered fluoride a communist plot," Rauch said with a smile. "And others must have thought it would cause chickens to lay bad eggs or something. When the newspaper reporter left the room during one meeting, we just voted it in but the public did not know until much later."

Rauch left the council at the end of his second term for two reasons. He needed to devote more time to his business enterprise, and he was being encouraged by George Jenkins, the local Democratic Party chairman, to step aside. Jenkins informed Rauch that another Jewish resident, Leon I. Schneider, wanted to run for mayor.

"George told me it would be difficult to elect two Jews to the council at the same time," Rauch said. While finding that line of reasoning offensive, Rauch agreed to pass up a third consecutive term in order to have more time for his business, but he expected to be back when the time was right.

Shortly after Rauch left the council in 1956, the new council caved in to opponents of fluoride and voted to discontinue its use. Rauch thought the council action was medically foolish even if it was politically popular. He quietly decided to work to reverse the decision when the opportunity arose. A decade later, Rauch again ran for the City Council and was elected easily. One of his first acts was to persuade his fellow council members to restore fluoride to the city's water supply. It is still there today.

Ironically, although Rauch twice was instrumental in getting fluoride added to the Gastonia water supply, he has never been given credit. In a 1977 news story commenting on the positive benefits of fluoride, the *Gastonia Gazette* (which had opposed the addition of flouride twenty years earlier) commended former Mayor Schneider for adding fluoride. That story ignored the fact that Schneider was, in fact, mayor when the City Council rejected fluoride.

Both amused and dismayed by the lack of facts in that story, Rauch never corrected the misstatements. "I didn't want to discredit (the mayor)," Rauch said, "so I never said anything publicly until now. It's no big thing, really, because what is important is that fluoride was added. But this is the opportunity to set the record straight."

It was Rauch's tenacity and vision on controversial issues such as fluoride and his interest in helping the less fortunate townspeople secure paved streets and recreational facilities that helped bring on the leadership role in the city's Human Relations Committee. The positive results of that choice are clear as one public service post led to another. The City Council work led to the Human Relations Committee service that led to a position of influence and power in the North Carolina Senate for twenty-four years.

Learning the art of politics on the City Council and working with the public on human relations served Rauch well in his later legislative service. "It was through my City Council and human relations work that I first became interested in the state legislature," Rauch said. The public record clearly shows that his services during those early civil rights days were beneficial. His leadership was both needed and wanted.

There is general agreement in the city that civil rights and the people of Gastonia are better off for Rauch's having served. As former retired Judge Ramseur said in an interview, Rauch didn't simply react to the negatives around him. He didn't wait for that. Instead, he acted positively as his conscience—and his courage—dictated.

Chapter 11 - The North Carolina Senate, Part I

When Marshall Rauch came to the North Carolina Senate, he was mistakenly perceived as a liberal Democrat. When most legislators were looking for ways to find more tax revenue, he was looking for ways to return some of that money to the people. He was, indeed, liberal on social issues because of his interest in improving human conditions but was quite conservative on fiscal matters. He possessed great leadership qualities and became one of the Senate's most effective and respected members.

Sylvia Fink, former NC Senate principal clerk.

Marshall Rauch's elevation from City Hall in Gastonia to the halls of the state legislature seemed to him a natural progression. His successful efforts at helping improve the plight of city residents as a member of the Gastonia City Council convinced him that he could do more of the same on a broader basis in the North Carolina General Assembly.

The political establishment in his home county, however, did not welcome his first campaign for a legislative seat. They preferred their own handpicked Senate candidate, not one with Rauch's independent streak. Their opposition only added to Rauch's determination to seek the office. He never doubted his ability to win or to accomplish his goals after winning.

Being a member of the North Carolina Senate, he felt, was heady stuff for a transplanted New Yorker, and he wanted to prove that he was deserving of the honor. But his maiden speech on the Senate floor, in the early days of his first legislative session in 1967, didn't go exactly as planned.

He was swelling with pride as the primary sponsor of legislation that he felt would provide more affordable electric power to small-town consumers. He was even more pleased that leaders of municipalities selling electric power to their citizens had come to him, a mere freshman lawmaker, to ask that he sponsor the bill that would allow cities across the state to sell power to people in newly annexed neighborhoods. What he didn't realize was that his bill didn't have a chance of passing, a fact that even those who asked him to sponsor it knew only too well.

The cities backing the bill came to Rauch in hopes of getting their case heard. They felt that was the most they could expect in that legislative year. In time, city officials felt, they would get the bill passed. Often that's the way good legislation gets approved—piecemeal. The process takes several years, and each time the bill gains a few more votes.

Because the electric-cities bill had attracted a lot of state-wide interest from big power companies (which were opposed to it) and from many municipalities (which favored it), the television cameras were on and the spectators' gallery was filled when Rauch rose at his Senate seat to explain the bill. It was his first big chance to do well in public view.

Carefully choosing his words on the worthiness of the bill and seeking to make a positive first impression on his Senate colleagues—and the television audience—Rauch was speaking eloquently when Senator Herman Moore, a friend from Mecklenburg County seated nearby, gave him a shock. Moore wrote in large letters on a legal pad and held it up for only Rauch to see: "Your fly is open."

"Well, I knew I couldn't just stop and shouldn't sit down at that very moment, so I kept talking," Rauch said. "But that note disrupted my concentration. I'm not sure what I said after that. I'm pretty sure I never made my main points about the bill. I know I finished speaking more quickly than I had planned. When I sat down, I looked and the zipper on my pants was not open."

The incident was Senator Rauch's welcome to one of the humorous rites of legislative initiation. Senator Moore, of course, thought his note was hilarious. So did Rauch—after he realized it was a joke. Years later, Rauch pulled the same stunt on another freshman, Senator Bill Goldston of Rockingham County.

The electric-cities bill was defeated in short order, but not because of an unopened zipper.

Rauch, however, learned an important lesson with that speech.

Tillie Wohl, Marshall Rauch's mother, as a teenager during a dance recital in New York in 1915. She was one of many family members with musical talents.

The Girard family siblings and their spouses. Standing (from left) are Marshall and Jeanne Rauch and Herbert and Phyllis Girard. Seated (from left) are Sam and Mimi Girard, Clarence and Ethel Girard Ross, and Cy and Dorothy Girard at Ingrid Rauch's bat mitzvah at Gaston Country Club, 1961.

Ingrid Helene Rauch Sturm (center) at her bat mitzvah at Temple Emanuel in Gastonia, March 1961. From left to right, brother John, father Marshall, grandfather Nathan, grandmother Ingrid, mother Jeanne, and brothers Peter and Marc.

Marc Fredric Rauch's bar mitzvah, May 1962. The picture is at the Rauch home, 1121 Scotch Drive, Gastonia, after service at Temple Emanuel in Gastonia. Front row: grandmother Tillie, brothers Peter and Marc, cousin Eric Gottlieb, baby sister Stephanie, mother Jeanne. Back row: grandfather Nathan, father Marshall, cousin David Gottlieb, brother John, sister Ingrid, uncle Newton Gottlieb, and aunt Jacqueline Gottlieb.

Nathan and Tillie Rauch, Marshall Rauch's parents, at their fiftieth wedding anniversary June 20,1965 at Grossinger's Hotel, New York

Peter David Rauch (seated far right) at his bar mitzvah at Temple Emanuel in Gastonia, September 1965.
From left: grandfather Nathan, Rabbi David Rabb, father Marshall, and (seated) uncle Herbert Girard.

Stephanie Laura Rauch's bat mitzvah in December 1974 at Temple Emanuel in Gastonia. From left are brothers Peter and Marc, sister Ingrid, grandmother Tillie, father Marshall, Stephanie, mother Jeanne, brother John, sister-in-law JoAnne, and grandfather Nathan.

Briss of Julian Ross Rauch, July 31, 1985, at 1121 Scotch Drive, Gastonia, North Carolina. From left are father Peter, grandfather Marshall, and Julian in the arms of his great-grandfather Nathan.

June 1987, Marshall Rauch received an honorary Ph.D. from Belmont Abbey College. Standing to Marshall's right is Dr. Mike Reedy, professor and athletic director of Belmont Abbey, a longtime close friend. A few years later Marshall received an honorary degree from Pfeiffer University at Misenheimer, North Carolina.

Marshall and Jeanne Rauch relaxing at Duck on the coast
of North Carolina, 1987, during a state Senate retreat hosted by
Senate President Pro-Tem Marc Basnight

Marshall Rauch holding his new grandson Elias
on the day Elias arrived in the United States,
September 22,1994. It was the first meeting of
Rauch and Elias who was adopted from Paraguay
by Rauch's son Marc and his wife Elaine.

In March 1995, debris from the burned 670,000-square-foot.Cramerton plant with the five Rauchs who had worked there (from left, Stephanie, Peter, Marc, Marshall, and Ingrid). Photo was made after the company had resumed full production at additional locations.

Marshall and Jeanne Rauch (seated center) at home with four of their five children and seven grandchildren on Passover, 1995. Standing at left is son Marc and seated below him is his wife Elaine and son Elias. Standing is daughter Ingrid with husband Larry; next is son John's family of Josh, Job, Johnny, and wife JoAnne. On the far right are son Peter with wife Vickie and their children Natillie and Julian seated with Lauren above.

Three generations of Rauch family at Marshall and Jeanne's fiftieth wedding anniversary, May 1996 at the Gaston Country Club. Front row from left to right: Josh, Stephanie, Julian, Jeanne, Marshall, Natillie, Lauren, Elias, and Elaine. Back row: Larry, Ingrid, Peter, Vickie, John, JoAnne, Johnny, Job, and Marc.

Marshall and Stephanie Rauch, May 1998, when she received her master's degree in counseling at UNC-Charlotte. At right is Chancellor James Woodward, a close family friend. Marshall was representing the UNC University Board of Governors of which he was a member.

Annual family beach vacation in June 1998 at Isle of Palms, South Carolina. From left to right seated: Charles Dewhurst, Marshall, Jeanne, and Julian. Standing: Marc, Elaine, Elias, Bonnie and Mike Reedy, Stephanie, Ingrid, Larry, Vickie, Natillie, Peter, JoAnne, Johnny, Lauren, Elliot Fox and Maxine, and Richard Dewhurst.

Rauch family gathering with Governor Jim Hunt and Gastonia Mayor Porter McAteen at the dedication of the Interstate 85 section through Gaston County in honor of Marshall Rauch, October 19, 1998

Marshall Rauch and Coach Dean Smith at the UNC Board of Governors banquet honoring Smith in November 1998 for his accomplishments with the university

Marshall Rauch with former UNC basketball players Charlie Scott (center) and Michael Jordan at the November 1998 banquet honoring Coach Dean Smith

Sisters Stephanie Rauch (left) and Ingrid Rauch Sturm during the dedication of the Rauch Sisters Stadium in Chapel Hill, April 2, 2001. The sisters donated money for the tennis complex at the University of North Carolina in Chapel Hill where each was a member of the under-graduate tennis team. The sisters are shown with their parents, Marshall and Jeanne Rauch and UNC athletics director Richard Baddour.

University of North Carolina
The Rauch Sisters Stadium

In appreciation of
Stephanie Rauch, class of '85
& Ingrid Rauch, class of '70
whose generosity made this stadium possible.

Dedicated April 2, 2001

A new generation entered the Rauch family in 2002 when the first great-grandchild was born. Jackson White is the son of Rauch's grandson, Josh. Jackson, at 23 months, is held by his mother at the family vacation in the summer of 2004. Shown with Jackson are grandparents John and JoAnne White, great-grandfather Marshall Rauch, and parents Josh and Marsha White.

It is that legislators can't—and shouldn't—expect to win every battle, and they shouldn't take themselves too seriously. Lawmakers need to know when to compromise for the good of all rather than the wishes of a few, and that often worthy legislation, like fine wine, needs to age and be given a chance to improve before being packaged.

In twenty-four years (from 1967 to 1991) of distinguished service in the North Carolina Senate, Rauch was successful in getting many of his bills enacted into law. Some were clearly ahead of their time in the eyes of many legislators. A few that were almost identical to proposals Rauch had introduced during the 1970s and 1980s were up for consideration and favorable votes in the late 1990s. It had taken that long for some of his ideas to win widespread approval.

That was particularly true of Rauch's plan to reduce tax burdens and strengthen drunk-driving laws. Bills that he sponsored on those issues in his first years as a senator didn't become law until 1997 or later.

Rauch's legislative years were rewarding as a result of the friendships he developed and the laws he helped enact. On the wall of his office at Rauch Industries, he kept photographs of close legislative and personal friends, including Senators Tom White of Kinston, Ollie Harris of Kings Mountain, Jim Ezzell of Rocky Mount, and Hargrove "Skipper" Bowles of Greensboro.

His accomplishments as a legislator were numerous, although most citizens were not aware of his involvement in some laws he helped to enact. For example, the plots of colorful flowers along the state's major highways are there because of legislation that Rauch helped his friend "Skipper" Bowles push into law. Revenues from the sale of vanity auto license plates pay for the planting of those flowers.

An alcohol treatment center in Chapel Hill, supported with public and private funds, exists because Rauch pushed for it in memory of Bowles, who first proposed such a center. Rauch sponsored the bill creating the center and later was the leading force behind another law requiring convicted drunk drivers to help pay for continuing research into the causes of and cures for alcoholism.

The movement toward self-service gas pumps, now commonplace across North Carolina and around the country, didn't just happen either. The gas pumps were installed more than a quarter century ago because of legislation that Rauch helped enact after heated debate.

Migrant workers in North Carolina receive better treatment today than they once did because Rauch cast a critical vote on legislation to improve living conditions in migrant-labor camps.

Taxes are lower today because Rauch worked to keep some levies off the books and reduce others. He supported a repeal of the intangibles tax on investments twenty years before that law was finally enacted.

His subcommittee vote for a bill to lower the tax on senior-citizen assets made it possible for the bill to become law. If he had voted no on that bill, called the Homestead Exemption Act, it would have died.

As a senator, Rauch was instrumental in changing the highway construction formula to increase the percentage of federal money going for road paving and reducing the state's share. He fought to stretch bond money for highway construction over a longer period of time than was originally proposed in order to get better bargains and higher quality work from contractors.

He headed a tax-fairness commission that recommended both reduction and simplification of state tax laws. However, his plan from the late 1970s to require a two-thirds vote of legislators before any tax could be increased still hasn't become law.

The only tax Rauch ever felt good about increasing was on cigarettes. But like his very first statewide bill on electric power, a high tax on cigarettes was, and still is, a losing cause in the tobacco-friendly North Carolina.

As a result of assistance Rauch gave Ted Kaplan, then a member of the North Carolina House from Forsyth County, the tragedy of the Holocaust gets official recognition by North Carolina each year, as does the celebration of Yom Kippur as a Jewish holiday.

The bill to recognize Yom Kippur occasioned an inside practical joke when it came over to the Senate. Though Rauch had paved the way for the bill, he was absent—delayed in New York by a snowstorm—when it came up in Senate committee. Without him there, Ted Kaplan came over from the House to explain the bill and speak in its favor.

Senators Kenneth Royall of Durham County and Harold Hardison of Lenoir County, two of the chamber's wiliest and most influential members, conspired to teach young Kaplan to respect Senate power. As soon as Kaplan finished speaking, Royall moved that the bill be given an unfavorable report. Hardison immediately seconded the motion, and without further discussion the bill was killed.

Kaplan was stunned but could hardly protest. He was not a member of either the committee or the Senate. He left the meeting room dazed and started across the legislative building to the House side. Before he could arrive there, a Senate sergeant-at-arms tapped him on the shoulder and said Senator Royall had summoned him back to the Senate committee.

When Kaplan returned to the meeting, Royall, having voted with the prevailing side, was able to make a motion that the bill be reconsidered. His motion passed. He then made a motion that the measure be given a favorable report. Immediately Hardison seconded the move. And as quickly as the bill had been killed, it was revived and approved.

Senator Royall then looked at Representative Kaplan and said, mischievously, "Mr. Kaplan, if you've never had prior reason to believe in resurrection, you have it now."

Rauch was one of the more

Senator Rauch with daughter Stephanie, age 7, in the Senate chamber, 1968 popular members of the state Senate during his tenure because of his outgoing personality, attention to detail, understanding of the subtleties of the legislative process, hard work, long hours, and personal integrity.

In an interview published in a Democratic Party newsletter early in his Senate career, Rauch said, "Religion and integrity are the two most important assets a businessman or a legislator should practice. If you practice both, they will bring you success in any endeavor."

It didn't take Rauch long to begin making a name for himself as a legislator. His personality and his ability quickly caught the eye of colleagues and the state media, which saw him as a future leader. Editorial writers around the state pegged Rauch as a man to watch. In a 1970 feature story during Rauch's second term in the Senate, the *News and Observer* of Raleigh was generous in its praise, describing him as a "tall, dark, and handsome Jew from New York" who was already making waves in the legislative halls.

"Can this man, with his background, survive as a politician and manufacturer of Christmas ornaments in a rural, agricultural, predominantly Christian state?" a reporter asked, then answered his own question with a resounding yes. "It's already happening," the story said and called Rauch a senator "who has parlayed a heady mixture of ambition, gregariousness, and plain, ordinary old horse sense into a million-dollar-plus personal business fortune and galloping political career."

That language may have been a bit effusive and premature, but it was not wrong. Rauch was not galloping at that point, but he had begun to trot.

Rauch entered state politics in 1966 following three successful terms as a City Council member and serving as mayor pro-tem in Gastonia. In his first state Senate campaign, Rauch pushed his own ideas and never intended for his candidacy to be interpreted as being against any opponent.

That's not how he was perceived by some Democratic Party leaders in Gastonia. They felt, because of in-bred political tradition, that he was too much of an upstart. The party officials didn't want him to run that year; they had other candidates picked out and tried to persuade Rauch to wait his turn. Rauch felt differently, and so did the voters who elected him by a wide margin in his first try for public office outside his hometown.

Prior to the November 1966 Senate election, one state senator had served Gaston County. A change in the district lines had put the county into a two-seat district with adjacent Cleveland County, which includes the city of Shelby. "I looked at the candidates, all of them lawyers, and decided if they could be senators, so could I," Rauch said.

Thirty-plus years ago Democratic tradition in Gaston County held that local party leaders routinely chose their nominees and determined who would run when. Rauch wasn't on anybody's list that year; thus, the Democratic insiders did not welcome his venture into the campaign.

Gastonia banker Allen Sims was the party's powerbroker during those years. Rauch went to see Sims to give him advance notice of his candidacy. "He told me I was a fine young man, but suggested that I not run that year because other candidates had already been selected by the party," Rauch recalled. "I was polite but reminded him I had not come seeking permission to run. I had come to tell him I was going to run.

"He wasn't pleased but said he wouldn't do anything to hurt my chances. But he didn't help me any, either. Lynn Hollowell, the party chairman and the incumbent state senator, was the designated candidate from Gaston. He was one of the old guard, a lifelong Gastonian, and I wasn't. But two senators were to be elected that year, so my candidacy was not against Hollowell."

Rauch campaigned hard in the Democratic primary in the spring of 1966, using his strong support in the Gastonia black community from his days on the City Council to good advantage and striking out on his own in Cleveland County, where hardly anyone knew him.

He also used his past connections with former Governor Terry Sanford to gain votes in Cleveland. Rauch had been a staunch Sanford supporter in the 1960 gubernatorial campaign and a supporter of Sanford's protégé, Richardson Preyer of Greensboro, in Preyer's 1964 unsuccessful run for governor.

Rauch's efforts in those two gubernatorial campaigns paid off in his own Senate race. Two Sanford and Preyer supporters who were particularly helpful in Cleveland County were Pat Spangler and Clint Newton, both Democrats with political clout who were happy to buck tradition with a fresh face like Rauch's.

He won the primary, finishing first in Gaston and second in Cleveland. He and Shelby lawyer Jack White became the Democratic candidates for the November general election.

Rauch continued to campaign hard that fall, working long hours and using his Sanford-Preyer connections to help spread the word of his candidacy. Two people Rauch met in that campaign who would become his friends for life were Ollie Harris, a Kings Mountain mortician who later would also be elected to the Senate, and Jack Hunt, a dentist from the rural community of Lattimore in Cleveland County. Hunt was later elected to the North Carolina House. Both helped Rauch gain voter support.

Rauch easily won the November election. He did well in all sections of the two counties except precincts in Cherryville and Mt. Holly. "Those two communities were hotbeds for the Ku Klux Klan, and I didn't do well in either place," Rauch said.

He also recalled one unpleasant experience during that campaign, an act of prejudice that both surprised and angered him but which he later accepted as part of the human condition. On the face of a Rauch billboard in Cherryville during that campaign, someone scrawled the word "Jew."

"I was obviously upset and talked about that slur with two of my friends, Buck Fraley and Grier Beam, executives at Carolina Freight Company in Cherryville," Rauch explained. "They suggested I just forget it. They correctly explained that I couldn't stop the thinking of people like that and shouldn't satisfy them with any display of anger.

"Buck and Grier gave me good advice. When a reporter asked me for a reaction to the defacing of my billboard, I just smiled and said that from the looks of the scrawl on that billboard I would guess the person who did it must be glad I wasn't Episcopalian because he wouldn't have known how to spell it. And that was the end of it."

Rauch's election made history. He was the first Jew elected to the state Senate in North Carolina.

When Rauch entered the legislative hall in Raleigh as a senator, it was the first time he had ever been inside the building. He was, he said, quite impressed that all the staff members welcomed him by name. His feeling of self-importance was lessened when he learned that those warm greeters had seen his photograph in the legislative directory just as they had every other member's.

The staff memorized every legislator's face and name. "I was not as famous as I first thought," he said with a chuckle. "I thought I was somebody important, and all they had done was see my picture in the legislative handbook."

That didn't rob Rauch of his pride in being elected, however, and the first official act he performed was to write his parents in New York on his personalized Senate stationery.

Neither of Rauch's parents was enthralled by politics, but the new senator knew both would be happy he had been elected to such an important job. Rauch also knew his grandparents, who came to this country a century earlier as Hungarian immigrants, would have been especially proud if they had lived long enough to see his election.

"I was in awe of virtually everything that first term," Rauch said. "I was not an integral part of anything. It takes time to learn. I was just happy to be there."

Rauch learned a couple of things that year. First, committee leaders have tremendous power and influence over bills. Second, lawyer members initially have a huge advantage over others because they're trained in ways to make laws work for them and against others.

"But after a few years, business experience gives business people an advantage," Rauch said. "Once you learn the process, experience in the business world provides an edge because you can apply those principles to what needs to be done."

Those early experiences also persuaded Rauch that North Carolina is wise not to impose term limits on its legislators:

> It takes a long time to learn to become effective. You need members with experience to understand the process and the guts to tell the professional staff how things ought to be done. Most of the staff has more

experience than the members, and if you limit terms, you make that situation worse. If members aren't doing a worthy job, vote them out but don't limit their experience and opportunity to perform worthy services just because of some arbitrary number of years. Term limits would give too much power to the staff because they would understand the process better than members with limited experience. Most legislators don't read all the bills. Only the most dedicated do. With term limits, the twenty most influential people in the legislative building wouldn't include more than five legislators. The other fifteen would be staff members and lobbyists. That could be disastrous.

Rauch may have been in awe of the system and his more experienced colleagues that first session, but it didn't stop him from showing his brashness at the first opportunity. Lieutenant Governor Bob Scott was the Senate's presiding officer and the one who appointed committee chairs during Rauch's first term. Rauch brazenly asked Scott for a chairmanship. He didn't get it. Freshmen members don't get such assignments unless they've done a lot of political favors for those making the appointments. Scott did appoint Rauch to the influential Appropriations Committee, which gave him a head start on exerting his leadership talents and put him in close contact with some of the more powerful lawmakers.

Rauch's forwardness in seeking a chair that first year caused his friend Jack Hunt to remember his first meeting with Rauch during that 1966 campaign. Rauch knocked on Hunt's door one evening, introduced himself, and said he was seeking support. Rauch and Hunt recall the experience somewhat differently, but they agree on the basics of what was said.

Rauch had been told that Hunt was a man with good political ties in Cleveland County. "I introduced myself, told him I was running and was seeking support. I told him I was from New York, but I was careful to let him know that my wife and children had all been born in Gaston County. I also told him that I was physically able to run my business and also handle duties in Raleigh and that I also thought I was smart enough to do both."

Hunt said that was the essence of the conversation, but he vividly remembers Rauch's exact words. "He told me who he was and what he wanted," Hunt said. "But the thing I most remember is that he said, 'You know, I'm a big old strong boy physically, and I ain't no damn mental lightweight either.' I was impressed with his self-assurance in that first meeting, and he has never disappointed me with his abilities as a legislative leader. He's one of the best I've ever known."

Rauch didn't talk much about religion in that initial Senate campaign, but he never shied from discussing it when asked. Obviously, as the ethnic slur on the defaced billboard showed, his faith was no secret. He was running as an individual, however, not as a representative of any group, religious or otherwise. He remembers one campaign trip to Cleveland County when a fellow plowing a field stopped his mule and asked if he was "Hebrewish." Rauch knew what the man meant and confirmed that he was. That was all the explanation necessary to gain another supporter and future friend.

While he was the first Jew to join the Senate, he was not the first member of that religious faith to serve in the General Assembly. Jews had previously been elected to the

Senator Rauch with daughter
Stephanie, age 17, in the
Senate chamber, 1978

153

North Carolina House of Representatives, and several have since been elected to the Senate. "I was pleased with the respect the senators showed me because of my religion," Rauch said. Discrimination, so far as Rauch was concerned, did not exist in the Senate.

In fact, at least two senators made special efforts to ensure courtesy. In the first instance, the Senate rules were amended to allow hats to be worn in the Senate for religious purposes. A ban on headwear when Rauch was elected prevented an Orthodox Jew from either offering a prayer or sitting in the visitors' gallery.

On another occasion during his first month of Senate service, a senator asked him to read a bill pertaining to the humane slaughter of animals to make sure there was no language that violated any kosher rules. "I thought it was really special that the senators would come to me on those issues and that they cared for my feelings and opinions," Rauch said.

Two of the senators Rauch became close friends with during his 1967 freshman term were Tom White and Jimmy Green, both hard-nosed Democrats from eastern North Carolina who had nothing in common with Rauch's background—nor, in many instances, did they share his views on legislation. The three learned to respect each other for their independence and diligence to legislative matters, even when they were on opposing sides of issues.

Tom White, a Kinston lawyer with a quick mind and keen understanding of the legislative process, was clearly the single most powerful senator in the state during Rauch's first years in the General Assembly. White headed the Appropriations Committee, the Advisory Budget Commission, and the Legislative Building Commission, among other things. "He ran the show," Rauch said. "Knowledge is power, and he had knowledge. He worked hard. His knowledge of Senate rules and of the state Constitution encouraged me to get more involved. Our backgrounds were absolutely different. He grew up as a rural, devout, Southern Presbyterian, and I was raised in New York as a Jew. But we became very close friends and remained so until his death.

"I respected him as much as any man I've ever known. He was a perfect gentleman and cared deeply for the people of this state." When White left the Senate, he gave his friend Rauch a hand-lettered sign that he had kept on his legislative desk. The sign said, "There is no limit to what a man can accomplish if he doesn't care who gets the credit." That, Rauch said, was the motto by which White lived.

Rauch's friendship with Jimmy Green, who later was elected speaker of the House and lieutenant governor, was also established that first year, despite their divergent political philosophies and backgrounds. They worked with each other on bills of mutual interest and respectfully opposed each other on other issues, particularly legislation involving tobacco, a product that provided Green his livelihood but one, which Rauch both then and now has no use for.

Their friendship remained intact until Green's death, even though Green encountered personal and legal problems after serving as lieutenant governor and making an unsuccessful run for governor. Rauch was steadfastly supportive of Green, refusing to abandon his friend as some others had done.

"He always treated me with respect, and he was always fair, even when we differed on issues," Rauch said. "He was always a man of his word, and I greatly respected him for that. To me, he has always been a loyal friend. You should never turn your back on friends when they're down. Friends make mistakes, but they are still friends."

Green called Rauch a dependable friend with high integrity. "He has always been a statesman every inch of the way," Green said in an interview from his hometown of Clarkton, in the eastern North Carolina tobacco heartland, shortly before his death. "He was one of the best and most able committee chairmen I ever served with. I applaud his honesty and his integrity. You never had to wonder where he stood on an issue when he gave you his word. He could say in a few words what bills were about, and you could believe him. During my first year serving with Marshall, I often wondered what a liberal Yankee like him was doing in the legislature, but the longer he stayed, the more conservative he became. He is a credit to this state. Of course, he didn't to it alone. His wife Jeanne was a big plus, too."

Rauch also received a crash course in the political arena early in his first term when he was called to the office of then-Governor Dan Moore, a man Rauch had not met and whom he did not support in the 1964 Democratic primary against Rauch's friend Richardson Preyer. "He knew I hadn't supported his candidacy, but he greeted me warmly and we discussed his legislative program and ways that I might help him," Rauch recalled. "I realized for the first time in that meeting that people in state government are just like regular people. They work for or against each other on certain issues, but they can remain friends and respect differing opinions." The Rauches and Moores later became personal friends after Governor Moore left office in 1969.

Governor Moore's daughter, Edith Hamilton, and her husband Edgar live in Shelby and remain friends of Marshall and Jeanne Rauch. "My father always thought a lot of Marshall and always spoke highly of him," Edith Hamilton said.

Edgar Hamilton also recalls that Governor Moore spoke of his fondness for Rauch. "I recall him often saying how impressed he was with Marshall as a legislator," Hamilton said. "He said Marshall was one of the most astute and mature freshmen lawmakers he had ever met. He watched Marshall's career and always felt he conducted himself in a smart manner. The governor was impressed with Marshall's abilities and his concern for the people of the state."

Rauch gave himself little credit for accomplishments during his first few years in the Senate, except for learning and listening, although in his second term he was named vice chairman of the powerful Appropriations Committee.

In Rauch's third term, beginning in 1971, his influence began to show. By that time, Bob Scott had been elected governor, with Rauch's support, and Wadesboro lawyer Pat Taylor, a man known for his quick wit and slow Southern drawl, had been elected lieutenant governor with committee appointment powers. Taylor earlier appointed Rauch chairman of a subcommittee on appropriations in 1969, the first of many important committee chairmanships to come his way.

Rauch learned another important political lesson that year. The 1972 governor's campaign was already taking shape, and Rauch made it known he enthusiastically supported his Senate colleague "Skipper" Bowles over Lieutenant Governor Taylor in that race. Bowles and Taylor would become the leading Democratic candidates in the gubernatorial primary. Rauch's decision to support Bowles cost Rauch a committee chairmanship the next year because Taylor shut him out of a leadership post. That temporarily slowed Rauch's climb to a position of power but didn't stop it.

Taylor discounted any perceived political punishment of Rauch for supporting Bowles by pointing out that he had appointed Rauch as chairman of the committee on Intergovernmental Relations. That sounded a lot more impressive than it was. There had never been such a committee before and has never been one since. The committee did little that year because Taylor gave it nothing of significance to do. As a result, Rauch better understood political realities and was ready to regain influence after the next election. He did just that.

Several critical issues stand out in Rauch's memory as those in which he played a pivotal role during that 1971 legislative session, even though Pat Taylor limited his power and influence. One was the Homestead Exemption Act, sponsored by influential Senator Ralph Scott of Alamance County, uncle of then Governor Robert Scott. The bill was designed to create property tax breaks for elderly homeowners. Despite Scott's power in the Senate, the bill was facing strong opposition because it would have slashed government revenue (and left more cash in the hands of senior citizens). Lieutenant Governor Taylor sent the bill to a three-member appropriations subcommittee, headed by Rauch, for an initial vote. When the subcommittee voted, one senator voted against the plan and one voted for it. Rauch broke the tie by voting in the affirmative, and the bill eventually became law. Senator Scott and Rauch became even closer after this mutual victory and supported much of each other's legislation.

Another bill that year also bore the personal stamp of Senator Scott. Scott wanted to strengthen the state Milk Commission, which regulated milk prices. Rauch was philosophically opposed to the commission on grounds that it helped inflate prices for consumers. But Scott had close ties to the dairy industry and was determined to help his dairymen friends, who he felt were being treated unfairly. Rauch said of that bill:

I had always been bothered by the fact that this state had the highest milk prices and the lowest cigarette prices in the country. But I knew the bill was going to pass, so I saw no need to publicly oppose it. There's no need to do that unless you're just looking for headlines. So I kept quiet as Senator Scott spoke on the merits of regulating milk prices. I remember his impassioned argument that if we didn't pass that bill, women and children in North Carolina would be forced to drink what he disdainfully called imported milk. I wondered about that, but was not ready to question the senior senator while he was speaking. I was concerned, however, about imported milk maybe coming to this state from foreign countries like China or Korea. I sure didn't think that was a good idea, and I voted for the bill. After the Senate session that day the bill passed, I walked over to Senator Scott and asked him privately where that imported milk would have come from. He smiled and said, 'Oh, Virginia and South Carolina.' I knew I had been had. The bill became law. The North Carolina Milk Commission still exists, and milk prices are still high in this state.

A third bill would have improved conditions for migrant workers. A new senator, Zeb Alley, a fun-loving mountain lawyer with an impressive war record and a big heart, sponsored it. Alley's bill would have imposed stricter health and safety laws for migrants, who were becoming an important factor in farm production across the state. Rauch thought the migrant bill was worthy and promised to support it. Rauch's eastern lawmaker friends pressured him to back away, because it would make things harder for farmers. Rauch wanted to support his farmer friends in the Senate, but he had made a commitment to Alley to support the plan and he felt it was needed for the benefit of migrants. Alley credits Rauch's support as essential to passage of that law. "He made a pledge, and he stuck with it against heavy pressures from the fellows Down East," Alley said. "He was a man of his word. He is just that kind of fellow. He earned the respect of his colleagues and the people for that."

Alley and Rauch have remained close friends through the years although neither now serves in the General Assembly. The mutual respect they share is clear. "He gives the appearance of a hard-nosed lobbyist," Rauch said of Alley, "but he is truly one of the most compassionate, never-forget-your-friends human beings I have ever known."

A fourth bill Rauch cited as important was one sponsored by Senator George Wood, a pork producer and businessman from Camden County, in the northeast corner of the state. Wood's bill called for the creation of a new system of self-service gasoline pumps so drivers could pump their own fuel for less money. Rauch favored the plan.

Though pump-your-own gas stations are common across North Carolina and the country today, that bill tore the Senate

Senator Rauch, Rabbi Yussi Groner, and Governor James Hunt in the governor's office during Hunt's second term, 1982

apart and prompted some of the most heated debates of the year. Rauch supported the gas pump bill as one that was good for consumers. By pumping their own gas, he believed, drivers could save a few cents per gallon. The oil industry opposed the idea, arguing that it would be dangerous to allow just anybody to operate a pump.

Both sides in the debate hedged a bit in their arguments. What Wood didn't explain was that if the bill passed, he planned to open some self-service pumps.

What the oil companies didn't concede was that they saw the plan cutting into their profits. On the final day of the debate, John Burney of Wilmington, a colorful senator and talented lawyer who represented the oil industry, walked onto the Senate floor carrying a pitchfork. He had a copy of Wood's bill lying on the fork's prongs. Holding his nose, Burney decried the merits of the bill, saying the proposal smelled so bad he wouldn't touch it but felt compelled to put it on the end of a pitchfork where other smelly barnyard items are usually found. Nonetheless, the bill became law and self-service pumps are now more popular than ever.

Perhaps the most significant pieces of legislation on Rauch's list in the 1971 legislative session were related to higher education. One bill created a new system of governance for the state's public university system. He supported the proposal to restructure the University of North Carolina by creating a single administrative board for all sixteen university campuses. Later, he became a member of that governing board. The other higher education proposal that Rauch also helped lead created the Medical School at East Carolina University.

"We needed another medical school," Rauch explained, "not necessarily at ECU, but that was the political reality of the situation. It was there or nowhere, so I supported it. I've never regretted that decision." Needed in eastern North Carolina or not, the ECU medical school has probably done more for the economy and growth of Greenville and Pitt County than anything else in the history of that part of the state.

Rauch recalls one humorous incident involving Dr. Leo Jenkins, the ECU chancellor and a colorful character whose political expertise helped persuade lawmakers to create a medical school on his campus. "A group of legislators involved in the budget process was touring the ECU campus one day on a bus with Jenkins standing at the front, extolling the virtues of his school and the many fine students there," Rauch said. "Just as he was talking about all the clean-cut, bright students there, the bus stopped for a traffic light and a disheveled teenager with holes in his jeans, uncombed hair, a beard, and dirty shirt crossed the street in front of us. We all saw him. Without even a pause, Chancellor Jenkins calmly stated, 'Obviously a transfer student from Chapel Hill.'"

Another legislative proposal was the vanity license plate bill conceived by his friend Senator Skipper Bowles, who the next year became the Democratic nominee for governor. Bowles wanted to improve the appearance of North Carolina's main highways and build on an idea for highway beautification that had been advanced nationally by Lady Bird Johnson, the wife of President Lyndon Johnson.

Facing a tight state budget, Bowles, with essential support from Rauch, conceived the idea of permitting motorists to buy personalized auto license plates with revenues going to beautify the roads. That's how the flowers and other plantings on major roads in North Carolina became a reality. "Each time I see some of those flowers along the highway, I smile a little bit knowing I had a small part in it," Rauch said. "But I have an even warmer feeling because it reminds me of my friend Skipper. He would be proud."

Bowles left public life after his 1972 defeat in the governor's race, losing to Jim Holshouser, the first Republican elected as governor in North Carolina in the twentieth century. Bowles' defeat by the little-known Boone lawyer and Republican member of the North Carolina House was the beginning of major changes in the North Carolina political landscape.

The election's outcome was a shocker. Of all reasons cited for Holshouser's victory, the main one was the national presidential ticket that pitted Republican Richard Nixon against Democrat George McGovern. Nixon's popularity and McGovern's lack of it built support for Holhouser and worked against Bowles.

That also was the year Jesse Helms was elected to the United States Senate, eventually becoming a nationally known symbol and powerful senator for the right wing of the Republican Party during the 1980s and 1990s.

Rauch didn't realize it at the time, but he was just beginning his ascent to a place of power in the General Assembly despite the political setback of his friend Bowles and the rise of the GOP in the state. The next ten years of his public service would be significant. He was just coming into his own.

Chapter 12 - The North Carolina Senate, Part II

This place won't be the same without Marshall Rauch. Only a few legislators could compete with his intelligence, vision, and integrity or with his commitment to sound government and a sensible tax policy. He deserves the title of Mr. Public Servant.

Raleigh journalist Paul O'Connor, after Rauch was defeated for reelection in 1990.

Views similar to those of newspaper columnist Paul O'Connor were commonly expressed in the North Carolina General Assembly following Rauch's surprising 1990 election defeat. Rauch was a legislative leader with nearly twenty-five years' experience, a bright and industrious businessman, known for genuinely caring about people, working hard, and getting things accomplished. The people in Gaston and Cleveland counties, indeed residents across the state of North Carolina, were without a powerful legislative voice when Rauch lost the election.

That election, marked by a strong Republican surge across the state, was successful for many GOP candidates, even those with no experience and little knowledge of the legislative process. Democrat Rauch was caught in the rising Republican tide.

In casting him aside, voters in Rauch's district gave up more than they perhaps knew in swapping his expertise for what former Alabama Governor George Wallace used to call the "melodious" voice of his opponent, a Charlotte television broadcaster who was seeking office for the first—and last—time.

The reaction of legislative and political leaders, as well as personal friends, was typified in a handwritten note to Rauch from Erskine Bowles, a Charlotte investment banker who would later serve as White House chief of staff for President Bill Clinton.

"What a shame for our state," Bowles wrote. "There have been few, if any, who have done more for the people of North Carolina than you. You have more to be proud of than most people. I just wish more people knew just how much you have done for our citizens."

The son of Rauch's former Senate colleague Hargrove "Skipper" Bowles, Erskine Bowles then added some solace born of his own experience.

"I've often felt that it was Jesse Helms' first tidal wave that beat my dad and now it looks like you are the latest victim of that kind of thing. It makes me sick. It is sad for our state. But from a personal viewpoint, I can tell you my dad's loss gave us time together we would never have had if he had won. Maybe this will give you time with your wonderful family that you would have given so generously to the state."

Bowles knew whereof he spoke. After his defeat, Rauch spent far more time with his family than he had during his years in elective office.

Gaston County businessman David Hoyle, who later served Gaston County in the state Senate, attributed the 1990 defeat to Rauch's own diligence in doing his job as a senator. "He chose to go to Raleigh and be an effective senator and do the right things for the state," Hoyle said. "He did his job there rather than go back home and be a politician."

Many people who sound good as politicians, Hoyle said, "are totally ineffective in Raleigh. Marshall was not one of those. His success in the General Assembly is what defeated him back home. He was in the legislature working instead of spending his time back home bragging about all he had done. The people who brag are usually the ones who don't accomplish much. Marshall just kept working, and he was a victim of his own success at election time. People just didn't realize all he had achieved."

Rauch took his defeat in stride. His record was such that he didn't need to second guess himself or wonder what he could have done differently. His only regret, he later explained, was spending so much money on his campaign. That was the first year Rauch had ever accepted campaign contributions. He did so at the urging of friends who feared the Republicans would make a big push to throw him out despite his entrenched position, experience, and almost a quarter century of service.

During his twelve terms in the Senate, Rauch cut a wide swath in his gradual climb to positions of power. In annual rankings of legislators for their power and influence by the non-partisan and nonprofit North Carolina Center for Public Policy Research, Rauch never finished below sixth among the fifty senators. Rauch was listed as the sixth most influential senator in the initial 1977 rankings and was never listed below fourth in any subsequent term. In 1990, at the end of his last term, he was ranked second only to the Senate president pro-tem in influence and effectiveness.

Rauch's legislative power actually began to be noticed as far back as 1973. It just didn't evolve as he expected or planned because a strange thing had happened in the preceding November election.

After "Skipper" Bowles won the Democratic gubernatorial primary in 1972, it was assumed that Bowles would win the November election. After all, Democrats had won every North Carolina governor's race in the twentieth century. Bowles and Rauch were confident, so confident that they began putting things in place for the next year's legislative session.

Rauch was both a personal friend and a strong political supporter of Bowles, and the two men began planning ways to implement Bowles' new programs, including strengthening public education. With Bowles' nomination came the choice of former Governor Terry Sanford's protégé Jim Hunt as the Democratic nominee for lieutenant governor who, if he won in November, would preside over the state Senate.

In the November election, Bowles lost to Republican Jim Holshouser, shocking Democrats and surprising Republicans. Afterward, North Carolina's political structure was significantly altered.

Although Republican Holshouser won the governorship, Democrat Hunt won the lieutenant governor's race. The stage was then set for the first General Assembly in almost one hundred years with a Republican as governor and Democrats in control of the legislature.

Rauch quickly learned that his hopes of becoming chairman of the Senate Finance Committee dissolved in the November voting. But Rauch's time would come. He spent the four years that Hunt was presiding officer in the Senate learning more about the politics and the process. He didn't get the Finance Committee chairmanships he wanted, but his reputation grew as a dedicated senator with greater potential.

After the 1976 election, Hunt moved up to the governor's office where one of his top priorities was to get a constitutional amendment adopted, allowing North Carolina governors to succeed themselves in office. That mystified Rauch.

"It was hard for me to accept it the first time I heard about the legislation that would permit a vote of the people and a constitutional change so that governors—including Hunt—could run for a second consecutive four-year term," Rauch said. "It amazed me that anybody would think of that while in office. However, politics means different things to different people, and Hunt did absolutely nothing wrong. It just showed his political ambition and his popularity at that time. Every major newspaper in the state endorsed the proposal. In fact, I ended up voting for it. I am happy to say it actually turned out to be one of the best things we did, because Jim Hunt proved to be one of the most progressive, dynamic, and successful leaders this state has ever had or is likely to have."

Leaders of the state legislature gave Hunt a choice. They agreed to approve either a bill allowing a vote of the people on gubernatorial succession or a bill authorizing a referendum on giving the governor the veto power, another proposal that had long been discussed as a means of strengthening gubernatorial power in the state.

It was an historic moment in North Carolina. For two centuries, state legislators had vigilantly protected their authority, but either of the proposals, if enacted, would diminish legislative power. North Carolina had long limited governors to one term and was the only state that denied its governor the power to veto laws passed by the General Assembly. Governor Hunt opted for gubernatorial succession rather than the veto power. In approving that Constitutional amendment, voters brought significant change to state politics. The amendment enabled Hunt to become the first North Carolina governor in modern times to succeed himself. And Hunt did it twice. After serving eight years, he sat out while Jim Martin served two terms as governor. Then Hunt was elected twice more. In all, the amendment allowed Hunt to serve a record sixteen years as governor—after having served four years as lieutenant governor.

Twenty years passed before the General Assembly got around to approving the second of the two proposed reforms: legislation authorizing a referendum on giving the governor a veto. In 1997, after winning reelection to succeed himself for a second time, Jim Hunt became the first governor in North Carolina with veto power.

With Hunt's rise to the governor's office in 1976, Rauch's Senate friend Jimmy Green, a tobacco warehouseman and political trench-fighter, was elected lieutenant governor. With that election, Rauch's Senate star was again rising.

At Rauch's first meeting with Lieutenant Governor Green following that election, Green made it known that Rauch would be chairman of the Senate Finance Committee. Also participating in that meeting were Senators Kenneth Royall and Harold Hardison, two experienced and savvy lawmakers who had been and would continue to wield power for another decade.

"I hadn't asked Green for the chairmanship, but I surely did want it," Rauch said. "There wasn't much discussion in that meeting about who would do it. Green just told me there would be a lot of work involved but he wanted me in the job because he was confident I could handle it. That was the first time, in the 1977 legislative session, that I really began to feel I was accomplishing something. I had been there paying my dues for ten years by then. My earlier years as vice chairman of Finance, where I learned from then Lieutenant Governor Jim Hunt and committee Chairman Senator Kirby, gave me a really good background for the chairmanship."

Rauch dug into his task, with Lieutenant Governor Green presiding over the Senate and Senators Royall and Hardison working as heads of committees on Ways and Means and

Appropriations, respectively. In those days and for at least the next decade, Royall was generally considered to be the state's best budget expert. Hardison was a tough partisan cut from the same eastern traditions as Green.

"That was a great experience," Rauch said of his close association with that trio. "They were highly motivated, worked hard, and understood how things were to be done. We were always able to work things out in harmony without any bickering even when we disagreed. I was really proud to be a part of that group."

Royall, who died in the spring of 1999, credited Rauch with much of the success of that legislative session. "Marshall is one of the most efficient legislators I ever worked with," Royall said in the fall of 1998. "He ran the Finance Committee like it was a business and had the respect of all his colleagues. He had great command presence and personality. I never questioned him much because I didn't need to. He had excellent judgment. When he spoke, people listened."

Former state senator Henson Barnes of Goldsboro was a young senator in 1977 when Rauch first reached a position of power and influence. "He was a big help to me," Barnes said of Rauch. "He taught me the importance of hard work and keeping your word. He is a loyalist. If he said he was on your side, you didn't need to check. He'd be there. His greatest strength is that he's a natural leader. It didn't matter if you were a conservative or a liberal; he worked on the merits of bills. His defeat (in 1990) was a great loss to the people of this state."

The experience Rauch gained in 1977, when added to what he had learned from Senator Tom White, his first mentor, gave him insight that most legislators would envy. As chairman of the Finance Committee, Rauch began work on what would be a series of efforts to lower taxes and reduce state spending. This wasn't the first time he had tried to cut state costs, but it was the first time he had clout enough to get it done.

In his very first Senate term, almost a decade earlier, Rauch had opposed a tax increase totaling $102 million. He said it was wrong for the government to increase spending on programs that were not essential or services that private citizens should

State Senator Jim Ezzell (right) confers with his close friend Senator Marshall Rauch
during a Senate debate. Ezzell was later tragically killed in an auto crash
in Raleigh. Rauch delivered a eulogy at the memorial service.

do for themselves, calling such moves a "squandering" of public resources.

Of the taxes added in 1969, he said, "The government was growing too fast because it was trying to do too many things that private industry needed to do on its own. We needed good roads, but they didn't have to be the best roads in the world. If we needed the best of anything, it ought to have been the best public education system in the world."

He also had spoken earlier against increased spending for prison cells. Instead of spending more money building prisons, he argued unsuccessfully, the state should be spending those dollars to reduce the need for prisons.

During Rauch's first legislative term, he showed his independence by proposing an idea that some of his colleagues thought was absurd. He wanted to open all state government meetings to the public so people could see what was happening and how their money was being spent. His plan got nowhere.

"I was just planting a seed for later," Rauch explained. "I knew it would come in time." He was proved right. Rules were later amended to open all governmental meetings with specific exceptions for personnel matters, land acquisition, and pending lawsuits.

Rauch also was an early advocate of tougher laws against drunk driving. In his first year in the Senate, Rauch sponsored legislation that would have revoked the driving privileges of anyone charged with driving while intoxicated if the driver refused to take a breath test. The proposal also would have suspended for ten years the license of any driver convicted a second time of drunk driving.

The next year, he sponsored a bill that would have mandated weekend jail terms for people convicted of drunk driving. "A drunk driver is just as dangerous as a person with a machine gun," he said, in arguing for his bills.

All those efforts died in the hands of trial lawyers in the General Assembly. That same year, he also proposed revoking the driver's license of any driver under age eighteen who had dropped out of school. "The farmers killed that one," Rauch said. "The farm lobby was powerful."

In the 1997 legislative session, thirty years after Rauch first tried to strengthen laws involving intoxicated drivers, lawmakers finally enacted statutes almost identical to those that Rauch had put forth in the late 1960s.

Rauch didn't have the influence in those early days that he did a decade later as a committee chairman when he succeeded in getting more of his ideas accepted. But as chairman of the Finance Committee, he gained a reputation for speaking out on bills, not sitting silently as the debate continued. His voice was heeded and his influence felt.

His influence and reputation for integrity also brought him a leadership post he didn't seek but was willing to accept. Rauch was named head of the General Assembly's first joint House and Senate Ethics Committee, where he dealt with the thorny issues posed by lawmakers who used their influence in both unethical and illegal ways to get things done for personal gain. It was not a post from which to win friends among legislative colleagues, but it was one that he agreed was essential to honest and open government.

"You never enjoy having to deal with those issues, but the committee's efforts were both important and significant," he said. "They had to be handled correctly without any hint of a whitewash. As the first chairman of that committee, I got the efforts started, and I'm proud of what we were able to do and of the steps aimed at helping to raise ethical standards. That kind of action is what gains respect for the legislature from the voting public."

Once he achieved a leadership position, Rauch was instrumental in getting passed a little noticed but meaningful measure that reduced the amount of tax citizens were paying on investments and other intangible wealth. The remainder of the tax stayed on the books for thirty more years, but Rauch led efforts that reduced the assessment by working for passage of a law that allowed notes payable to be deducted from accounts receivable in calculating the intangibles tax. He later proposed outright repeal of the intangibles tax, but that was not passed until 1997, after he left the Senate. But he was the one who got the repeal discussion started.

When studies showed that North Carolina was paying more than its share of the costs of building federal highways, Rauch went to Washington to seek reimbursement from the Department of Transportation. He was warmly received, but his arguments fell on deaf ears. He came back and persuaded North Carolina to restrict the practice of paying more than its share of highway costs in order to get faster funding of road projects.

Two freshmen legislators who worked with Rauch on those highway studies later became influential lawmakers themselves. One was Representative Dennis Wicker of Lee County, who served as lieutenant governor from 1990 to 1998 and was a Democratic candidate for governor in 2000. The other was Representative Martin Nesbitt of Asheville, who later became chairman of the House Finance Committee before moving to the Senate.

Despite all the talk about highways and taxes, money was not the hottest topic of the 1977 legislative year. That distinction went to a politically charged proposal to change the United States Constitution by including an amendment granting equal rights to women.

That issue caused emotional distress for Rauch just as it did for many other legislators. Rauch had an earned reputation for encouraging fairness for both women and minorities. He had women and black supervisors in his manufacturing plants long before it became politically correct. He also had strong political support from women's groups and other proponents of gender equity. However, he was part of the Senate leadership of Green, Royall, and Hardison, who opposed the ERA for philosophical reasons.

Rauch's biggest problem with the ERA was that he considered it little more than a symbol for rallying political coalitions. He felt the proposed amendment would not make any difference in guaranteeing equality and that such a law was not needed to bring about fairness that could only come from the heart. He also had genuine concerns that the amendment would create serious problems for the military services and for other institutions because people didn't understand its ramifications.

He recalled one anecdote that showed how supporters' emotions clouded their thinking. A fellow senator, a female, sharply criticized Rauch for not supporting the amendment. "I just don't see how a person of your race cannot support something like this that will help so many people," the woman said to Rauch. Ever polite but direct, Rauch reminded the colleague that Judaism is a religion and has nothing to do with race.

Part of the problem with the ERA, Rauch concluded, was that many of the amendment's supporters didn't know what it meant or would do. Even worse was his suspicion that some of them didn't care. They were making political statements, not sound government policy. Rauch was pressured by both sides in the ERA debate, especially by liberal Democrats, both women and men. He held firm to his belief that passage wouldn't help anybody much but could hurt many by either establishing unrealistic rules or creating false hopes.

The ERA vote in the North Carolina General Assembly was crucial to the national campaign for the amendment because, at the time, proponents needed only the approval of one or two more states to reach the two-thirds required for ratification. The

North Carolina House had approved the amendment. Its fate lay in the Senate, which normally was more conservative on social issues. Each side lobbied long and hard for votes; several members switched back and forth during the debates. It was a cliffhanger. Proponents feared they were two votes shy of a majority on the eve of the Senate vote, and they brought out all their troops.

One ERA supporter who called Rauch urging him to vote for the amendment was a surprise even to Rauch, but it showed the depth and breadth of the support and the desperate efforts of proponents. "A few days before the vote, the phone rang in my office and when I answered someone on the other end of the line said the White House was calling," Rauch said. "And in just a few seconds, President Jimmy Carter came on the line and asked me to vote for the ERA. I remember very well telling him I was distressed to tell my president that I couldn't honor his wishes. But I didn't vacillate. I told him plainly and honestly that my mind was made up to vote against the amendment." If a personal call from the president of the United States couldn't persuade Rauch to change his mind, nothing could. He was solidly in the opposition camp.

He had some other influential North Carolina names on his side, most notably then U.S. Senator Sam Ervin and North Carolina Supreme Court Chief Justice Susie Sharp. Both had spoken out in opposition to the amendment. With twenty-six "no" votes committed against the ERA in the North Carolina Senate—one more than was needed to defeat it—the die seemed cast, but there was still room for political posturing.

The voting procedure was prearranged in what Rauch recalled as one of the most dramatic Senate exercises in his experience. The plan was carefully drawn. Senator Robert Jordan, a moderate Democrat from Montgomery County who had ambitions for higher office, wanted to go on record as a key ERA advocate even though he knew the amendment was heading for defeat. Opponents gave him that opportunity, knowing that he was supporting a losing cause.

On the day of the ERA vote in the Senate, Jordan was given permission to make the motion that the ERA be approved. The

Senate's presiding officer, Lieutenant Governor Jimmy Green, despite his opposition to the amendment, agreed to give Jordan that opportunity because he knew the gesture was purely symbolic.

As planned, the moment that Jordan made his motion for approval, Rauch stood at his Senate desk and made a motion that Jordan's motion "do lie upon the table," invoking a parliamentary maneuver that under Senate rules was frequently used to kill measures. A motion to table was not debatable. In a matter of seconds, Rauch's motion was approved, twenty-six votes to twenty-four. The maneuver had worked as planned, with Jordan making his political stand public and the ERA going down to defeat.

The Equal Rights Amendment has not been revived in recent years. It has never been ratified by enough states to make it a part of the federal Constitution. Senator Jordan later was elected lieutenant governor but subsequently lost a campaign for governor. Among the legislative achievements Jordan claimed in waging those two campaigns was his strong support for the ERA.

As a member of the winning side in the ERA debate, Rauch's influence continued to be felt throughout that session. The next election, however, would throw some stumbling blocks in his path to continuing power.

The adoption of gubernatorial succession four years earlier also enabled the lieutenant governor to seek a second consecutive term. Rauch's good friend, Lieutenant Governor Green, opted to seek another four years in office. His Democratic primary challenger was a young Gastonia lawyer named Carl Stewart Jr., also a close friend and political associate of Rauch.

The candidacies of Green and Stewart put Rauch on a political tightrope. As a close associate of Green's in the Senate, Rauch felt an obligation to support Green for a second term. Stewart, however, was a young man who Rauch felt had great potential for leadership. Stewart had served admirably as speaker of the North Carolina House, had been a friend of long standing, was from Rauch's hometown, and was a person Rauch had helped politically and financially in his early days of law practice by directing legal business his way.

"That caused me a great deal of consternation," Rauch conceded. "Green was my Senate friend who had shown his faith in me through important committee assignments and had always treated me fairly. But Stewart was also my good friend whom I knew well, was very proud of, and whose career had been helped and shaped by my own efforts. I was in a real dilemma. I talked with Jimmy Green, and he told me to do what I felt was right. I hated to go against him, but I felt I belonged with Carl and I supported him in the campaign."

It was a losing effort for Stewart, whom Green defeated in the primary of 1980. It also resulted in a loss for Rauch in the next session of the North Carolina Senate, where Green had political debts to pay and Rauch wasn't a creditor. When it came time for committee assignments, Rauch was passed over as chairman of the Finance Committee. That post went to Senator Conrad Duncan, a lesser-experienced lawmaker from Rockingham County. One of the reasons Duncan got the job was he had worked for and contributed financially to Green's campaign.

While Green owed a political debt to Duncan, he also knew Duncan could use some help with the Finance Committee. Therefore Green named Rauch vice chairman and expected him to shoulder most of the committee's workload. Duncan seemed content with the title because Rauch always gave Duncan credit for the committee's output. The next year, Green renamed Rauch chairman of Finance and put him back in the official seat of power.

Rauch found himself in a similar situation four years later. This time it was Senate colleague Robert Jordan running for lieutenant governor against Carl Stewart. Rauch again supported Stewart who lost again. But Jordan, knowing the importance of the Finance Committee's work, picked Rauch as co-chairman, despite Rauch's lack of political support for Jordan. Rauch was given the full chairmanship the next year.

Rauch called his work with and service as chairman of the Senate Finance Committee both satisfying and rewarding during the decade of the 1980s. That doesn't mean his actions were always popular with some voters who lacked an understanding of how the political and legislative processes worked.

For example, the Appropriations Committees in the General Assembly are those who vote how to spend tax money. It is the Finance Committees that have to find the revenues for Appropriations Committees to spend. When the time comes to increase taxes, Finance Committees must bite the bullet.

"The Finance work is essential and important," Rauch said, adding a smile when he thinks of the spending rather than the

Senator Marshall Rauch listening to floor debate, March 1987

collecting of tax money. "I've known buildings to be named for people who provided appropriations for facilities, but I've never known a building to be named for anyone who levied the tax to pay for them."

Rauch spent uncounted hours working on tax issues during his Senate career. In addition to the achievements already cited, there were two other examples of tax issues worth noting.

The first was his chairmanship of a Tax Fairness Commission that recommended changes in the state tax structure, resulting in tax cuts for lower-income taxpayers and increases for those in the upper-income brackets. That work, Rauch recalled with pride, helped people who needed help the most. As chairman of the Tax Fairness Commission, Rauch led efforts that exempted the state's poorest people from income taxes.

That single tax reform bill that Rauch guided through the legislature eliminated approximately 480,000 low-wage earners from the income tax rolls. Until that bill became law, any family of four with a gross income of as little as $6,000 was required to pay income taxes. Rauch led the effort to change the law and raised the tax cutoff to $13,000. "Any family of four earning such a meager income certainly couldn't afford to pay taxes and certainly didn't deserve to be forced to pay," Rauch said of the change. "It wasn't fair, and we made it fair to those who needed the most help." The hundreds of thousands of low-wage workers may not have known who saved them those tax payments, but their gratitude ought to go to Rauch.

Rauch learned from his earlier efforts on a study commission relating to criminal justice that commissions can be little more than window dressing unless the people working on them have legislative clout. With Rauch as chairman of the Finance Committee, the Tax Fairness Commission was able to get its proposals through the General Assembly. That was not true with the Jail Study Commission.

As a member of the Jail Study Commission in his first year in the Senate, Rauch and his colleagues visited jails and prisons across the state. They put forth fifteen specific recommendations for legislative consideration. "Lawyers in the legislature killed fourteen of the fifteen proposals," Rauch said. "I learned then that commissions are sometimes just eyewash and, as often as not, nothing of value happens. I was determined that wouldn't be the case with the Tax Fairness Commission."

The second exemplary tax issue in which Rauch was involved near the end of his career is one he looks on with both satisfaction and amusement. The state was struggling for revenue in the 1989 legislative session. Republican Governor Jim Martin, who like all gubernatorial candidates had been elected without any hint of a tax increase, put forth a massive revenue-enhancement package that would have added taxes on a multitude of items. Martin wanted a one-cent sales tax increase to support educational enhancements including pay raises for teachers and other state employees and a gasoline-tax increase to pay for road construction.

Rauch balked at the dual additional taxes, saying the state didn't need both and that there were better ways to build roads and improve education. Governor Martin was displeased with Rauch's position, but the veteran senator stood firm. As Finance chairman, Rauch persuaded his legislative colleagues to reject Martin's plan and instead approve the gas-tax increase for roads with some of the increased revenue earmarked for teacher pay and public school improvements.

In his rebuttal to Rauch's proposal, Governor Martin publicly accused Rauch of "highway robbery" for wanting to use some of the gas-tax increase for projects other than roads and for passing over the other tax increases. Rauch didn't budge, and his firmness showed that his influence overpowered the governor's. The gas tax was approved, but the sales tax increase wasn't.

"In business, you sometimes have to use creative financing and that's all I did with the governor's package," Rauch explained. "I didn't think the state needed all those taxes at one time. At the very worst, if I had been proved wrong, we could have added the sales tax the next year and saved the taxpayers money for a little while longer. I saw no way for the people to lose."

Rauch's amusement over the memory of that debate stems from his recognition that years later Governor Martin got most of the credit for the highway-tax plan that Rauch had implemented over Martin's strenuous objections. "All in all, he did an excellent job, was a gentleman I was proud to become friends with, and was and still is a credit to North Carolina," Rauch said of Martin.

As hard as Rauch worked against most general tax increases in the decade of the 1980s, he pushed equally hard for special fees designed for specific humanitarian purposes. One was a $10 fee added to the cost of marriage licenses, with the money going exclusively for educational programs to help reduce and prevent child abuse. Rauch said that legislation was requested by Charles Dunn, then director of the State Bureau of Investigation. Dunn had worked in the area of child abuse. Concluding that the fee was a worthy one, Rauch helped push it into law.

An even stronger cause for Rauch as a powerful state senator was the creation of the Bowles Center for Alcohol Studies at the University of North Carolina at Chapel Hill. Rauch's good friend and former Senate colleague Skipper Bowles had long advocated improved alcohol treatment programs and was working on the establishment of a new treatment facility in North Carolina when he became fatally ill with ALS, more commonly known as Lou Gehrig's disease, in the mid 1980s. The disease took Bowles' life, but in his final days, he elicited from Rauch the pledge to continue his efforts to help people afflicted with alcoholism.

Rauch was determined not to let Bowles' dream die. As Finance Committee chairman in 1985, Rauch proposed a joint public-private partnership to create the treatment center by making it a part of the UNC hospital complex in Chapel Hill. Rauch was instrumental in securing $4.5 million in state money to start the center, which he suggested would be named in memory of Bowles. Those state dollars and private contributions from the Bowles family and other donors were the beginning of what is now a nationally recognized research and treatment center.

While there is still no known cure for alcoholism, the Bowles Center has shown through research that certain forms of treatment have positive effects on persons who abuse alcohol and are unable to stop drinking without special medical assistance.

The center, among other things, has developed drugs that reduce the craving for alcohol.

While proud of helping establish the Bowles Center, Rauch wasn't convinced the operations of the center were being adequately funded. He felt people who contribute to the problem of alcohol abuse could and should do more to help with research. In the 1987 legislative session, Rauch conceived a creative way to enhance research revenues. He sponsored a new law, which he labeled an "abuser fee," that added $25 to the cost of restoring a driver's license to persons convicted of drunk driving but needing limited driving privileges to get to and from work. That extra revenue was earmarked for the endowment at the Bowles Center. Rauch set the ceiling on those fees at $5 million on the belief that it would be well into the twenty-first century before that total was reached.

He was wrong. Rauch's original $5 million ceiling on the limited driving fee was reached in less than a decade. Rauch had not realized so many people convicted of driving while intoxicated would be seeking those special privileges after their criminal convictions. Thus, in 1997, when the extra fee was about to go into the state's general fund, Rauch intervened, even though he was no longer a legislator. Rauch sought through legislative contacts to raise or eliminate the ceiling so the money from convicted drunk drivers would continue to flow into alcohol research.

In adopting its new budget in 1997, the North Carolina Senate omitted raising the $5 million ceiling as Rauch had been told would happen. Rauch wouldn't accept that and immediately began working with Republican Representative George Holmes, co-chairman of House Appropriations, to get a ceiling increase included in a special appropriations bill. He then went back to some key senators who agreed to help. Rauch's efforts paid off. The ceiling was raised to $10 million in the final days of the 1997 session. That act alone will mean another $5 million in coming years for research into the causes of and cures for the disease of alcoholism.

As Rauch's efforts on behalf of the Bowles treatment center show, after his defeat in the 1990 Senate race, he did not stop working for issues he believed were beneficial to people of the state. "If we can determine ways to prevent alcohol or other drug problems," Rauch said, "it will be one of the greatest things ever done for mankind. I couldn't just accept not continuing to help."

After his Senate defeat, Rauch's friends repeatedly urged him to run for public office again, either for the state legislature or the Gastonia City Council, where he began his public service career more than forty years earlier. He always respectfully declined. He would continue to work for his community and state, he told his friends, but not as an elected official.

Rauch's legacy to the state and its people will be in the form of legislation that he helped enact, ranging from tax reform to alcohol research. In a more tangible way, in the fall of 1997, Governor Jim Hunt asked the Board of Transportation to recognize Rauch's public service by designating a twenty-mile section of Interstate 85 in Gaston County, from near Charlotte to Kings Mountain, as the Senator Marshall Arthur Rauch Highway. The board unanimously voted to take that action on October 3, 1997, as a way of honoring Rauch for his "dedication to the citizens of his community and the state of North Carolina." The dedication ceremony was held October 19, 1998, with Govenor Hunt and other state officials present.

When he talked about his desire to dedicate the highway to the former senator and public servant, Governor Hunt made clear his appreciation of Rauch's work in behalf of the people of the state. The governor said:

> He has just been one of the most progressive businessmen who helped lead this state to a position of distinction. He has consistently been conservative on fiscal matters by insisting on efficiency as a way of keeping government from becoming too big. But at the same time, he has been deeply committed to the improvement of the educational system and to having a transportation system that is functional. He has always been there for better schools and better highways and for a long time has been a champion of making this state a better place for its citizens. He has helped move us forward, sometimes at great

personal sacrifice. But he did it because it was right and he wanted to be a part of making improvements. His leadership has been marvelous. He has served us well. That's why I wanted to recognize him with the dedication of that section of highway in his honor. We ought to do things like that for people who have done so much for us. Marshall Rauch deserves an honor like this, and a lot more.

At the ceremony, Hunt called Rauch a "great North Carolinian and legislator who cares about people and who always felt he should give something back to the people and the community he served." Rauch called the highway dedication "a very meaningful and proud moment" in his life.

Rauch often expresses appreciation for the many honors that he has received from his public service and philanthropy, but he is quick to say he has gained much more from his public service than public recognition. He becomes philosophical in talking about his service in the state Senate. It is, he said, a

State Senator Ollie Harris (left) and Senator Marshall Rauch pay tribute to members of the United States military, past and present, at the dedication of the Veteran's Memorial at the State Capitol in Raleigh. Harris and Rauch were state Senate colleagues as well as close personal friends.

special bond developed among colleagues.

There is just something unexplainable about having been a part of the North Carolina Senate for so many years. Perhaps members of the state House get the same feeling, but the fact that there are 120 members of the House and only 50 in the Senate probably precludes the solid friendships that senators develop. This fact was driven home to me most recently on June 3, 1998, when I visited the Senate to be present at the passage of a resolution memorializing the late Senator Ollie Harris, one of the closest and best friends I've ever known. It was a tribute well deserved and beautifully done.

When I visited that day, I had a chance to see many Senate friends who have been closer to me than any group I have ever known. It brought back many great memories, passing laws that were truly meaningful, stopping legislation you didn't believe in, and amending legislation because you felt you could help make it better. Working with so many people so closely for so long, you realize you're not always right, even if you think you are. But this makes you a more able and effective legislator. I now realize how strong that bond is because we were working for the same thing, even when we disagreed, and that was for the love of our state and each other.

As unsettling as his defeat for re-election was, however, Rauch didn't let it change his approach to dealing with his constituents and friends. A particular incident in the spring after his election loss, in fact, makes clear his continuing approach to life and brings a smile to his face in recalling his father's response to the Senate defeat.

It was in April 1991 following his ballot box loss the preceding November. Rauch and his father ate lunch every Wednesday at John's Grill in Gastonia, a fifty-year-old eatery owned by his friend Jim Heracklis, because that was the day each week the owner and his wife Marie served salmon patties.

After finding a vacant booth, Rauch began his customary

rounds shaking hands with other diners, as his father grew increasingly impatient. It was as if he was still running for the Senate. His father suddenly had enough of the hand shaking. "Hey, big shot," the elder Rauch called to his son, "come on back here and sit with your father. If they were really your friends, you wouldn't have lost the election."

Chapter 13
Business: A Contact Sport

Marshall noticed a man sitting across the aisle on the airplane and began a conversation just as a way of being nice. That's how it all started.

Jeanne Rauch, recalling how some unwise business dealings began.

Marshall Rauch was interested in nothing more than friendly talk in the late 1960s when he struck up a conversation with a man across the aisle on a flight from Charlotte to Nassau. He now knows he would have been better off if he had kept quiet. That sociable encounter led to events that produced a huge financial loss in the biggest error in business judgment Rauch ever made. It wound up costing him about $3 million and years of personal anguish.

With quiet fortitude and a deep concern for his good reputation, Rauch endured a long struggle to overcome the misadventure. He ultimately brought the episode to an honorable end, but only because he was able to draw great emotional support from his wife and family, his friends, and his religion.

Marshall and Jeanne Rauch had been looking forward to their Nassau trip in the spring of 1968. He had been working long hours and was anxiously anticipating a change of pace. She, too, was well aware of his need for a break. They arranged for responsible care for their children and headed south for a vacation in the warmth of the Caribbean. They made only one promise to each other: to avoid all talk of business. This excursion was to be solely for relaxation and pleasure.

Rauch, however, is nothing if not gregarious. After more than twenty-five years in North Carolina, his New York accent was still apparent, but his friendliness and outgoing manner were pure Southern charm. He had never met anyone he considered a stranger. That's why he initiated an exchange on the flight that fateful day.

The man introduced himself as a real estate broker. Once the plane landed in Nassau, neither Rauch nor his wife thought any more about the man until they met him again in the hotel restaurant the next day. There was more friendly banter.

"He was a real charmer," Rauch said of the broker. "Smooth and convincing." Not surprisingly, their talk quickly turned to business, including real estate opportunities that sounded both realistic and profitable. But nothing of consequence occurred.

Out of the encounter in the ensuing years came a growing relationship in which the broker often called at the Rauch home in Gastonia. His visits were brief but cordial.

Then one day the broker mentioned he was interested in starting a modular-manufacturing venture and was looking for investors. He asked if Rauch would be interested in becoming one of them. As he talked, the opportunity seemed more inviting. There appeared to be a ready market for the company's products.

At first Rauch was reluctant. This business was outside his field of expertise. He knew the textile industry but didn't know much about construction. The broker recommended a third investor, a wealthy North Carolina entrepreneur who had experienced considerable success.

On reflection, Rauch now realizes he should have been wary of the overtures. But despite his uncertainty, he found his new acquaintance persuasive. The broker already had laid the groundwork for the corporation. All Rauch had to do was put up $33,000, sit back, and enjoy the returns. Despite his second thoughts, Rauch agreed to invest.

While Rauch was busy with his own business enterprise and with matters in the North Carolina Senate, the new company seemed to be doing well. He received regular reports and felt good about them.

Consequently, the corporation started substantial borrowing to finance its growth and increase its profits.

Getting the bank loans was easy. Before long, however,

problems arose, and Rauch began to learn how painful it would be to pay them off.

Over time and as he insisted on knowing more financial details, Rauch began to have other misgivings. His instincts were seemingly coming true. Instead of getting reassurance, he got more surprises.

Rauch asked his own company financial vice president Don Walser, a man he trusted for his expertise as well as his integrity, to examine the corporation's financial records. That examination confirmed his worst fears.

"I discovered for the first time that there were some situations that were even worse than I imagined. The business was obviously in financial trouble, which endangered the notes held by our banks," Rauch said. However, he still assumed that both business associates would honor their share of the corporation's debts.

Rauch then found himself in court for the first time in his life. He became a co-defendant with the real estate broker in an unrelated civil suit filed against the two of them.

"I knew after the first day we would lose," Rauch said. "The evidence was overwhelming against us. On the second day, the broker complained that he had a toothache and was going to the men's room. I haven't seen him since. He went to the men's room and never came back."

Meanwhile, the banks were clamoring for payment of their loans, which were significantly past due.

"My best recollection is that all three of us, the real estate broker, the entrepreneur, and myself were all equally responsible for the corporate notes because we had personally guaranteed the loans," Rauch explained. "Also, unfortunately, my best recollection is that in the final settlement neither of them participated in paying off the notes, so I was compelled to do so."

Rauch faced millions in outstanding bank loans. Under pressure to enforce federal lending rules, First Union Bank had begun efforts to collect from him.

When he realized his financial problems, he voluntarily resigned his seat on the local board at First Union to avoid causing the bank any embarrassment and to eliminate any hint of conflict of interest. Through his long-time Gastonia attorney Mack Holland, Rauch pledged to repay the loans and told First Union he would give the bank a payment schedule within thirty days.

Holland drafted the payment schedule and presented it to the bank. Even so, the next day First Union filed a civil suit against Rauch, seeking to collect $1.7 million. Following the First Union suit, First Citizens Bank filed a similar suit. First Citizens' executive George Broadrick, a Charlotte business and civic leader and a long-time friend, told Rauch that his bank had an obligation to sue after First Union did. Rauch told Broadrick that he understood and accepted First Citizens' position.

When news of the bank suits made headlines in Raleigh newspapers, Rauch went to leaders of the North Carolina Senate and offered to resign as chairman of the Senate Finance Committee. He met with Lieutenant Governor Jimmy Green; and Senator Ken Royall, chairman of the Senate Appropriations Committee; and Senator Harold Hardison, chairman of the Senate Ways and Means Committee. They asked whether Rauch had done anything illegal or morally wrong. When Rauch said no, Royall said, "Then we won't accept your resignation."

Many of Rauch's friends and some of his legal advisers suggested that he simply declare personal bankruptcy and walk away. While that may have been a possibility, he refused to consider it. "Bankruptcy was never an option as far as I was concerned," Rauch said. "I didn't *want* to do that. I *didn't* do it. I *couldn't* do it."

He eventually settled some $3 million in debts. He received some concessions from the banks, but believes the lenders fully recouped the original principal.

The repayments devastated him personally as well as financially. To repay the debt, Rauch had to make many sacrifices, none easy but all essential. He remortgaged his home. He borrowed from his company, which at the time was solely owned by him and his family. He borrowed the total cash value of all his life insurance.

He transferred to the two banks fifty-five acres of prime real estate along Interstate 85 between Gastonia and Charlotte.

(Ironically, in 1998 the North Carolina Department of Transportation named a nearby stretch of that roadway the Senator Marshall Arthur Rauch Highway in recognition of his many contributions to the state and its people.)

Rauch also transferred to the banks twenty acres of land he owned adjacent to the city golf course near downtown Gastonia and a half interest in 200 acres he owned close to the Gastonia city limits. He also turned over to the banks all the stocks he owned in public companies.

"I gave the banks virtually everything I owned," he said. Though the assets Rauch deeded over were all he had, they were not enough to cover the debts.

He also went to his sister and her husband, Newton Gottlieb, to ask for a loan. They never hesitated to help. Rauch borrowed $300,000 in bonds from them and used the bonds as collateral for a loan that covered the remainder of his debt. The bonds were returned to the Gottliebs two years later when Rauch paid off that loan.

"That was by far the worst couple of years of my life," Rauch said. "I put up everything I owned to get out of that financial mess. I told my lawyer I felt like mashed potatoes. I didn't sleep much for a long time.

"I didn't and couldn't run away from the debt. I had an obligation to repay it. It took a great deal of strength and faith to come through it and keep going. And I couldn't have done it alone. Jeanne and my children gave me the strength that only a caring family can give. Friends responded not only with sympathy and kindness, but also offered personal loans and even volunteered to work for me with no pay or salary, if that would help."

Also Rauch called on his religion, and is convinced that prayer helped him maintain his composure and gave him the strength to go on.

"I learned some important lessons in that," he said. "Never expect anyone to make easy money for you. Never take your family or true friends for granted. And never forget your religion. Slow but sure will always win the race. I had never been a plunger until that business venture and I haven't been since. I was broke, but I just wouldn't accept it."

In the late 1970s, Rauch learned that the real estate broker was living in Florida. He threatened a lawsuit to recover the debts the broker owed. He collected $150,000, a small fraction of the total, and by agreement gave two-thirds of that to the two banks.

The settlement of the bank debt didn't end Rauch's relationship with officials of First Union Bank, especially C.C. Cameron, First Union's former chairman and chief executive officer who after retirement became the budget officer for newly elected Republican Governor Jim Martin.

As the governor's budget officer, Cameron often met with members of Rauch's Senate Finance Committee on matters related to state revenue.

"Shortly after I took that job," Cameron recalled, "Marshall, while serving as a state senator, told me he had something in his craw he wanted to discuss with me. He talked with me about the financial problems he had encountered and how he felt the bank treated him. I couldn't really remember the details, but I checked into it, and he and I had a long talk about it.

"I explained that what our bank did was what any other bank would have done under the circumstances. We shook hands, and he told me he was comfortable with it. That was the end of it. As a senator, he never once let those past difficulties interfere with his professional relationship with me in the Budget Office. I respect him for that."

Cameron conceded that First Union had put the squeeze on Rauch in ways that might have seemed unfair at the time. "Those were some bad years for real estate," Cameron said. "We were at times maybe a little tough on some customers, but that was just the way it was. Marshall Rauch and I have been great friends, and he's one of the finest and most dedicated individuals I've ever known. He has been willing to make tough decisions and still get along well with everyone. I have high regard for him."

In the decade of the 1990s Cameron and Rauch both went on to serve on the prestigious Board of Governors that oversees the sixteen-campus University of North Carolina higher education system. For several years Cameron was chairman of the board, and Rauch was chairman of its Finance Committee. Their working relationship in behalf of the university and the state was cordial and professional. Neither man mentioned the past debts or the bank's treatment of Rauch.

When Cameron sought to be elected chairman of the UNC board, he turned to Rauch for help. He asked Rauch to nominate him. "He asked me to do it, and I did," Rauch said. "Our past problems were never mentioned. That is history. And I thought Cliff would be a very capable chair and would add prestige and dignity to the office. Cliff Cameron is one of the outstanding men I have known, and his accomplishments in business, politics, and education have been of exceptional and permanent benefit to the people of North Carolina."

Rauch later could chuckle about how First Union had treated him, but the bank had less reason to laugh. In February 1996 Rauch Industries was sold to Syratech Inc. of Boston for $48 million, with a majority of the money going directly to Rauch and his family.

Not long after the sale price was publicly reported, Rauch got a call from a First Union bank officer who obviously was unaware of Rauch's previous experience in repaying the bank loans. The banker said he would be very interested in "helping" Rauch with any investments he might want to make. Rauch chose other venues for his investments.

Over time, Rauch has become more philosophical about his unprofitable business ventures. He had the inner satisfaction of knowing that despite the hardships of repaying the debts, he had done the honorable thing. With a clear conscience, he was able to rebound and to continue building his business and public service careers.

Chapter 14
Fairness & Facts

The voters gave me the privilege of serving thirty years in elective office, six years on the Gastonia City Council and twenty-four in the North Carolina Senate. I might have served longer and in higher offices had it not been for the unusual circumstances that arose in my 1990 campaign for reelection to the state Senate.

Marshall Rauch, looking back on the unhappy campaign
that brought his political career to an unexpected end.

By 1990, Marshall Rauch had come to love politics and public service almost as much as he did his business. And he had proved he was as good at one as he was the other. He liked people and liked making laws and public policy decisions that improved their lives. Unlike many of his fellow citizens, he viewed politics positively and saw it as the art of the possible in interpreting and executing what he believed to be in the best interest of the people of North Carolina.

After serving twenty-four years, he was the North Carolina Senate's senior member and, in working with five different governors (Dan Moore, Bob Scott, Jim Holshouser, Jim Hunt, and Jim Martin—three Democrats and two Republicans), he had earned a reputation for integrity and sound judgment. As chairman of the Senate Finance Committee, he was a highly visible member of the Senate leadership and a power to be reckoned with.

When he filed in 1990 for reelection to a thirteenth Senate term, he admitted to entertaining higher office ambitions. His business was doing well, and his sons and daughters had shown they were capable of managing it. He thought it might be time to consider running for governor in 1992 or maybe for the United States Senate. In his long service to the people of the state, he thought he had gained the personal experience and laid the political groundwork essential to seeking either office.

That was why he was so startled and in time deeply hurt by the unexpected outcome of that year's tumultuous political events. Almost overnight, the perception of him among many voters turned from positive to negative, and his many years of faithful service were discounted.

In the spring of 1990, *The Charlotte Observer* began publishing a series of stories about the toxic wastes contaminating Crowder's Creek in south Gastonia. The newspaper called it "the most polluted stream in North Carolina." Seeking to identify the source of the pollution, *Observer* reporters asked the state's environmental management agency for the names of industries known to be dumping wastes into the creek. High up on the list was Rauch Industries Inc., cited for ninety-one violations of wastewater regulations over a period of twelve years.

The pollution stemmed from a malfunctioning wastewater-treatment plant that had been dumping poorly treated sewage into the creek. The old plant had been completely replaced by a newly engineered, modern treatment facility, but the pollution represented a serious breach of state regulations by a company headed by a high-ranking state official. Journalists smelled a story. The environmental management agency said the company had never been fined for any of the violations, but assured *Observer* reporters that no one at Rauch Industries had sought preferential treatment.

The violations were attributable to the rapid expansion of Rauch Industries and to changing state regulations. The company had become the world's largest producer of satin and glass Christmas decorations. Its annual production had grown dramatically during the 1980s, exceeding not only the capacity of its water-treatment plant but also the state's water-treatment rules.

In those years, Rauch had more on his mind than the management of his business. Each year, it seemed, the state's legislative sessions grew longer. As chairman of the state Senate's tax-writing Finance Committee, he was in the thick of efforts to avoid a mounting state budget crunch. He also was weighing his future political options. Newspaper stories about his bid for reelection to the Senate often noted that he was likely to be a candidate for governor in 1992.

Notices from the state environmental agency in Raleigh about suspected water-quality problems at his Gastonia plant had been sent to Rauch's corporate offices, even though he wasn't there. Once Rauch learned of the pollution problems, he set about solving them.

The solution had been expensive. The plant's manufacturing process sent a mixture of ammonia and silver nitrate wastes coursing through the sewage-treatment plant along with other liquids. Treatment methods that in previous years had been accepted by the state were no longer allowed. In its haste to accommodate rapid growth in production, Rauch Industries had not kept up with changing environmental rules.

Rauch made no excuse for the violations. "We were wrong," he said. "Once I realized the seriousness, we took action." That action included building new waste-treatment facilities at a cost of $750,000 and committing $200,000 a year to operate them. The company hired an additional environmental engineer and sent two experienced employees to Gaston College, where they earned licenses to operate waste-treatment plants.

After the initial newspaper stories—and long after the new treatment plant was put into service—state environmental officials announced they were recommending that Rauch Industries be fined $17,927. Some of Rauch's friends suggested that politics had played a part in the fine because Republicans then controlled the governor's office and Rauch was a powerful Democrat with higher ambitions. Clearly, publicity about environmental-rule violations wouldn't help a candidate in a campaign for state senator, much less for governor or the U.S. Senate.

Instinctively Marshall Rauch understood that. Fearing that the environmental sanctions would damage his candidacy, in August 1990, he withdrew from the Senate race, saying he needed to spend more time with his business. But friends and party officials counseled otherwise. Finding a candidate to replace him at that late date (ninety days before the election) would be difficult, party leaders said. They cited Rauch's long string of successes in winning elections and pleaded with him to reconsider. So did colleagues from around the state, who said the state Senate needed him. About a week later, after a flurry of newspaper stories about whether Rauch was in or out of the race, he reentered the campaign.

Rauch never claimed politics was behind the state fine and never pulled strings to win favorable treatment from state agencies. As soon as the fine was assessed, he paid it in full. As rare as such fines were, records show that after they were levied the amounts were often reduced. Rauch didn't ask for a reduction. He paid the full amount to avoid what he feared would be an appearance of favoritism because of his public office.

In fact a year earlier, in his role as a state senator, Rauch had supported a tough new law that, under certain circumstances, would put polluters in jail. If that law had been on the books at the time of his violations, he candidly told colleagues during debate on the measure, he probably would have been guilty, even if he had had no personal knowledge of the problem. Still, he favored the new law and voted for it.

For those and other reasons, Rauch was certainly never perceived across the state as an opponent of environmental-protection. Two of the state's most influential environmental lobby groups, the North Carolina Conservation Council and the Sierra Club, endorsed him for re-election in 1990. They endorsed him because of his previous support of clean-air and clean-water legislation and for his record of accomplishment in maintaining both.

In returning to the race after having withdrawn, Rauch was perhaps naive to expect the pollution issue would go away, even though he had done what was right and put his company in compliance with the new regulations. A public official operating a business with even a hint of environmental difficulty was an inviting political target.

Not all the coverage of Rauch's candidacy was negative. One news story that fall pointed out an example of Rauch's influence and his ability to help his district, but it was buried on the inside page of his hometown newspaper, *The Gaston Gazette.* It showed that as a result of changes in state law that Rauch had helped engineer, the non-metropolitan counties would get a better break in the distribution of state sales tax revenues, which previously had stayed mostly in the counties where they were collected. The change meant that counties such as Gaston, Lincoln, Cleveland, and Rutherford, which made up his senatorial district, would receive an extra $5.5 million annually to support the programs of local government, as would similar counties across the state.

Unfortunately for Rauch, there were too few of those stories. As the fall campaign unfolded, many other news reports and editorials referred in one way or another to the pollution issue that continued to dog the Rauch candidacy.

On election day, November 6, Rauch was defeated. He finished fifth in a six-candidate race for three seats in the state Senate. Two of the three winners were Republicans who had never served in the legislature, where seniority and experience were critically important. One had never sought public office and would not seek reelection.

Of all the campaign coverage that year, Rauch cited the newspaper stories and editorials in *The Charlotte Observer*, which had tens of thousands of readers in his senatorial district, as the most damaging. He ran well in most Gaston precincts but poorly in the other three counties, Lincoln, Cleveland, and Rutherford, where voters did not know him as well.

Most of *The Observer* stories were written by Ann Doss Helms, a reporter in the newspaper's Gaston County bureau. Helms had good contacts and news sources, because she often reported on environmental issues involving Rauch Industries before the company knew about them. She stoutly denied that any of her tips came from Republican informants. "They were calling me to ask where I got my information," she said. She told them all of it came from official documents.

Helms defended the integrity of her work. "I was just reporting facts from the public record," she said. "I had no ulterior motive. There were no personal motivations behind my stories. There was never any 'get Rauch' angle. I was aware he was upset with the stories, but he was always a gentleman when we spoke and was never rude or unkind. And there was never a suggestion that he had personally done anything improper."

Rauch was especially sensitive to *The Observer's* coverage because Rolfe Neill, a longtime friend, was then the newspaper's publisher and had written Rauch personal letters encouraging him to run for governor and subtly offering to help. After the election, Neill wrote Rauch offering consolation for his defeat.

Compounding the effects of the unflattering newspaper coverage was a heavy Republican turnout on election day. That was the year that incumbent U.S. Senator Jesse Helms, a white Republican, defeated former Charlotte Mayor Harvey Gantt, a black Democrat, in a campaign laced with racial overtones. The Helms-Gantt contest attracted national attention and drew record numbers of voters to the polls. Helms beat Gantt statewide with 52.6 percent of the vote but in Gaston County he outpolled Gantt by 64 percent.

That also was a year in which local, state, and federal tax controversies had aroused a strong anti-incumbent mood among many voters. Rauch was not the only Democratic incumbent to lose that senatorial district. His friend, Ollie Harris, a nine-term incumbent from Kings Mountain in Cleveland County, also lost.

The only incumbent to survive in that senate district was Democrat Helen Rhyne Marvin of Gastonia, who ran third in the field of six and won by only 1,368 votes out of nearly 100,000 cast. Rauch finished fifth with 46,581 votes, 2,806 short of the total needed to win a seat.

In addition to stories about his company's environmental record, Rauch also feels he was hurt by his decision to withdraw as a candidate and then return to the campaign. "I suspect the early withdrawal and then getting back into the race made me seem weak to some voters," Rauch said. It also gave rise to persistent rumors that if Rauch won, he might step down after the election to seek higher office and allow the Democratic Party to appoint a successor.

"But it was the coverage of those past environmental problems that already had been corrected that I think hurt me the most," Rauch said.

Years later Rauch could accept the unfavorable press treatment and his ultimate defeat as part of the price a private businessman pays to participate in public life. However, he strongly felt that the press had an obligation to make fairness equal to the facts in its coverage of political campaigns.

If Rauch had won that 1990 Senate race, would he have later run for governor or the U.S. Senate? "I was seriously considering it," he said. "But we'll never know with certainty. With that defeat, it didn't matter because my chances were gone regardless of what I might have wanted."

Though Rauch was deeply disappointed, in time he recognized that all things happen for the best. Had he won another term in the Senate, he might not have had time to care for his father. Four months after that election, his father, then ninety-five and living alone in New York, called to say, "You have been trying to take charge of me for a long time. I think that time has come." Rauch went to New York the morning his father called and had him comfortably settled in North Carolina that same evening.

After the defeat, others began recognizing Rauch for his services, even if the voters did not. In 1990, Rauch Industries was named winner of the Senior Master Entrepreneur Award, given to one North Carolina company each year by Ernest & Young, Merrill Lynch, and *Inc.* magazine. That same year, *Business North Carolina* magazine selected Rauch as its Entrepreneur of the Year.

Those awards didn't heal the wounds of the campaign, but they did bring some redemption. The awards were based on existing achievements, not past problems long since solved. Had that been the case with the environmental coverage during the 1990 campaign, a biography of Marshall Rauch—and perhaps the history of North Carolina—might have been quite different.

Chapter 15
The Board of Governors

*Rauch has been a valuable university supporter as well as
a worthy critic. I always knew that he would accept things based
on merit and fact. He was a very wise and astute board member.*

UNC President Emeritus William Friday

*Rauch is someone who can just naturally work with people.
It would be to his and the university's benefit if he could continue
as a member of the Board of Governors because he understands the
history of both the university and the legislature. He is an asset
to the state and has been a valuable member of the board.*

UNC President Emeritus C.D. Spangler Jr.

His stunning defeat in the 1990 state Senate election did not force Marshall Rauch off the public stage for long. At the very next session of the state legislature, his former colleagues in the North Carolina Senate appointed him to the prestigious Board of Governors that supervised the sixteen-campus University of North Carolina system. It was an especially good fit for someone with Rauch's previous experience in the legislature and his lifelong interest in education.

"I will concede that in that first year I really missed serving in the General Assembly," Rauch said. "But I also had served on the Senate's Committee on Higher Education for twenty-four years and felt I had an understanding of the university's needs."

In addition to his service to higher education as an elected official, Rauch had for many years been involved with the state university system as a parent. Three of his children were graduated from UNC Chapel Hill. Further, Rauch had been a strong supporter of athletic programs at UNC Chapel Hill, even though many years earlier he had been a student and basketball player at Duke.

As evidence of his support of athletic programs at Chapel Hill, a framed caricature of UNC Chapel Hill basketball coach Dean Smith hung on the wall of the reception area at Rauch's company offices in Gastonia. Coach Smith gave it to Rauch with the inscription: "Best wishes always to some of my favorite people, the Rauches."

Rauch also had an historic interest in the Board of Governors. As a state senator in 1971, Rauch participated in the heated debates that restructured the state's higher education system and created the board as its overseer. The goal was to end twenty-five years of intense politicking and budgetary end-runs by the state's senior colleges and universities in pursuit of special favors from the legislature.

The restructuring was intended to enable the state to avoid the duplication of expensive higher-education programs and build a comprehensive system that would meet rising demands for higher education services. Little did Rauch know then that one day he would be an important player in the operation of that restructured system.

Until 1971, the Consolidated University of North Carolina, which originally included UNC Chapel Hill, North Carolina State University, and UNC Greensboro, was thought by its rivals to enjoy higher prestige and more favorable treatment by the legislature. Led by East Carolina University, several other colleges and universities overseen by the state Board of Higher Education openly lobbied the legislature for special programs and larger budgets to expand their operations.

Every year, feelings of envy, suspicion, and resentment rose higher among friends of the university, supporters of the several other schools, and their representatives in the legislature. When the jealousies threatened to erode public support for all of higher education—an asset that had fueled North Carolina's twentieth century rise to industrial and economic prominence—the governor (Robert Scott) and key legislators proposed to place all sixteen senior institutions under the aegis of The University of North Carolina. A newly created Board of Governors would supervise the enlarged university.

Though born out of bitterness and anger, the restructuring won the support of North Carolinians and the admiration of many other states to become a model for public higher education systems. One of those who made the restructuring work was William C. "Bill" Friday, a son of Gaston County who had served sixteen years as president of the Consolidated University and, after the restructuring, became president of the enlarged university. Friday served as the university's president from 1956 to 1987. His calm leadership restored public confidence and generally quieted the storm.

When Friday retired, C. D. "Dick" Spangler Jr., a wealthy and well-respected Charlotte builder, investor, and educational leader with roots in nearby Cleveland County, succeeded him. Spangler's crisp, decisive leadership—while different from Friday's in style—helped to put operations of the state university system on a more business-like basis and laid the groundwork for steady improvement in both the quality and the quantity of programs offered, especially among the five institutions that served mostly African-American students. Spangler was president of The University of North Carolina in 1995 when the institution celebrated the bicentennial of its opening at Chapel Hill in 1795.

For nearly thirty years, Rauch worked closely with Friday and Spangler, either as chairman of the Finance Committee of the state Senate or later as chairman of the Budget and Finance Committee of the university's Board of Governors. Both Friday and Spangler praised Rauch's performance as a legislator and a board member.

Friday recalled Rauch's support for the new governing board and his understanding of the university system. Rauch's university loyalty, however, didn't mean he rubber-stamped money requests without seeking and getting answers on needs as well as wants within the sixteen separate institutions. Rauch understood the institutional and regional interests that were often at issue in university finances and tried to balance those against the overall needs of the state.

When Spangler succeeded Friday in 1987, Rauch was at the height of his power as chairman of the Senate Finance Committee. Together they helped mold the university's biennial budget, which amounted to more than $2 billion.

Rauch's relationship with Spangler went back many years. In the early 1970s, Spangler and W.T. Harris, another corporate executive from Charlotte, sought Rauch's help as a state senator in adding kindergartens to the state's public school program. "He welcomed the idea and was instrumental in getting $250 million to start that extra grade for preschoolers," Spangler said. "He is a major reason that we have public kindergartens in this state."

When Rauch joined the Board of Governors, Spangler considered him a natural for chairman of the Budget and Finance Committee. "Then and now he acts and looks like a senator ought to act and look, distinguished and smart," Spangler said. "He wants to be thought of as the person who very carefully looks at the economic circumstances of an issue. That's important. He does it well."

Rauch's first day as a member of the Board of Governors caused a moment of unintended embarrassment. He was the first Jew ever chosen for the board, but no one provided a proper Bible on which he could be sworn in. As a result, Rauch didn't take the oath of office at his first board meeting. He waited until the next meeting when he brought his own Bible, a gift from his parents when he was elected to the state legislature.

Rauch says he wasn't surprised and was not offended when no one remembered to provide an appropriate Bible. It had happened several times before in his public life, and he had forgotten to bring his personal Bible, as he had done at other such occasions. After that incident, however, the university purchased such a Bible and has made it available as needed.

President Spangler said he was embarrassed by the Bible incident, even though it was unintentional. It had not occurred to any member of the university staff that Rauch needed a different Bible, Spangler said. "I don't think of Rauch as being Jewish," he added. "I look at him as an individual, not as a member of a group," a compliment to Rauch's even-handedness in public life.

Spangler more than made up for the missing Bible bit by writing a letter to Rauch's father Nathan, a former chemistry professor at Columbia University in New York, who was then in his nineties. The letter said: "It was a fine day for The University of North Carolina when your son was elected to its Board of Governors. As a state legislator, he was a great friend of this university, and he will be an influential and valued member of the governing board. You obviously have been a great influence on your son, and I am writing to express my gratitude and admiration."

The elder Rauch was especially proud of the fact that his son had been elected to that post. "My years in the Senate didn't impress my father very much," Rauch said, "but because he had been a chemistry professor at Columbia University, he was extremely proud of my association with higher education."

Rauch was elected to the UNC board under a process that ensured the board would include members from different political parties, races, and genders. Of the members elected by the legislature, half were nominated by the Senate and half by the House of Representatives. That was the procedure Rauch helped to write into law in 1971–72 because it looked like the most sensible arrangement.

By the turn of the century in 2000, after seeing the system operate from the inside, he was no longer assured there wasn't a better way. "I thought at the time [in 1971] it was the best system possible," Rauch said. "Changes were needed to reduce so much political interference, and what we did seemed wise back then. But that may no longer be the case, because it is too easy to create coalitions among certain board members. I believe the state would be better served without these little cliques."

By 2004, others were agreeing with Rauch's views. The state legislature by that time had begun looking into ways to restructure the Board of Governors to make it more receptive to state needs and less susceptible to political whims.

Even so, Rauch was pleased to accept an appointment to the UNC board. He said he was proud to be a member and still felt that the new structure, even with its inherent weaknesses, was better than the previous one. His frustrations, however, were apparent.

For more than forty years, he had run his own business as the chief executive and, for most of those years, the sole owner. Then he served for twenty-four years in the state legislature, where he was part of an inner circle of power brokers who could decide what was needed and what was possible and get it done. He was an activist.

He found that the UNC Board of Governors operated differently. Usually, the university president and professional staff worked out most of the important decisions ahead of time and asked the board to approve them. That was not the Rauch style.

"In the legislature, there was always something going on," Rauch said. "There were inquiring people working for what they thought was right and getting things done. The Board of Governors works like most other boards, and many times does little more than adjust what the staff presents. I found the process painful. It's a wonderful place to serve with wonderful people, but as a former legislator as well as a chief executive of a company, I guess I had been doubly frustrated at times."

Despite these frustrations, Rauch served conscientiously and was hardly a shrinking violet in expressing his views, sometimes against great odds. That's one of the reasons former president Friday called Rauch a worthy critic.

"He always did his homework in the Senate and on the Board of Governors," Friday said. "He'd call for and seek out information. Then he would study it. He was always thinking and studying. He has always listened well and stuck with the facts. That's one reason his whole life has been an entrepreneurial success story. I can offer only praise for his work."

Rauch never served on the Board of Governors when Friday was president, but during the Spangler administration, he did not hesitate to oppose the president on occasion, a fact that both men regarded as a result of their philosophical rather than personal differences. Both had earned reputations for expressing strong views in the corporate world, and those characteristics spilled over into their public lives.

An example of Rauch's independent thinking concerned issues involved in a large bond allocation. Rauch lost that battle, but not for lack of effort, though he was badly outnumbered.

The controversy arose after the 1993 session of the legislature. The North Carolina House, then led by Speaker Dan Blue, an African-American Democrat, agreed to add $12 million to the UNC budget as part of a $300-million bond proposal. But the extra money was to be spent, in the language of the appropriations bill, "on the most pressing needs" of the university system.

The Board of Governors gladly accepted the extra money, but it was not until later, to Rauch's surprise, that he and other board members learned that all the extra dollars had been verbally earmarked for the five historically black universities, regardless of other campus needs. As chairman of the board's finance committee, Rauch did not agree to allocate the extra $12 million to just five campuses. He felt all sixteen campuses had "pressing needs," as the legislation had specified.

Rauch was convinced that an arrangement had been struck between the university administrators and Speaker Blue, without the knowledge or approval of the Board of Governors. The agreement was that Blue would support the total university package only if the Board of Governors would agree to spend the extra $12 million on the historically black campuses while ignoring other needs.

The plan upset Rauch because special consideration was being given to certain campuses without a vote of either the Board of Governors or the General Assembly. Former Governor Jim Martin, also a member of the Board of Governors, agreed with Rauch and attempted to divert some of the $12 million to other campuses, but when the Martin plan was put to a vote before the board, only Rauch and Martin supported it. The other thirty members went the other way.

However, differences of opinion never interfered with Rauch's personal relations with Spangler, Rauch said. "I have absolute respect for the man and for his commitment. He gave the university much more than he ever received. In fact, he always gave back his salary and then some. He's a very capable executive, and we just had honest differences of opinion on a few issues. He has proved to be an outstanding leader in education, business, and philanthropy, not only for North Carolina, but also for Harvard University, where he currently is president of the Board of Overseers."

Later, after Spangler retired as president of the university, Rauch was disappointed at the way the Board of Governors handled arrangements for buying a new airplane to be shared by the university's new president, Molly Broad, and the university's health-services system. Spangler had supplied his own plane while he was president.

As finance chairman, Rauch was not made aware of plans to buy or lease a plane. The staff had been told to proceed with the plan without the knowledge of his committee. Not surprisingly, once word of the plane deal leaked, the press made it "Molly's" plane.

"That created an unnecessary mess and an embarrassment to the new president," Rauch said. "If we had done it openly, there would have been no controversy. The way it was handled created an unnecessary flap in the newspapers. Unfortunately, the newspapers didn't have the facts because it had not been discussed openly in committee."

At the board's June 1997 meeting, however, it was Rauch, in his role as finance chair, who explained the need for the plane, supported its purchase, and with a full set of facts at the ready, easily eliminated any opposition to the purchase. That didn't mean, however, that he agreed with the way the purchase had been pursued.

The appreciation for Rauch and his service to the UNC board was made abundantly clear at the June 1997 meeting when an endowed professorship was created in his honor. Fellow board member Derick Close and his sister Crandall Bowles donated $233,000 for the professorship at Elizabeth City State University. The endowed chair was to be known as the Marshall A. Rauch Distinguished Professorship in the Department of Biology. The Close-Bowles contribution was added to money donated by C.D. Spangler Jr. and additional money available from the state to total $500,000. Rauch was given the privilege of helping to decide the field of study for the professorship.

Close said he and his sister, the wife of Erskine Bowles, former chief of staff to U.S. President Bill Clinton, created the endowment as a way of showing their appreciation for what the university system had done for them and as a way of honoring Rauch for his many years of public service.

Rauch had no notice that the honor was coming, and the announcement left him close to tears. "It was an absolute surprise," he said. "I had no idea that was going to happen or that they thought that highly of me. I was honored and pleased. I knew I did not deserve it and was completely overwhelmed."

As he expressed gratitude for the professorship, Rauch also used the occasion to praise retiring UNC President "Dick" Spangler for being the catalyst for such endowments. It was Spangler's family foundation that launched a program to create endowed chairs at campuses of the public university system. Either personally or through his foundation, Spangler has donated more than $20 million for endowed professorships or other programs on the sixteen campuses. In addition, he returned his state salary to UNC every year he served as president. Rauch felt Spangler's gifts set an example for others who wanted to support higher education in the state.

All UNC board sessions were not as joyful as the one in which the Rauch professorship was announced. On another occasion, Rauch was caught in a political power play among rival cliques on the board. In 1995, the state Senate rejected the bid of board chairman Travis Porter, a Durham lawyer, for reappointment to the board. Some senators were upset that while serving on the Board of Governors, Porter had represented UNC coaches in contract and salary negotiations with the Chapel Hill campus. The senators thought that was a conflict of interest and under-mined public confidence in the board.

Porter's defeat left the board chair vacant. Five other members, including Rauch, emerged as possible successors. The other four were retired Charlotte banker C.C. Cameron, New Bern real estate executive Joe Thomas, Hendersonville lawyer Sam Neill, and Rose Hill pork-industry executive Lois Britt.

Cameron had locks on the votes of the board's eight Repub-licans because he had served as state budget director for former GOP Governor Jim Martin. The other twenty-four votes were scattered—or so Rauch believed. That was before Ben Ruffin of Winston-Salem, an R.J. Reynolds officer, a minority board member, an astute Democrat, and former special assistant to Governor Jim Hunt, started rolling his political dice.

Ruffin called a private meeting of three of the candidates—Thomas, Neill, and Britt—to discuss strategy. Cameron was left out because he had the Republican votes. Rauch was left out because he had opposed the deal to spend $12 million on the historically black campuses.

In Ruffin's private meeting, an agreement was struck. Britt won a promise that all the women on the board would vote for her, including Rauch's former Gastonia Senate colleague Helen Rhyne Marvin, who upon leaving the Senate had also joined the Board of Governors. "By that time I had lost all the women's votes, the black votes, and the Republican votes," Rauch said. "My chances for the board chairmanship were gone."

Sam Neill won the chairmanship by promising to serve out Travis Porter's unfinished term and not seek reelection. Rauch never sought the chairmanship again, but a year later nominated and helped to elect Cliff Cameron as chairman.

Rauch said he supported Cameron in 1996 because at the time he felt the former Charlotte banking executive was the preferred candidate. In July 1998, when Ben Ruffin opposed Cameron, Rauch was no longer in the chairman's corner. That election literally went down to the wire with neither candidate ensured of victory until the last vote was cast.

Cameron's supporters had lobbied Rauch for weeks prior to the vote but couldn't win his support. When a clear split developed among members of the board, Rauch was asked if he would accept the chairmanship as a compromise candidate. Many members assured Rauch he would have their votes if he would accept the chairmanship.

As late as midnight on the day before the vote, political operatives on the board were still trying to persuade Rauch to accept the post. One member who was committed to Ruffin said he would switch to Rauch if Rauch would run. Not wanting to be part of a last-minute political deal within a divided board, Rauch declined. When the election was held, Rauch supported Ruffin, who won by a single vote.

Despite his frustrations, Rauch says he enjoyed serving the

university system. He remembers one special ceremonial event in late 1998 as one of his most enjoyable as a board member.

Not surprisingly, it involved two of the best known athletic figures in the state and nation: Dean Smith and Michael Jordan. On November 12, 1998, Rauch's longtime friend Dean Smith was scheduled to receive the University Award, an annual honor given by the Board of Governors in recognition of illustrious service to the university and higher education. Rauch was chairman of the awards committee.

Although reluctant to accept the prize, Smith was honored at a banquet attended by more than 300 university officials, alumni, and supporters. When the award was presented, Smith said in his modest way that the "true champions of the university are the staff, family, friends, and former players who have helped me reach success."

To Rauch "that evening was one of the most memorable in my life. It was a chance to honor a man who truly deserved the award and an opportunity for many people to come together and express their feelings about him. Dean Smith has been my friend for more than thirty years, and it made me tremendously proud to be a part of awarding him that high honor."

Among Smith's former players present to offer their congratulations were Charlie Scott and Michael Jordan. Scott was the first African-American to play basketball at UNC Chapel Hill, and Jordan was considered by many as the greatest basketball player ever to attend the university. Smith recruited both. Scott said of Smith: "How do you thank someone who has been the most inspirational person in your life? Coach Smith is not only my coach, he is my mentor, my idol, and my hero."

Jordan was equally eloquent in expressing his feelings about what Smith had meant to both the university and to Jordan personally. "When I came to the university," Jordan said, "I think you saw two people, my mother and father [as major influences]. When people see me now, they also see Coach Smith."

Jordan, through his basketball talents, and Scott, as the first African-American to play for UNC, helped open doors for many other athletes who have found opportunities that may not have existed except for the presence and influence of Dean Smith,

Rauch said. "It was a wonderful occasion. I sat next to Michael Jordan for several hours and found him to be a patient, warm, and modest person. It was an amazing contrast to the aggressive, driving competitor I had admired on the basketball court."

Rauch's term on the UNC Board of Governors expired at the end of 1999. It was another chapter in a public service career that was both long and fruitful. Events like the one creating a professorship in his honor and honoring a great man like Dean Smith are memories he says he will cherish forever.

Chapter 16
The Big Fire

I guess I've been through a lot. When the fire hit, I just kept going. It never occurred to me to do anything else. I think that's a tribute to what my mother and father instilled in me.

Marshall Rauch, on his feelings about the disastrous fire
at his company warehouse in October 1994.

Business was right on schedule for Rauch Industries of Gastonia until that fateful night in October 1994. Production was up, orders were about to be shipped, and the 665,000-square-foot warehouse was packed with finished goods to be delivered to the nation's retailers over the next thirty days. In fact, Marshall Rauch was sitting at home that very night with his wife Jeanne thinking and talking about how smoothly the business was going. Their sons Marc and Peter and eldest daughter Ingrid were more involved in the business than ever—and doing their jobs well. At age seventy-one at the time, Marshall Rauch was thinking about eventually moving out of his leadership role at the company he had founded and letting his children take over.

Then the call came in the early evening of October 19. Son Peter was on the phone. Not to panic, Peter said, but the company's garland production and warehouse facility in nearby Cramerton had sustained some fire damage. Cramerton is a small town eight miles east of Gastonia where Rauch lived.

The blaze was out, Peter said, and while damage was the most severe in the company's forty-two-year history, it was not a major disaster. No one was hurt because all company employees had been evacuated from the building. The Cramerton Fire Department had declared the fire safely contained, Peter said, and for that reason suggested there was no need for his dad to come to the plant until the next morning.

In more than forty years in the business, making crochet thread, kite string, and now Christmas ornaments by the millions, Rauch had encountered several small fires at his plants, but never one that was serious or one that caused personal injury. In fact, during his entire time in business, Rauch had never filed a fire insurance claim. Damages from previous fires had not exceeded the company's $10,000 deductible coverage.

Even as he advised his father not to come to the fire, Peter knew the advice would be ignored and that his dad would not be long in arriving. Peter also knew that with a fire that put the lives of his employees and a large share of the company's annual production at risk, his father could not stay away.

Less than fifteen minutes after receiving the call, Marshall Rauch arrived at the company facilities in Cramerton. It was, indeed, the worst fire in the company's history, but there was no blaze when Rauch arrived. He was relieved it wasn't worse. Little did he know that in a little while, it would be far worse than any fire he had ever witnessed.

Jeanne Rauch recalled that night's anxiety, although she wasn't at the site. "I didn't go to the scene because Pete had said when he called that it wasn't all that bad," she remembered. "But Marshall didn't come back as soon as I expected. I thought he would call once he got to the scene, but he didn't. Then I turned on the television and saw it was an inferno. It was horrifying."

Rauch didn't call Jeanne when he got to the warehouse because he didn't have a chance. When firefighters thought they had the blaze extinguished, they shut off the automatic sprinklers because water from the sprinklers was damaging finished merchandise. Fire officials concluded—incorrectly, it turned out—that the fire was out even though they had never seen a blaze like this one. More than 100 million Christmas ornaments were packaged in folded boxes stacked inside corrugated shipping cartons. Flames had filtered into and around the stored merchandise that was stacked up to fifteen feet high. A fire that appeared to be under control was not.

Within minutes of Marshall Rauch's arrival, flames erupted again, this time far worse than before. Sprinklers couldn't be activated quickly enough to keep the flames under control. A major disaster was in the making. Fed by breezy October winds, the flames spread rapidly. They leaped over the warehouse's open aisles that acted as air tunnels. Quickly the firefighters realized they were losing the battle.

Reinforcements from surrounding fire departments were summoned. Every fire department in the county came, as did firefighters and equipment from as far as Charlotte in the adjoining county. In an hour or so, approximately 350 firefighters, rescue workers, and police officers were at the scene. The people of tiny Cramerton were witnessing the worst blaze in the county's history.

Traffic was halted for blocks, except for newly arriving fire-fighting equipment that snaked its way through the maze of hoses that were running from every hydrant near the plant. Fire hoses crisscrossed every street.

The night sky was a maze of red, orange, and blue flames. Heat was unbearable, so intense that spectators were ordered to remain at least fifty yards away. Firefighters in heavy gear moved as close as possible, putting their own lives in danger as they struggled against the stubborn blaze that just wouldn't stop.

"We don't know how the firemen were able to get as close as they did," Rauch said. "They were courageous and dedicated. They did all they could." As the flames spread, soot and debris covered houses, cars, and people as far away as two miles from the plant site.

Before that night was over, the Rauch Industries warehouse was a massive pile of ruins. Nothing was left. The fire was so stubborn, in fact, that it smoldered for ten days even with continuous monitoring by firefighters and private security forces.

The fire became a calendar benchmark for people of the town. They talked of the "Rauch fire" and used it to mark events in their lives, like natural disasters. People remembered where they were and what they were doing when they heard about "the Rauch fire."

"It was absolute devastation," Rauch said of the blaze. That night and the ensuing weeks of recovery were among the worse times of his adult life. The initial blaze caused an estimated

$200,000 in damage from both the fire and sprinklers. But after the blaze flared anew, the far more damaging flames consumed everything.

Damage to the destroyed building and its contents was estimated at $44 million. Insurance covered financial losses, but no payment covered the personal trauma inflicted on Rauch, his family, employees, and customers. Partially offsetting the tragedy, however, was the response from friends, business associates, customers, suppliers, bankers, the insurance carrier, and even competitors. Those responses were a tribute to Rauch's family, the company's reputation, and the generosity of all those offering help in time of need. It was, Rauch says, tremendously heartwarming.

Rauch and his family remained at the fire scene throughout the night as firefighters worked feverishly to douse the flames. Nearby churches set up facilities for food and coffee for those fighting the fire. "Everybody did all they could that night," Rauch remembered, "but it was to no avail in containing the fire. Everything was gone."

Amid the smoke and ashes, however, Rauch began to witness the goodness of his fellowman and the kindness that people can bestow. The insurance carrier, AIG, was on the scene the following day to begin its work. Without being asked, NationsBank, Rauch's primary banker, voluntarily increased the company's line of credit. Wal-Mart, the company's largest single customer, offered help. Friends called and offered to pitch in to resume production. Competitors around the country called and offered assistance.

"I was very touched by the outpouring of help and support," Rauch said. "NationsBank was outstanding, as were many others. People sometimes give a bad name to big companies like Wal-Mart but, based on my experiences, that's undeserved. They proved it in their response to our disaster. They went beyond what might have been expected, and I appreciate it. All our customers were really wonderful. They sympathized with us and understood our problem. Without exception, they all willingly agreed to accept what merchandise we would make available. Many of our buyers from the early days had become vice presidents or other officers in the companies we now served, and they trusted us."

The fire was not only devastating to Rauch and his company, but it was terribly expensive for retail customers such as Wal-Mart, Target, and Kmart, who were expecting the major portion of their glass and satin Christmas ornaments to come from Rauch within weeks of the fire. Rauch's company had 70 percent of its annual production inventory stored in the Cramerton warehouse when the fire struck. Because of that loss and the short period between the October fire and the Christmas sales season, there was no time to manufacture replacement inventory or for retailers to buy from other companies that had not anticipated the need for last minute orders.

"Our customers lost tens of millions of dollars because they didn't have enough merchandise for their shelves," Rauch said. "We were able to ship only about 40 percent of the normal supply."

Financially, Rauch Industries was able to weather the fire losses because insurance coverage was adequate. However, operating profits were drastically down in the remainder of 1994 and in the following year because of the extra costs incurred making up for the fire losses.

As chief executive of his company, Rauch had never personally handled insurance coverage. He delegated that to his vice president and finance officer, Don Walser. Walser is a slow-talking native of Lexington, North Carolina, with an accounting degree from Pfeiffer University and an abundance of good-business sense. He had worked with Rauch for twenty-five years, and the two men trusted each other in every business endeavor.

Once he discovered the huge fire losses and the disaster coverage his company had, Rauch was more appreciative than ever of Walser's ability and judgment. The fire insurance contract Walser had written with AIG called for full replacement cost of the building, replacement of all machines and raw materials at existing costs, replacement of burned finished products at current sales prices, and reimbursement of costs for normal business interruptions.

"I was satisfied when I saw our contract with the insurance company," Rauch said. "If the company had said to me the morning after the fire that I could have written any contract I wanted, I'd have taken the one we had. I didn't know what coverage we had until then, but I knew Don Walser and he had done exactly as I knew he would. Don and I remain great friends, and today, when we no longer work together at Rauch, are still in another business venture as partners and serve together in community services."

While insurance claim processing began immediately, it would be many months before initial settlements were reached and more than a year before the company realized a full settlement on the burned building itself. In fact, final settlements were not made until after Rauch and his family sold the company in early 1996.

Insurance carrier AIG's rapid response included sending an adjuster to visit Rauch. The company didn't just send one adjuster; it sent a team. Each adjuster was said to represent a

Remains of the Rauch Industries Cramerton production plant and warehouse after it was destroyed by fire, October 1994 (photo by Gaston Gazette)

specialty: building, raw materials, machines, finished goods, and supplies.

"I knew immediately I was out-manned and could be in over my head with all those people, so I told them to hold off until we could hire our own adjuster to make sure we were balanced," Rauch recalled. He did just that—and all participants finally did agree that total insurance payments would be $44 million.

Despite the loss of the fire and its accompanying headaches, Rauch and his family realized they didn't have time to feel sorry for themselves. They had work to be done—in a hurry. Rauch Industries had been unable to supply its customers for the 1994 sales season because of the fire and couldn't afford to fail them again the next year.

The company began its recovery immediately. "I knew if we didn't get production back up for the 1995 season, it [our business] would be all over," Rauch said. "Customers understood that first year, but they could not take a second year of no deliveries."

Good news came quickly. Within weeks of the fire, Wal-Mart increased its order for 1995 over 1994. Rauch interpreted that as a sign that Wal-Mart trusted that his company would soon be back to full speed. It also showed Wal-Mart's appreciation for previous experience with Rauch.

"Not only did Wal-Mart increase its order for the next year," Rauch said, "but the company also offered financial help if we needed it. That was a wonderful gesture on its part. I was and still am most appreciative. That was just one more incentive for us to get into production quickly. That was a great offer by Wal-Mart. I've never forgotten the company's willingness to be of service to us."

In the first six months of 1995, Rauch and his family opened five temporary plants in vacant buildings to replace the destroyed Cramerton warehouse. Used for both production and warehousing, the new facilities were in rented space in Gastonia, Shelby, Charlotte, and Lumberton. It was an expensive relocation, but Rauch believed it was essential to his company's revival.

None of the 136 employees at the Cramerton plant lost their

jobs. All were offered positions at either the main Rauch plant on U.S. Highway 321 at Forbes Road in Gastonia or at one of the new temporary sites. By the end of the 1995 manufacturing season, Rauch Industries production was back to where it had been before the fire.

To get production up, Rauch and his managers organized a team effort with each individual having responsibility for at least one phase of operations. As each step in the process was accomplished, Rauch marked off the responsibility from the list, but he kept an original list available so everyone could see the progress being made at each planning session. "My main job was just to keep morale up," Rauch said. "Each person on the team knew what was expected, and it was done. It worked wonderfully well."

The Cramerton site had a long history as a cotton mill long before Rauch Industries bought it. It had once been a primary plant for the giant Burlington Industries of Greensboro, which operated it under the name of the Mayflower Mills. Burlington had abandoned the location years earlier, and the building had fallen into disrepair by the early 1980s.

In the early 1980s, as part of an effort to reduce transportation costs, Rauch had rented part of the old Mayflower plant as warehouse space. Rauch Industries had high inventories for nine or ten months each year and then worked long hours to make deliveries in October and early November.

As Rauch increased its rental space in the Mayflower plant, Burlington put the building on the market for $2.75 million. There were no immediate takers. Burlington real estate manager Marvin Baugh of Greensboro offered it to Rauch at roughly half the original asking price: $1.5 million. Rauch considered it a bargain, even though it would cost another half million to repair the roof.

Burlington later sold most of the open land nearby which has since been developed into residential property as part of the Cramer Mountain Country Club by Rauch's close friend, former state Representative Graham Bell. "Marshall Rauch is a great guy, and I have a lot of respect for him as an individual and as a businessman," the now-retired Baugh said.

Rauch Industries used the Mayflower building only as warehouse space for several years, but in 1987 it moved its garland production operation to the site. From that date until the fire, Mayflower had been used for both manufacturing and inventory storage. It was perfect for the busy shipping season with thirty-three bays for loading trucks.

Rauch still gets nostalgic when he discusses the fire and its effect on him and his company:

> It was very emotional and still is. I would walk through the ruins after the fire and get tears in my eyes, not so much for the bricks and mortar but for the people and the entity that was there. But I never once even thought of quitting and never really took the time to feel sorry for myself. I didn't sleep much for a long time after the fire and would wake up at night thinking we had another fire. It was traumatic and still is when I think about it. I still remember what my son Marc said the night of the fire. He said that if something like that had to happen he was glad it didn't occur until after Pop (Rauch's father) had died. That would have devastated him.

The elder Rauch had died ten days before his ninety-ninth birthday, less than three months before the fire.

No one has been charged with causing the blaze, although four different criminal investigations have concluded that the fire was man-made. No determination has been made whether it was an accident or intentionally set.

Fire investigators say they have not given up on finding the exact cause of the fire and the person responsible. Rauch and his family say they are still hopeful that the mystery can be solved. But with the passage of time their optimism wanes.

Chapter 17
Faith & Tzedakah

*To me, Judaism and family are synonymous, intertwined
into everything I do, enhancing the significance of everyday life
and being the base of my support and strength.*

Marshall Rauch, on the influence of religion in his life.

When Marshall Rauch discusses the importance of personal
religious faith, his voice drops and he grows introspective. The
free-flowing laughter and outgoing manner that permeate his
general conversation disappear. To him, personal faith is
serious, powerful, and meaningful.

> My faith in Judaism has given me everything I am and
> have. It has given me strength when I couldn't get it any-
> where else. Even so, I'm not always truly observant. There
> are certainly times when I don't follow all the 613 *mitzvahs*
> [a term denoting both commandment and good deed].
> But my religion is an extremely important part of my life,
> intertwined in all I do with my family, in my business,
> politics, civic work, and my treatment of others. I enjoy
> what it does for me. A main goal at this time in my life is
> to build the Rauch Foundation. There is no doubt in my
> mind that my religion has driven me to start that effort
> and is driving me to make it a force for helping people.
> Religion is in my everyday life. It's part of who and what
> I am.

One need not look far to see that Rauch's actions match his
words.

Almost every morning, the eighty-one-year-old walks along
the golf course behind his home for physical exercise and
spiritual enhancement. Afterwards he pauses for a time of
private meditation and prayer in which he either performs

a ritual of Orthodox Jews (facing eastward into the morning sun, wraps himself in his *tallis* and *tefillin* and reads selected passages from his prayer book) or he reads and studies the histories and laws of Judaism. It is a quiet time that has become as important to him as food or sleep.

The *tefillin*, sometimes called *phylacteries*, consist of two small boxes of parchment containing four Hebrew passages that adhere to a decree found in Deuteronomy. They symbolize the Jews' emotional and intellectual belief in Judaism.

Rauch considers himself a Reform Jew but one with traditional leanings. "I'm not what some might call modern and am not about to change," he said of his approach to his faith. He engages in his morning Orthodox-style prayer ritual, because it takes him closer to the religious beliefs of his ancestors. It also brings him close to G-d* on a daily basis.

The heart of the Jewish religion, based on the writings of scholars, is best reflected in the prayers of Judaism. This is a belief Rauch adheres to in his daily life.

Rauch has always maintained his faith, but his true devotion has come as he has matured and increased in age and life experience. "I didn't take religion as seriously when I was growing up as I do now," he conceded. "I always had faith, but I think the older you grow, the more involved you become."

In addition to his daily devotional, prayer is also a part of Rauch's daily life. He cites personal experiences of his faith and the belief that prayers are answered and can bring wondrous results.

"Prayer means two things to me," he said. "In the formal reading of prayers, you have a learning experience that is a part of subjugation. But prayer also gives you a chance to speak personally with G-d, although there are no specific answers on a daily basis. Seldom do you know directly that prayers are answered, but I have known."

To illustrate, Rauch explained a personal experience. In 1995, his oldest son Marc, then forty-five, was diagnosed with colon cancer. Both an internist and a pathologist studied the results of

* *Jews prefer not to spell out the word God because they consider it defiling.*

medical tests and agreed that malignant tissue was present.

"I earnestly prayed that Marc would be healed and I asked G-d for a perfect healing," Rauch said. "I prayed every day, several times a day during that period. Then a wonderful thing happened. One morning on my walk, I prayed again as I walked alone. It was a beautiful, sunny morning when I began the walk, but as I was about halfway through my rounds, a sudden thunderstorm came up. It was a beautiful, cleansing rain. I just kept walking. A strange and pleasing feeling came over me as I prayed in that rain."

In the days immediately after Rauch's walk that morning, additional medical tests in Charlotte and at Duke Hospital revealed no sign of colon cancer in Marc Rauch. "I never mentioned to anyone—until now—the feeling I had after those prayers that morning. But I knew. That was one of the most wonderful moments of my life. I know my prayers were answered. I sincerely feel G-d heard me."

Rauch's recognition of the importance of religious faith came during his service in World War II as he engaged in combat against the Germans in France. Recalling those cold, wet months in infantry combat, he declares that his faith deepened in a hurry during that first night on the front lines, with German soldiers shooting at him. That faith has held firm ever since, growing stronger through the years.

All Jewish holidays are particularly meaningful for Rauch and his family, and all are observed. Each Passover, the Rauches celebrate the annual Seder dinner as a special family reunion. And on Friday nights, the Rauch family comes to Jeanne and Marshall's home for traditional Sabbath prayers and dinner. In his days as a state senator, Rauch was instrumental in passing laws honoring Jewish heritage on holy days.

Rauch also concedes that faith played a major role in his recovery from some costly and embarrassing business ventures in the middle 1970s. Faith sustained him when he went through some tough personal struggles a few years earlier.

As his faith grew stronger, so did his activism among Jewish groups. By the early 1990s, he had become a member and participant in four Jewish synagogues, ranging from the liberal

Reformed to the traditional Orthodox.

Rauch's daily private meditation and prayer were rekindled through his friendship with Lubovitch Rabbi Yossi Groner, who came from New York to serve the Lubovitch movement in Charlotte where Rauch is a member. He also has been a member of the conservative Temple Israel in Charlotte for forty-five years and the reformed congregation in Boone, North Carolina, near his mountain summer home at Banner Elk. For more than fifty years he has been an active member of and participant in Temple Emanuel in Gastonia where he was married, where two of his sons were married, and where his children and grandchildren were *b'nai mitzvahed.*

Founded in the 1920s by what was then a small but determined group of Jews in Gaston County, Temple Emanuel has special significance to Rauch because it has been a part of his family for more than seventy-five years. One of the founders was Frank Goldberg, father of Rauch's wife Jeanne. Temple Emanuel was started as an Orthodox synagogue but over time slowly emerged as a reformed house of worship. For some forty years, the temple held both Orthodox and Reformed services.

For Rauch, religion and family are inseparable.

My whole family, including the grandchildren, participates in and benefits from Judaism. But it's true that at this stage in our lives, I'm more involved than my children are. One definition of a Jew is a person whose grandchildren are Jewish. That means it takes a lot of effort over several generations for the real purpose to be fulfilled. But if a grandfather teaches his child and the child teaches the grandchild, the faith will go on forever. I don't really see how a person can exist without religious faith. Religion makes us stronger and better people. All good things that have happened to me or that I have done have found their beginnings in my religion.

Rauch's religious beliefs have changed his lifestyle, including his dietary habits. Today he abstains from all pork and any fish without scales. "I'm not truly kosher," he said, "but I am observant of certain kosher practices because they are not only symbolic but also help provide me with discipline. We all need that in our daily lives. Discipline makes us stronger and better people."

Discipline was certainly part of the religious life of his parents and grandparents. As a child in New York, Rauch recalls his grandparents Isaac and Esther Rauch strictly adhering to their Orthodox faith. "They walked to services on the Sabbath and on High Holy days," Rauch recalled. "That was my introduction to the importance of faith and discipline."

While Rauch's religious faith is a serious subject, he laughingly recalled one anecdote involving his religion and his first campaign for election to the North Carolina Senate. In that 1968 campaign, which was before Rauch began keeping some of the kosher laws, he visited City Market, a country store in Cherryville, with Basil Whitener, then the Democratic congressman from the Gaston-Cleveland district.

As they entered the store—owned by Bedie Stroupe Fraley, who was widely admired as the mother of Rauch's friend Buck Fraley—Rauch was hit by what he vividly remembers as a distinctive odor that he had never before encountered. Congressman Whitener immediately recognized the smell and complimented Mrs. Fraley on having prepared a fresh batch of livermush, a mixture of ingredients from the slaughter of hogs, but best left unspecified. Livermush is usually served fried and is considered a delicacy by some Southerners, although fewer with each passing year. At the time Rauch didn't know what livermush was, but to him the smell was certainly distinctive.

Ever the politician, Congressman Whitener asked for his usual livermush sandwich with mayonnaise. Mrs. Fraley asked Rauch if he'd also like such a sandwich. Wanting to appear hospitable in the heat of a campaign, Rauch answered affirmatively.

"It was awful," he recalled. "To me, it was dog food. I knew the only way I could get it to my stomach was to eat quickly in hopes the taste wouldn't last as long. I gobbled it down in a hurry, hoping it would stay down.

"Well, Mrs. Fraley was so impressed that I ate that sandwich so fast, she promptly made another and handed it to me. I had to eat it, too. I didn't want to lose votes because she had strong political connections in that area. But I will never forget that taste. From that day forward, I have never eaten livermush and never will again."

Rauch and his family are Ashkenazi Jews, descendants of Jewish groups that came to this country from Europe. Rauch's grandparents came to the United States from Austria-Hungary; Jeanne Rauch's parents came from Latvia. The other division of Jews in the United States is Sephardic Jews, people who came to America from Spain. Sephardic Jews arrived first, some leaving Spain as early as 1492, during the reign of Ferdinand and Isabella.

As Rauch's faith has grown through the years, so has his concern about unfairness toward all minorities. He was one of the original participants in the 1960s civil rights movement in Gastonia and across North Carolina.

His generosity in assisting people in education and business endeavors has been widespread and has come primarily from his belief that justice calls for helping others, especially those who are trying to help themselves.

His faith in this regard basically comes from his belief in and following of Hillel's Rule. Abba Hillel was a noted rabbi and scholar, the most prominent spiritual leader among the Jews of Palestine from 30 BC until his death in 10 AD. An authority on the interpretation of Jewish law, Hillel was known for his humility and love for his fellowmen. Many of his writings are similar to the later teachings of Jesus.

Hillel described the meaning of Judaism in simple terms. "What is hateful to thee, do not unto thy fellowman; this is the whole Law; the rest is mere commentary." Hillel's writings and teachings became the foundation for the Golden Rule.

Hillel's teachings have become one of the major guides for practitioners of Judaism through the centuries. The B'nai B'rith, the oldest and largest international Jewish service organization, has its origins in Hillel's writings. The B'nai B'rith Hillel Foundations maintain religious and cultural centers at hundreds of universities in the United States and dozens of campuses in other countries. Upwards of 200,000 Jewish students and faculty members are involved in Hillel Foundations programs.

In his writings and teachings, Hillel admonished Jews that if people are unkind or uncharitable to you, do not respond in kind. Rather, he taught, work for justice and charity. Those two words in Hebrew are synonymous, although there is no specific word in Hebrew for charity. Justice ought to be the foundation of all good deeds, according to Hillel.

"To me," Rauch said, "*tzedakah* (which in Hebrew means *justice*) is especially important in all that I do. Working for justice and helping provide help for those willing to help themselves is a wonderful philosophy for life."

Rauch's strong religious faith, his belief in Hillel's Rule, and his family upbringing have combined to help make him an unusually successful businessman and public servant. These three factors have created the driving force behind his desire to build the Rauch Foundation into a viable and worthwhile charitable organization that will spread good works for generations to come. "My faith is what's behind this effort," he proudly explained. "It's part of what I am and what I stand for."

As Rabbi Bernard Martin, Hillel professor of Jewish Studies and chairman of the Department of Religion at Case Western Reserve University, has written in his book on prayer, faith must exceed words or promises to include good works. It is not enough, according to Judaism, to profess G-d in words. G-d must also be loved through deeds. Rauch embraces this belief. His benevolent actions and willingness to help others have spoken far louder than mere words.

Jewish commandments, furthermore, are not only to be obeyed by today's believers but also transmitted to future generations. Rauch's creation of a family foundation clearly manifests his hope and dedication to extend *tzedakah* into the future. It is up to others to carry on what he has started.

Chapter 18
The Children's Views

*I shall never forget that first time I spent the night in the
Rauch home. When I climbed into bed, (Marshall) reached down
and kissed me on the cheek and told me he loved me. That was the
first time anyone had ever done that or said that to me.
It was a wonderful feeling to be wanted.*

John White, adopted Rauch son who became part of the family
when he was fifteen, more than forty-five years ago.

John White's two most vivid childhood memories stretch across
extremes.

One is anything but pleasant: a deceased mother he never
knew, an absentee father who struggled unsuccessfully for work
and against alcoholism, and the inadequate care from two aged
and ill aunts whose resources were woefully lacking for even
minimum human comfort. Early on he concluded that his best
ticket toward a better life was to excel in sports. He worked at
that—hard.

The other memory is as close to storybook perfect as it gets.
In the late 1950s, John White was on Gastonia's Ashley High
School basketball team and was admired by a community-
volunteer coach with a big heart. The coach offered encouragement and advice. Then he offered yard work as a token source
of income. Next came invitations to dinner. Then came the
opportunity to spend the night with the coach's two young sons.
Finally, he was asked to spend the summer and, in short order,
to officially become part of the family.

That volunteer coach was Marshall Rauch. That's how John
White, an athletically gifted kid who faced, at best, an uncertain
future because of a disadvantaged home environment, became
a member of the Rauch family. He still is an important part of
the family as a recently retired successful stockbroker, father,

grandfather, brother, and son. Marshall and Jeanne Rauch proudly describe White as their son, even though they aren't his biological parents and have never legally adopted him. "He's our son," Rauch said. "That's the way we've always looked at him since he came to live with us and join our family. We've never thought of him in any other way."

"Without them, I would never have had a mother or father," White said. "A child's parents are the two people who raised him, not those who gave him birth. Marshall and Jeanne Rauch gave me a home and raised me. They are my mom and dad. He has been a wonderful, loving father, and she has been a beautiful and caring mother. They saw I had no parents, took me in, and have been my parents for more than fifty years. You could say, really, that I was born when I was fifteen and came to live with the Rauch family. What I now have, I owe to them."

The Rauch's four biological children share the feelings that Marshall and Jeanne Rauch and John White have for each other. "Making John a part of our family is probably the greatest thing Pop has ever done," says third son Peter. "It has been a wonderful thing for all of us. I don't ever remember a time when he wasn't part of our family." Peter was a preschooler when John White entered the Rauch family circle.

"He became the big brother that I never had when he came to live with us," oldest daughter Ingrid Rauch Sturm said. "We all love him dearly and are proud to have him as part of our family."

Second son Marc and youngest daughter Stephanie offered identical assessments of their family's close relationships. And when one speaks of the Rauch family, f-a-m-i-l-y is the operable word. Clearly, Marshall Rauch is the patriarch, but togetherness and collective love are central themes in virtually all the family members do.

Except for Ingrid Sturm, who with her husband has lived in Las Vegas since 1996, all the other siblings see or talk with their parents almost every day, sometimes more than once. All the others live only short distances from their parents. Family lunches or dinners together are routine.

The generous decision by Marshall and Jeanne Rauch to take

John White into their home and make him a part of their family was extended to another generation of the family in the fall of 1994.

After unsuccessfully trying to have children of their own, Marc Rauch and his wife Elaine Lyerly, who owns a successful advertising, public relations, and marketing agency in Charlotte, decided to adopt. They chose an international adoption, preferring a child from South America. This choice was based on the belief that so many children there needed good homes and had little hope of success in that part of the world.

In July 1994, Elaine and Marc flew to Paraguay to meet their son and begin the legal proceedings to bring him home. Joyfully they learned the courts granted them legal custody. But within hours of getting that happy news, they also received an unexpected word from back home that Marc's grandfather, Nathan Rauch, had died.

"It was a bittersweet day," Elaine Lyerly said. "Amid all the excitement of becoming parents, we had to return home because of the death of Nathan. All the paperwork was not yet completed, and we were not allowed to bring [our son] home with us that trip."

On a subsequent trip to Paraguay, Marc and Elaine were handed their seven-month-old son in a hotel lobby. They named him Elias in memory of Nathan Rauch's brother. By the turn of the twenty-first century, Elias Rauch was a bundle of energy, adored by his parents, grandparents, uncles, and aunts. Not until later would Elias be able to learn how he came into the bountiful Rauch family instead of being left, in all likelihood, to roam the streets of a poor South American town.

As one who, over a forty-plus-year span, built a business from ground zero into the world's largest manufacturer of glass and satin Christmas ornaments, Marshall Rauch has been reluctant to relinquish control of family finances. His wife and daughters expect and prefer it, and his sons accept and appreciate it. Nobody in the family complains or has hinted at any desire to change the arrangements.

"We're his fifty-something-year-old kids and he still manages our money," Marc Rauch said. "But he has such good common sense. He has almost always been right. He's successful, and we're not looking to change anything."

"If it makes sense, he'll just do it," Stephanie Rauch said of her father. "He has always given good advice and fixed things for us. Sometimes I think maybe I've created problems just so he could fix them and give me more attention."

"He does things his way with the finances and investments because he always has," Jeanne Rauch said. "He has handled all the family business affairs well, and we all understand and respect that."

The Rauch siblings readily concede, however, that by their standards their father at times can be frustratingly fastidious with money. The patriarch, they say, is more likely to spend money on someone else than on himself. The family standard of living is clearly above average, but it's not lavish. There is no flaunting of the family wealth.

The Rauch home, the fourth for Marshall and Jeanne in their fifty-eight years of marriage, backs up to the golf course at the Gastonia Country Club, where all in the family are members. The home on Sherwood Circle is equipped with an indoor pool and exercise room and is located on what neighbors agree is probably the most scenic site in the neighborhood. It is not extravagant, yet it is spacious—ideal for large gatherings inside or on the large deck. It has two bedrooms along with an office and large family room. It's a home built for large social gatherings.

As a businessman and state senator, Rauch was always labeled a sharp dresser, but he never was flamboyant. His children still tease him about wearing aged and tattered gym clothes instead of new ones they give him. He has, however, on occasion spent $300 for a shirt or a pair of shoes and later said such acts were foolish mistakes because the expensive clothes were no better or more comfortable than those he normally buys for much less.

Rauch routinely asks for senior citizen discounts when he dines at restaurants that offer that amenity, yet he is known for giving gifts, often expensive ones, to friends and associates as well as to family members. He has given away hundreds of thousands of dollars through the years and will give away millions more once his family foundation is in full operation.

His philosophy about money, he readily admits, is the result of early lessons on the importance of savings and frugality driven home by his parents, who remembered the financial struggles of the Great Depression. Rauch's wife and children tease him about his spending habits, but they've long since stopped suggesting that he change. "That's just the way I am," Rauch says. "That's the way I learned about money, and I don't plan to change."

Rauch made his money the old-fashioned way through hard work, long hours, frequent travel, and a low salary in the formative years of his companies. The work and hours slowly but surely paid off since the 1960s, even with some severe, albeit temporary, setbacks along the way.

His wife and children all respect and admire him for his efforts as both a parent and a business executive. His success has meant their financial success, and without hesitation, they all give him full credit. Rauch not only has provided well for his children and grandchildren, but he also has treated them with respect and loyalty—sometimes, they say, when they probably didn't deserve as much as he gave.

John White, sixty-three, and his wife JoAnne have three sons: John Marshall, the oldest; Job, the youngest; and Josh, who is married to Marsha and has a son, Jackson. John and JoAnne live in Gastonia, just one block from his mother and father, and their children all live in Gastonia.

Peter D. Rauch, fifty-two, and his wife Vicki have two daughters and one son: Natillie (named after her paternal grandparents Nathan and Tillie Rauch), Lauren, and Julian. The family lives in the Gastonia home formerly owned by Marshall and Jeanne Rauch, the home Peter grew up in. In 2004, Natillie and Lauren were both students at UNC Chapel Hill, and Julian was a freshman at Appalachian State University.

Julian was graduated from Ashbrook High School in 2003 and had the thrill of kicking two field goals and one extra point in the last seconds of three successive playoff games that brought his school the state 3AA football championship in 2002. He was voted the Most Valuable Player in the state championship game.

Marc F. Rauch, fifty-five, and wife Elaine Lyerly live seven miles away at nearby Cramer Mountain with their son, Elias, their only child.

Youngest daughter Stephanie Rauch, forty-two, lives in Cramerton with her partner, Eileen Sweeney, and Eileen's son, Stuart Anderson. In 1998 Stephanie earned a master's degree in counseling at UNC Charlotte. She has opened her own counseling office and now is in the last year of a doctoral degree in multicultural counseling.

In early 2004, Marshall Rauch, sons Marc, Peter, and John, and daughter Stephanie all moved into a newly purchased office, a converted residence, on Union Road in Gastonia. Stephanie maintains her counseling office in one room, while her father and brothers deal in financial matters.

Oldest daughter Ingrid, fifty-six, and her husband Larry Sturm have no children and live in Las Vegas. "When I was a child, I thought my dad was perfect," Ingrid says of her father. "Now I know he isn't perfect, but I see him for the man he is. He's generous, fair, thoughtful, sentimental, religious, charitable, family oriented, extremely bright, and rational. He is a leader who has good values and always sets a good example. He's easy to talk to and willing to listen and learn. He never expects anything in return for what he does. I try to do things the way he would in most cases. How much closer to perfect can you get? He's as close as a mere mortal can be."

However, his vivacious oldest daughter says there have been more than a few occasions when they have disagreed, both philosophically and politically. Ingrid is, by her own admission and her father's characterization, a feminist. Her dad, she says, was once quite chauvinistic, as were the other men in the Rauch family. As an employee of Rauch Industries, Ingrid remembered what she called unfair—if unintended—gender-based decisions by her father and brothers.

For example, when she initially expressed an interest in joining the family business in the late 1970s after more than a decade in an independent, successful career in New York City, her brothers' first question was whether she would like to be their secretary. Needless to say, that didn't sit well with the sister who had been an account executive with an advertising agency in New York City.

Ingrid went to New York in 1970, immediately after graduating from UNC at Chapel Hill with a degree in French. Earlier she was graduated from the MacDuffie School for Girls in Springfield, Massachusetts. She went to New York, she says, for two reasons: she wanted to prove she could succeed on her own, and she was determined to marry a Jewish man. She did both although she met her husband at a health spa in Florida instead of in New York where they both lived.

Ingrid says her father was initially slow to accept her as an equal in the business, because he looked upon her as his daughter instead of a mature woman. However, she quickly added, he gradually changed and provided her an opportunity to start a new division in specialty products within the family company.

"He told me that Marc and Pete were each vice presidents of sales and manufacturing and that I needed to develop the advertising specialty division," Ingrid said. "I really think he wanted to keep the three of us apart and minimize any friction and competition among us."

She also recalled an incident when her two brothers were asked to participate in an important business decision while she was excluded. After an apology from her father, Ingrid showed her displeasure by using his credit card to purchase a Rolex watch, which she still wears. She also laughed about the day she drove her new red Corvette to the company offices, causing employees to joke that her dad must have made her angry again so she bought the car to get even. That was the case with the watch, but not the car.

One of Ingrid's most memorable political disagreements with her father came during his state Senate tenure in the middle 1970s when he voted against approval of the Equal Rights Amendment, a move that helped ensure its defeat.

"He was a chauvinist then," Ingrid said. "But I understood why. It was mainly because his father was like that before him. That's the way he was brought up. That's the way the world was at the time. He said one of the reasons he voted against the ERA was that his constituents were opposed to it. He rationalizes well, and it's hard to argue with him.

"Sometimes my father still finds it hard to change in certain ways, as do many people," Ingrid said. "But I give him a lot of credit for the improvements he has made. He just grew up in a different era. I don't think any decisions he or my brothers ever made were malicious or with any intent to hurt my feelings. They were more often than not done by omission and simply lack of enough thought."

Perceived chauvinism aside, Ingrid offers only glowing assessments of her dad. She and her husband moved to Las Vegas when Rauch Industries was sold. Larry Sturm owned a car wash facility when the couple lived in Gastonia, and Ingrid worked in the family business. Like her siblings, Ingrid is in frequent—sometimes daily—contact with her father concerning family and financial matters. The Sturms live in the planned community of Summerlin some twenty minutes from the Las Vegas strip where both have retired.

Marc and Peter Rauch agree with Ingrid's assessment of the wisdom of their father, except, of course, for the gender issue. "I didn't realize until I was thirty that I wasn't perfect because he gave me such a sense of security," Marc said.

"He was a great leader who could handle a crisis better than anyone I knew," Peter said. "When we were young, he worked hard and long hours, but he was always there when we needed him. Family is important to him."

As adults, brothers Marc and Peter have become best friends. They worked together at Rauch Industries for more than two decades. They play golf together regularly and are with each other almost every day.

However, they were not always so close. Growing up, they had intense sibling rivalry. "We both had big egos and were very competitive," Marc says with a nod of agreement from Peter. Regular fistfights took place between the two, some even after they were full-time Rauch Industries executives. "Even into their twenties," their father says, "and even when we'd go to temple for worship, I'd have sit between those two to keep them from aggravating each other."

"He finally put a stop to it," Peter says of his dad. "We had so much respect for him that all he needed to do was talk with us." There have been lots of talks through the years.

"Marc and Pete were ten times the trouble John was when they were growing up," Rauch said, recalling a "forty-eight-hour party" the two sons once threw while their parents were away. "Pete hired a band and brought its members to the house when he was in high school and Marc was in college. Marc came home to join in the celebration. It lasted forty-eight hours while we were away, and we didn't learn about it until much later. Years later we discovered that a table broken at that party was glued back together."

"Marshall always said that if he could just keep Pete out of jail until he was twenty-one, he'd turn out all right," Jeanne Rauch said with a laugh. "He was right."

"I was a lousy kid," Peter said. "I raised a lot of hell and did a lot of things I now regret. I knew I would straighten up some day, but I'm sure I worried my parents, and they must have wondered if I ever would. I was the black sheep in the family growing up."

Marc agreed with Peter's self-assessment, adding that in most cases whatever problems one of them had, the other had either already experienced or soon would.

Marc once spent the night in a Myrtle Beach jail after being arrested for "mouthing off" at a policeman. In one five-week period, Peter wrecked three cars: his own, his mother's, and a rental car she was leasing because hers was wrecked.

Marc joined the family business after graduating from UNC at Chapel Hill in 1971. Peter attended Lenoir Rhyne College in Hickory, but left the school twelve academic hours short of graduation.

In 1975, Marc was making $200 a week when Peter started at $150. Both had worked at Rauch Industries during high school when their father paid them a percentage of the minimum wage, based on their age, as one way of teaching them the importance of earning a salary.

Although Marshall Rauch wanted his sons working with the company, he never promised them they would have lifetime jobs.

"He told us if we screwed up, he'd pay us $200 a week just to stay away," Peter said. "Fortunately, he never had to do that."

Marc was in charge of sales for twenty-five years, and Peter was head of manufacturing for fifteen years before the company was sold. Both planned to remain with the new owners for three years, although that soon changed. Ingrid left the company when the sale was completed, as did Stephanie.

Marc and Peter Rauch remained with the company only several months after it was sold in early 1996. They left because they didn't like the way the new owners dealt with employees. In resigning, each gave up an annual salary of $300,000, which they had been guaranteed for three years. Both said their frustrations were not worth the pay.

In late 1996, the brothers formed Rauch Brothers LLC. in hopes of resuming ornament manufacturing once their non-compete agreement with their former employer expired in 1999. However, at this point, their future business plans still are uncertain. In the meantime, the brothers are spending much of their time on the golf course. The sale of Rauch Industries affords them that luxury.

"Pop had a great plan for us when we first began to work with him," Marc said. "He physically separated us in two different areas of the business, which kept us apart so we wouldn't keep fighting. But over time, we stopped all that foolishness and are now best friends."

Stephanie Rauch grew up as a teenage tennis star and won several state junior tennis titles and later won the North Carolina Open championship. She was offered tennis scholarships at both North Carolina State University and UNC Chapel Hill. After graduating from UNC Chapel Hill, she turned professional and for two years held international world rankings in both singles and doubles. She played in tournaments in England, Austria, Israel, France, Yugoslavia, Australia, and Mexico before realizing, she said, that her skills would not take her to the top of the profession. Recurring knee problems also didn't help her chances for success.

She returned to Gastonia and worked two years in the family business in the late 1980s before deciding to make her mark elsewhere. She moved to Vail, Colorado, where she worked as a ski and tennis instructor, then moved back home to begin part-time work with the family business while she pursued a degree in counseling at graduate school.

Stephanie and Ingrid have not given up the game of tennis. The sisters donated $50,000 to the UNC Education Foundation (also known as the Rams Club) for construction of the Rauch Sisters stadium court at the campus tennis complex off Highway 54, just east of Chapel Hill. Moyer Smith, the former Education Foundation director, says the "generous gift" from the Rauch sisters gives UNC Chapel Hill a tennis facility that encourages national competition because it is one of the finest on any university campus in the United States.

All the Rauch children are good athletes, as was their father. Stephanie may be the best athlete in the family. Since retiring as a tennis pro, she has taken up golf and now competes with her brothers while pursuing her own counseling career.

Son John White played basketball at Wake Forest University, where he was on the freshman team before transferring to Catawba College in Salisbury, where he played on the varsity as a scholarship athlete. Both Marc and Peter were varsity players in high school. Ingrid was on the varsity tennis team at UNC after playing a variety of sports in boarding school and participating in Junior Olympics as a swimmer.

Like her older sister and her brothers, Stephanie credits her father with much of her success in sports and life. "I grew up feeling like a princess," she said. "I've always been a worrier, but I really have nothing to worry about. I've always felt protected, mostly because of an ideal father and mother. My father is a wonderful example of how to live. He is a motivating force. I love what he has done for me. He's not perfect, but he's ideal."

Ingrid and Stephanie said they don't remember their parents ever being angry with them, and were always willing to listen to their concerns. "They had a great philosophy," Ingrid said. "I think they felt if they never acted surprised at anything we told them, we would tell them everything. And I think we did, at least until I went to college, and Mom asked me *not* to tell her everything."

Marc and Peter can't say the same about their parents, but admit it was because of their own actions. "He always wanted to know everything," Peter said of his father. "He always said he'd do anything to help us if we just kept him informed. He always commanded and demanded respect. That's the way he handled problems."

The brothers recall one particular incident that proved to be embarrassing to their father while he was campaigning for the state Senate. At the time Peter and Marc frequented a well-known poker house near Gastonia. Peter's car was seen at the house during police surveillance prior to a raid on the house. News stories about the raid highlighted the fact that police at the scene of illegal activity had seen Senator Rauch's son's car.

"That embarrassed him," Peter says. "It hurt him. He just told me not to let the public exposure get me down, but that I should let him know about those things before the reporters started asking questions."

All the Rauch children say that while their father was the parent who demanded respect, it was their mother who was the disciplinarian in their early years because Rauch was often away on business or political activities. While dad was the important one for the future, it was mom who was in charge for the present. "Mom was always there to help when we needed it," John White says.

> They both have been wonderful to all of us. But I cannot forget the many kind things he has done for me. I was so insecure when he took me in. He gave me confidence. I doubt I could have ever done anything without him. He's a person you respect because he's so honest. It's like that first night I spent at the Rauch home; when I went to bed, he reached down and kissed my cheek and told me he loved me. No one had ever done that for me. I knew he was something special. That meant so much to me then and still does.

Rauch recalled that, on reflection, his relationship with his children had differed over the years, depending on what was happening in his life. He said:

> At my eightieth birthday party at the Gaston Country

Club, with the entire family there along with some close friends, I heard my daughter Ingrid talk about a number of things I had done with her when she was a teenager. They were really great. I remember them well and obviously she did too: from a weekend in New York where she came in from MacDuffie, her prep school in New England, and we went out dining and dancing, to a special trip when I took her to Florida for a long weekend. I realized that I had done things with Ingrid that I didn't do with any of my other children. And sometimes they remind me of certain trips I had talked about but never taken.

In 1967 my life completely changed when I became a state senator and stayed involved with the Senate until 1991. Those were wenty-four years when the other children were growing up, and between politics and our expanding family business, I admit there were things I talked about doing with the other children that I never did get to do. The children still remind me of it, and they are right.

Chapter 19
Extended Family

*The highest Degree of Charity is to aid a person in need by offering
a loan, gift, or scholarship, or by entering into a partnership
with him, or otherwise provide an opportunity, so that
the person may become self-supporting.*

Moses Maimonides, 1135–1204, rabbi and philosopher.

This admonition about benevolence doubtlessly has had special
meanings for large numbers of Jewish philanthropists, but it's
unlikely that it has meant more to anyone than to Marshall Rauch,
who has embraced it as a part of his everyday life. He has adopted
the philosophy of the ancient Jewish rabbi as words and deeds
to live by.

There are growing numbers of persons and organizations that
can attest to Rauch's good works based on Maimonides'
(pronounced my-MAHN-ih-deez) words. And there will be many
more in the years to come. Using the Eight Degrees of Charity
from Maimonides as his springboard and accepting the eighth
as the most important, Rauch has provided financial and
mentoring assistance to dozens of individuals and groups in the
decades of the 1980s and 1990s.

That was just the beginning. Starting in the mid-1990s, his
ultimate plan called for creating a private foundation bearing
his family name and committed to providing an avenue for
spreading good works and some of his personal wealth to people
and organizations in need. Rauch started his foundation in 1994
with an initial contribution of $400,000. He and his family have
added to the total each year since the sale of his company,
Rauch Industries. The goal is to build a foundation valued at
$10 million.

In addition to the foundation resources, Rauch and his wife

Jeanne in the late 1990s donated $1 million for a new education building at Gaston Community College as well as provided multiple scholarships and professorships at campuses within the state's public university system.

While Rauch's success in business and his personal wealth have given him the ability to help others, it was Maimonides' writings that gave him the incentive to do so. Maimonides, whose writings have influenced Christian theologians as well as Jewish leaders through his attempts to harmonize Judaism with the teachings of Aristotle, formulated thirteen articles of faith that make up the basis of the Jewish religion. He also proposed the Eight Degrees of Charity, each successfully more an approximation of perfection. Maimonides' Eight Degrees of Charity are these:

First is to give but give resentfully, however minimal.

Second is to give cheerfully, but give less than one should.

Third is to give, after being asked.

Fourth is to give without being asked.

Fifth is to give where the recipient knows the giver, but the giver does not know the recipient.

Sixth is to give where the giver knows the recipient, but the recipient does not know the giver.

Seventh is to give where the giver and the recipient do not know each other.

The **Eighth**, and highest degree, is to aid a person in need by offering a loan, gift, or scholarship, or by entering into a partnership with him, or otherwise provide opportunity, so that the person may become self-supporting.

To Marshall Rauch, the Eighth Degree has become the First Degree. It is this opportunity to help others help themselves that has become his personal goal. The beneficiaries are numerous, and with the foundation in place their numbers will multiply.

"I've always felt that by helping those who are really trying to help themselves, my own assistance and service will go further and last longer because those people won't quit," Rauch says. "The recipients are sure winners. They're going to stick with it with some help. That's what I've tried to offer. I hope I've helped and that recipients will someday be able to do the same for others."

Those who have been touched by Rauch's generosity all say the only thing he has ever asked in return is for them to reach out to others as they are able when the needs exist. No one—not even Rauch—knows exactly how many people have been recipients of his benevolence or how much money he has given to help others.

Certainly his wife Jeanne and his sons and daughters aren't aware of the numbers. Nor have they inquired. "It has never bothered me that he was doing these things, because I knew he just had the strong desire to do it," Jeanne Rauch said. "He has been very generous in helping those who needed it if they were willing to help themselves. He could be given the title of caregiver."

Some of those who have received a helping hand from Rauch have become close friends. Others, Rauch hardly knows and has seen only a few times, but offered assistance when he learned of their need. Here is a sampling:

Michael Holton

Michael Holton was like a lot of talented professional athletes whose ability to succeed in sports far surpassed his ability to manage his personal life. Bountiful paychecks from the National Basketball Association (NBA) often cause many problems for poor kids who learn to dribble and shoot basketballs much more quickly than they learn to handle money and the life of a celebrity.

Holton was caught in that cycle. After a successful college career at the University of California at Los Angeles, he became a professional and was chosen in the third-round of the 1984 NBA draft. He had up and down years as a journeyman player for four teams: the Golden State Warriors, Chicago Bulls, Phoenix Suns, and Portland Trailblazers.

In 1989 he signed with the newly franchised Charlotte Hornets and thought he was on easy street with a new team and a huge salary. Fan adulation ran as high as his emotions. That's how he was invited to speak at a Salvation Army Boys and Girls

Michael Holton and his wife Lashell at her graduation from UCLA in July 1999.
Marshall Rauch befriended Holton when he was an NBA player, helped Holton get
his first job after his playing days had ended, helped him get coaching jobs,
and has been a financial adviser and good friend to his family.

Club banquet in Gastonia in his first year as a Hornet. He was
introduced by Marshall Rauch, a businessman he did not know.
What a fateful event that turned out to be.

"We kind of hit it off, just sitting and talking at the banquet
before I made my speech," Holton recalled. "I was impressed
that he seemed so genuinely interested in me. At the end of the
program, he told me he'd like to get to know me better and
suggested I call him so we could talk further. I did that a couple
of weeks later because he had seemed so sincere. We met for
lunch. Then we met again just to talk. Pretty soon a very special
friendship began to develop."

Indeed, it was the beginning of a special friendship that Holton
now calls "heaven-sent." It came at just the right time for the
pro athlete. Rauch became a friend, counselor, financial adviser,
and a father figure to Holton who, despite outward appearances,
was heading for disaster in his personal and financial life.

Despite Holton's salary of $400,000 a year as a Hornet, money
was a problem. He had never learned financial management and

was having problems with both investments and debts, largely because of multiple credit-card use. Then came a back injury and things got progressively worse. Holton was released by the Hornets and sent to the Continental Basketball Association (CBA), where he hoped to work himself back into the NBA.

As his financial and athletic problems mounted, Holton, like many big-time athletes with whirlwind lives, began to feel sorry for himself. Then came what could have been a final blow. He flunked a drug test with his CBA team. "I called Marshall first to tell him," Holton recalls. "I didn't call my father or mother. I called Marshall. I knew he would care. He said 'we' would get through it. I knew he would help me."

Rauch did help. He encouraged Holton to get drug treatment. He also worked with him on proper planning and management of his finances. When Holton came out of treatment, he was welcomed back to the CBA and enjoyed another productive year on the basketball court. After deciding to retire as a player in 1991, Holton returned to UCLA to complete work toward the degree he had begun pursuing in 1979.

After earning his degree, he worked for a year as a clothing salesman, but was never able to achieve the same happiness he had had in sports. Rauch offered Holton advice and encouraged him to get into coaching, no matter the financial sacrifice. Holton's first collegiate job was at Pasadena City College, where he was

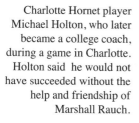

Charlotte Hornet player Michael Holton, who later became a college coach, during a game in Charlotte. Holton said he would not have succeeded without the help and friendship of Marshall Rauch.

paid a mere $1,500 a year for coaching plus a modest salary as a teacher.

Despite a huge drop in income, Holton persevered because Rauch advised him not to give up and to prove that he had the talent to get better jobs. Since Holton's first coaching job, Rauch has been a constant friend and adviser in what has become a successful coaching career at a Division I school in the National Collegiate Athletic Association. He is now head coach at the University of Portland.

"He has been like a father to me," Holton said from Los Angeles, when he served as a top assistant at UCLA after assistant coaching jobs of one season each at the University of Portland and at Oregon State University. "He has given me guidance I needed and confidence I didn't have. He has helped in so many ways. I'm scared to think what I might have become if he had not been there to help me. He is truly heaven-sent. I never had any extra money growing up, and I didn't know anything about how to handle money when I got into pro athletics. He has taught me how to manage my finances. He showed me how to get out of debt. He has offered counsel and advice in my jobs. I still don't make any significant decisions in my life without consulting Marshall first. That's how important he is to me and what he means in my life."

Rauch said he "saw something in Michael that convinced me he had the potential to overcome his problems. Time and again he has proven me right."

With a wife and three children, Holton often dreamed of becoming a head coach of a Division I NCAA basketball team. He and Rauch talked often about that, by phone and in person. In an interview in 2000, Holton said:

> One day I will be a head coach, and I know he'll be right there with me. He has been there for me so often, to help and guide me in the right direction. If I can someday be for someone just a fraction of what he has been for me, my life will have been worthwhile. He has always helped people because of his big heart. I am grateful he apparently saw something in me and chose me to be one he wanted to help. He is a very special person, both

patient and kind. All he has ever asked in return is for me to help others.

Holton's dream of a top coaching job became reality on April 2, 2001, when he was named head basketball coach at the University of Portland, following numerous conversations and advice and counsel from Rauch. Three weeks later, Rauch flew to Portland to help Holton celebrate his new job. His prediction that he would become a head coach and that Rauch would be there for him came true.

J.W. Isenhour

As a North Carolina State University tennis coach and physical education professor, J.W. Isenhour had no idea when he recruited Marshall Rauch's athletically talented daughter Stephanie to the Wolfpack tennis team in the early 1980s what that would mean for him and his family. Rauch saw in Isenhour a dedicated coach with high character, but one who also was struggling to make ends meet for his wife and two teenage sons on a salary of about $20,000 a year.

"Except for my mom and dad who taught me values, no one has ever done for me as much as Marshall Rauch has," Isenhour says. "His help significantly improved our family's life. The Lord has blessed me by bringing Marshall Rauch into my life. And I know I'm just one of many he has helped."

As a tennis coach looking for talent, Isenhour had followed Stephanie Rauch's early successes on the tennis court and recruited her to play for N.C. State. Stephanie had won many tournaments in North Carolina and elsewhere during her high school years. "I looked at her only as a recruit," Isenhour recalled. "I didn't know anything about her parents or her father's financial situation. They just always seemed cordial and interested in helping her get better."

Isenhour coached Stephanie for two years at N.C. State and was impressed with her talent and determination to improve. She was voted the Wolfpack's Most Valuable Player. In the fall of 1981, Isenhour drove from Raleigh to Greensboro to watch her compete in a women's tournament. That turned out to be an eventful day for the Isenhour family.

"After the tournament, Mr. Rauch came up to me and invited me to come to his home for dinner because he wanted to talk about a few things," Isenhour says. "I assumed he wanted to discuss Stephanie's tennis playing. What happened next was just simply unbelievable to me."

After dinner, Rauch told Isenhour of his appreciation for the help he had given Stephanie and added that he had heard Isenhour's family had been looking for an affordable home because their small apartment was overflowing.

He told me he wanted to help me. A friend of our family, Peggy Hogan, who worked on the staff of the General Assembly where Marshall was a state senator, had commented to him that we were looking for an affordable home. He said he'd like to help. He asked me to look for a home I could afford the mortgage on, and he'd like to help me with cash enough to get in it. He said he'd make me an interest-free loan that I shouldn't begin repaying until my sons were out of college. They were only about ten and twelve years old at the time. I couldn't believe he'd do that. There were no strings attached. He would get nothing more from me with that loan than if he hadn't offered to do it. I just couldn't believe that was happening.

In March 1982, Isenhour found a home in North Raleigh for $65,000. A down payment of $20,000 was required to lower the monthly payments to an amount the Isenhours could afford. Rauch made him an interest-free loan of $24,000, enough for the initial payment and $4,000 for repairs. Initially, Isenhour was scheduled to begin repaying the interest-free loan once his sons finished with college. But when time came to begin the repayments, Rauch changed the agreement. Instead of accepting money, Rauch asked Isenhour to show records that he was putting the repayment amount in mutual funds for the benefit of the Isenhour family.

Shortly after getting the Rauch loan, Isenhour resigned as an N. C. State tennis coach, but continued to teach physical education. When Isenhour resigned his coaching job, Stephanie Rauch transferred to UNC Chapel Hill to play varsity tennis, but she continued personal training and coaching from Isenhour.

Isenhour is the son of textile mill workers in Concord,

northeast of Charlotte. He was a good athlete and became a coach and sports instructor more out of love for athletics than for financial gain. "There is no way I would have ever been able to afford to buy that house without Marshall Rauch's help," Isenhour said. "He genuinely improved my life and the lives of my family. I will forever be grateful and appreciative. He made a difference in my life, but wanted and expected nothing in return. I realize there are lots of others with his personal resources, but they don't do what he has done to help others."

When Isenhour retired from N. C. State in the spring of 1997 and was given a certificate at the UNC Board of Governors meeting in May, Rauch, a member of the governing board, greeted him with a huge hug. "He hugged me in front of the whole group and said a handshake wasn't enough," Isenhour says. "That's what makes him different."

Kathrinn Fitzpatrick

Kathrinn Fitzpatrick was a single mother of three working in an entry-level summer job at the Bowles Center for Alcohol Studies on the campus at UNC Chapel Hill. She was struggling to stay in pharmacy school. It was on a muggy but typically beautiful spring day in 1995, the day of the official dedication of the Bowles Center building, and as a staff member, she was invited to attend the ceremony and luncheon.

At the luncheon, she chose to sit in the empty chair beside a distinguished, tanned, and sharply dressed man whom she had never met and who introduced himself to her as Marshall Rauch. She had never seen or heard of him until that moment. During their luncheon conversation, Rauch asked Fitzpatrick if she were in school, about her family, and her job at the Bowles Center.

From speakers at the program that followed that luncheon, Fitzpatrick learned that Rauch was a former state senator who was instrumental in enacting legislation creating the alcohol treatment facility in memory of Hargrove "Skipper" Bowles, his former legislative colleague and close friend. When the ceremony was over, Rauch and Fitzpatrick shook hands and said good-bye. In parting, Rauch told Fitzpatrick if he could ever help, she should let him know.

"I didn't think much about that comment at the time," Fitzpatrick later recalled. "But I had the distinct impression he was really serious and not just making idle talk." Several months later, with personal resources running out, Fitzpatrick wrote Rauch to ask if he might give her some leads on possible student loans. He did that and a lot more.

"He sent me $500 of his own money for the next semester and told me it was an interest-free loan," Fitzpatrick said. "And he did that every semester until I finished pharmacy school. He never asked for anything in return.

"I've never even seen Mr. Rauch except at that luncheon two years ago," she said after graduating in 1997.

> He's a very caring, thoughtful, and wonderful person. He's a man of his word and someone you can count on. He just told me he liked to help those who are trying to help themselves. He does what he says and is the kind of person you'd be proud to have as a member of your family. The interest-free loan allowed me to stay in school. But he has also helped beyond that. Through phone calls and letters he has given me moral support. And both he and other members of his family sent clothes and basket-ball tickets to my children. He just does nice things for people.

After Fitzpatrick finished pharmacy school, Rauch agreed to supplement her salary as a pharmacy technician until she found a full-time job as a pharmacist which would pay her enough to support herself and three sons. "His help and his words of encouragement never cease," she said. "My boys and I are truly blessed by his presence in our lives. I think when Mr. Rauch and I met at the Bowles dedication luncheon that the good Lord started a small miracle that has been nurtured by faith and hard work. For me, it has become a very large miracle."

In February 1998, Fitzpatrick was hired as a full-time pharmacist near her home in Chapel Hill. The first person she called to thank was Marshall Rauch.

Mark Bibbs

Mark Bibbs grew up in Gaston County. From his early years

he had heard about a successful businessman in Gastonia named Marshall Rauch, but he had never met Rauch until one day in the spring of 1990. As a student government leader at UNC Chapel Hill, he went to the North Carolina General Assembly in Raleigh to seek passage of legislation that would put a student representative on the board that governs the state university system.

"I will never forget that day," Bibbs recalls. "I discussed the proposed legislation with him, explaining that I felt a student ought to be represented on the board. He listened, thanked me for coming, and shook my hand when I left his office—but when he took my hand, he put $100 in it. He knew I was from Gaston County, and I guess he knew I could use the money."

Under Rauch's leadership, the students' legislative proposal became law, and Bibbs became a student member of the UNC Board of Governors. That was the beginning of a long and warm relationship between Rauch and Bibbs. After Bibbs was graduated from UNC, he enrolled in law school there and called Rauch for advice on getting some student loans. "He offered to help with personal money," Bibbs explained. "He said he believed in me and did it out of the goodness of his heart."

By the time Bibbs, who now lives in Wilson, North Carolina, entered law school, Rauch was out of the state Senate and was himself a member of the UNC governing board. Rauch and another board member, Tar Heel native and philanthropist Walter Davis, who made money in Texas oil and other investments, jointly agreed to help Bibbs with law school expenses.

They weren't willing just to give him money: he would have to adhere to some rules. Rauch and Davis requested two things: a written budget outlining how he would use the money and regular reports on his grades. Bibbs provided the budget, but declined to turn over his grades, causing Davis to withdraw his financial help. Rauch picked up the Bibbs' tab on his own.

"I like Mark Bibbs," Walter Davis said, "but he promised to allow us to see his grades and then decided he didn't want to do that. The grades were part of my commitment, and when he chose not to fulfill his promise, I felt no obligation to fulfill mine."

Bibbs concedes he declined to pass along his grades as originally promised. The grades were respectable, but not tip-top. Rauch forgave the grade commitment and made regular payments based on the Bibbs budget.

After reviewing my budget, he sent me money every month. He provided me with about $5,000 a year for three years. I couldn't believe it. I had never known anyone who was so generous. He's the most considerate person I've ever met. He's full of compassion. I've asked him how I can repay the debts, and he just says that he hopes someday I'll show the same kindness to someone else. I've promised him I would. He's truly a phenomenal guy and friend.

Gloria Majors

Gloria Majors was a frequent visitor at Temple Emanuel in Gastonia. She isn't Jewish but attended synagogue services with friends who were. She first learned to recognize Marshall Rauch while she was working as a waitress at the Gaston Country Club but became better acquainted with him at the synagogue where he is a member.

Majors knew that Rauch had some connection with the administration of the public university system and, one night after a temple service, she asked him if she could use him as a reference on her application for a nursing school scholarship. He said sure, but he had a better idea:

I was stunned. He asked me if I'd allow him to give me a scholarship. All he wanted to do was help. He wanted nothing in return but my own commitment to succeed and improve myself. From January 1996 until May 1997, he sent me a check for $500 every month to help me pay rent. I was working two jobs before his offer of assistance came, because I was helping with expenses for my college son. His kindness allowed me to stop one of my jobs and concentrate on nursing school studies. Without his help, I don't know what I would have done, but I doubt I would have been able to finish nursing school. He saw I was struggling. He knew I was serious about my studies and wanted to help. I will always be grateful to him. He has said the only repayment he ever expected is that some-day maybe I can help someone else.

256

THERE IS NO CHARGE
FOR THIS BOOK

After you read this book, if you would like
to help support **The Rauch Foundation,
Inc.**, please send any contribution you
wish to:

Rauch Foundation, Inc.
1309 Union Road
Gastonia, NC 28054

After obtaining her degree, Majors no longer needed Rauch's financial assistance. But thanks to his help, Majors began working in August 1997 as a nurse. She often remembers his kindness, not only in giving financial assistance but also in believing in her ability to complete her nursing degree and to pass her licensing exams.

Janet Thomas

By the 1990s, Janet Thomas was a busy and successful Charlotte lawyer whose courtroom expertise involved criminal defenses and serving the needs of young people. She had a special affinity for at-risk young people who needed help to get on the right path in society and stay there. Three decades earlier, she had been one of those young people. A special person had helped steer her in the direction to success. That person was Marshall Rauch.

Thomas grew up in a blue-collar family in Bessemer City, where Rauch's business was located, and, as a financially struggling high school student, obtained a second-shift job in Rauch's manufacturing plant. It wasn't the job that convinced her that life could improve with extra efforts. It was a Rauch speech.

"He came to my high school to make a speech," Thomas said, more than thirty years after hearing that speech. "His topic was motivation. That speech gave me encouragement and caused me, for the first time, to look at myself and think of going on to college. Before that, I never imagined that I could or would be able to go to college."

The inspiration didn't stop with the speech:

After the speech he got to know me in his plant, and he kept encouraging me to improve myself. I know I would not have gone to college without Marshall Rauch. I was scared to leave home at the time, but he helped me prepare my college application. He gave me hope and courage throughout my years at Sacred Heart College [in Belmont about twenty miles from her hometown]. He offered me financial help, but I wanted to show him I was independent. But he kept up with me and then encouraged me to go to law school. I wouldn't and couldn't have done it without his providing me the motivation to go on. He has helped me in so many ways, but the most important was his encouragement and his emphasis on keeping motivated. For twenty-seven years, he has consistently kept in touch and been a mentor and friend.

When Thomas obtained her law degree and opened her one-person practice, Rauch sent clients as a way of ensuring she had income as she was getting established.

"No words can adequately express what he has meant to me and done for me," Thomas says. "I don't know why he took such an interest in me. Maybe it was because he felt I was motivated to improve myself. But whatever the reason, I shall forever be grateful. He didn't have to help me. He did it because he wanted to."

Dr. Kenneth Sadler

Growing up in Gastonia, Kenneth Sadler had heard of Marshall Rauch, but he had never met Rauch until he was preparing to enter dental school in the fall of 1971. Sadler had no resources for dental training, but his parents, like so many others who knew of Rauch's willingness to help those trying to better themselves, suggested that he visit Rauch in search of advice on securing scholarship aid.

"He was kind enough to help arrange for me to get a scholarship to Howard University and also to help me obtain a B'nai B'rith scholarship," Sadler said of that initial meeting. Now a dentist and health-maintenance administrator in Winston-Salem, Sadler completed dental school at Howard because of those scholarships. "But that's not all he did for me," Sadler continues:

> I needed some other financial help during my years of dental study, and he kept sending me money, which he called an interest-free loan until I graduated and could repay the debt. He was very generous in that help, providing thousands of dollars to cover living expenses. When I got my degree and asked him about a repayment schedule, he told me I had already repaid him by just

succeeding in school. He wouldn't take any repayment. If it had not been for Marshall Rauch, I don't know how I could have reached my goals of becoming a dentist. It would be impossible to express my gratitude. And all he has ever asked in return is that I do well and maybe one day I can help others.

Rauch's assistance to Sadler has been more than direct financial help. As Sandler says, "He remains a good friend to this day and has been a big help in giving advice on investments and supplying business acumen. His help and friendship have been invaluable. He is altruistic to the highest degree."

Tony Byers

Marshall Rauch knew two things about Ida Byers, a kind and caring woman in Bessemer City in the late 1960s. She baked wonderful pies, and she had a son named Tony who had outstanding athletic abilities. Rauch enjoyed Ida's baking, but he was more interested in Tony, whose life needed some direction.

Rauch provided Tony a part-time job at Rauch Industries and made regular trips to watch the young man play basketball in high school. Tony and Rauch's son Pete, about the same age, became buddies and frequently spent nights together. When Tony finished high school, his athletic skills were ready for college basketball but his weak academic record caused most coaches to look elsewhere.

To prevent Byers' basketball skills from being wasted, Rauch contacted his friend Dean Smith, coach at UNC Chapel Hill. Smith suggested Vincennes Junior College (now a university) in Indiana, which willingly accepted the new recruit. For Byers, it was a great choice. In 1972, he led Vincennes to the national junior college championship with a 33-0 record. Among the fans at the final game in Kansas was Ida Byers, whose trip was arranged and paid for by Rauch.

By the time Byers had finished his two years at Vincennes, Coach Smith had decided against offering scholarships to any junior college players. But Wake Forest's new coach, Carl Tacy, was eager to have Byers on the Deacon team. Byers was good enough to average 21 points a game in his junior year at Wake

Forest and get his picture on the team's media booklet the next year, when his scoring average as a hot-shooting guard was 18 points a game in a 13-13 season. Byers didn't earn a degree at Wake Forest, but later as an assistant basketball coach at Belmont Abbey College, near his home, he completed work toward his degree.

Byers continued to struggle with personal problems and was unable to make it in the National Basketball Association. He worked for several years as a long-haul truck driver, but by the late 1990s had settled into a local trucking company driver's job in Lansing, Michigan. He describes his friendship with Marshall Rauch:

> My dad died when I was eleven. It made me feel good that someone like Marshall Rauch would take such an interest in someone like me and come to my high school games and help me with college choices. I looked to Marshall Rauch as a male figure and a father. He was a positive role model for me. His advice helped get me into Vincennes and into Wake Forest. He was always willing to help me and that has meant a lot. Even when I made mistakes, he was always there. He never turned away. He reminds me of a pastor, always willing to listen and help.

Ida Byers supported her son's assessment of Rauch, too. "Oh, Lord, he just helped and kept on helping in so many different ways," she said. "He has done so many beautiful things for our family and treated Tony just like his own son. He's a wonderful person."

Patsy Ezzell

A warm and caring friendship developed between Marshall Rauch and state Senator Jim Ezzell of Rocky Mount when the two served together in the General Assembly. They shared many philosophical views, but a strong personal bond was evident in their mutual respect and admiration for each other.

Rauch has always had a special affection for people who have overcome hardships. Maybe that was one thing that drew him to Ezzell, whose quadriplegic problems resulting from a birth defect had not stopped him from becoming a lawyer, judge, and state senator.

One of the saddest and most traumatic phone calls Rauch ever received was in the early morning hours of January 31, 1991, when he learned that Ezzell had been killed the previous night when his car slid off a rain-soaked Raleigh street after the opening day of that year's legislative session. Ezzell, who was not wearing a seatbelt when his car careened down an embankment, was thrown from the vehicle and fatally crushed when the car rolled over him. His only passenger, his wife Patsy, was securely strapped in her seatbelt and was not injured. Patsy Ezzell describes the relationship she and her husband had with Rauch:

> Marshall is a very dear friend. As soon as he heard of the crash, he called and asked what he could do to help. I told him I needed him. He and Jeanne came that very day. He called every day for months afterwards to give me encouragement and advice. He is a wonderful, giving person who has helped so many people in so many ways, some without even knowing he was the benefactor.

Rauch delivered a moving eulogy at Ezzell's funeral in Englewood Baptist Church. His concern for his friend Ezzell and his family didn't end with the funeral or the daily phone calls in the months after the service. He has become a financial counselor and adviser for Patsy Ezzell. Her assets in the late 1990s were far greater than when Rauch first began giving her advice following her husband's death.

"I just don't make any major financial decisions without first running it past him," she says. "He has been wonderful to me. He is one of the smartest and kindest people I've ever known. He was a true friend of Jim's, but he has also been that to me."

Gayle Kersh

Gayle Battley was a financially struggling eighteen-year-old waitress, one of two jobs she held while taking part-time college courses in 1971. She also was talented. Marshall Rauch noticed her astuteness the first time she took the Rauch family dinner order. She didn't write any of the orders down but got them all right. That impressed Rauch, and he told her so. He made several more trips to the restaurant in the next few weeks, each time becoming more convinced that the young woman had potential for success far beyond taking flawless dinner orders.

Rauch learned from Battley that she had graduated from Hamlet High School in Richmond County and come to Charlotte in search of a degree at UNC Charlotte, only to drop out for lack of money. She worked one full-time job as a secretary at a textile company in Gastonia, worked as a waitress at night, and attended classes at Gaston Community College.

Rauch offered her a job at his own company. Battley turned him down because she was scared to take a chance on another job. Shortly afterward, Rauch visited the textile company where she worked. When she learned that company was in financial trouble, she accepted work as a computer operator at Rauch Industries. Personally and financially, that was the smartest move Battley had made at that point in her life.

Battley is now Gayle Kersh, wife of highly successful Gastonia lawyer Danny Kersh, and former owner of her own company that marketed specialty ornaments in both Gastonia and Blowing Rock. Rauch helped her start her company. It is one of many ways he has helped her succeed in the last twenty years.

From that initial job as a computer operator at Rauch Industries, Kersh became Rauch's personal secretary at the company, worked as his legislative secretary when he served in the state Senate, and accepted his advice and financial assistance while starting her own ornament business.

I don't know where I might be today if it had not been for Mr. Rauch's help and advice. I guess I don't even want to think about that. But he afforded me opportunities that I never even dreamed of having and that I would never have had without him. He and Mrs. Rauch have been like a father and mother to me. He had always treated me like a daughter and even treats my husband as a son. He is an extremely caring and giving person, and his concern and help have certainly made things easier for me. He is an outstanding person, determined to help give people a chance to help themselves.

During her early years with Rauch Industries, Rauch financed Kersh's tuition at Sacred Heart College, where she earned a business degree. Then he helped her start her business. "That's just the way he is," she explained. "He enjoys helping people and he certainly helped me with education, with my training on how to function as a business person. I am very appreciative for all he has done for me. I know he has done similar things for lots of other people. He's a wonderful person."

Baron Davis

While Michael Holton was an assistant coach at UCLA, he introduced Marshall Rauch to a young Los Angeles point guard that UCLA was recruiting. Holton called the young man, Baron Davis, the best point guard in that year's class of college freshman. Rauch saw Davis several times that year, including at Durham, when UCLA came east to play Duke.

Near the end of his freshman season, Davis tore ligaments in his knee and required surgery that might have ended his playing days. Rauch responded by writing Davis an encouraging letter, telling him to hang tough, to stay in there. Davis made a strong comeback—and he kept that letter.

At the end of his sophomore year, Davis made himself available for the NBA draft and was chosen by the Charlotte Hornets. Immediately he got a welcoming phone call from Rauch, who offered to help ease the transition from Los Angeles to Charlotte.

Arriving in town as a rookie, Davis said he was "lonely and really had nothing to do, and had nobody to turn to. He (Rauch) was there, giving advice—about basketball, about finances, about everything."

During Davis's first season in Charlotte, the Rauch home was his home away from home. The Rauch family made him feel welcome there—by Marshall, by the children and the grandchildren. Davis and his fiancee, Elizabeth Edmond, spent Thanksgiving with the Rauch family.

In February, when Baron's father, Walter Davis, died one day before he was to see his son play in the NBA for the first time, Marshall Rauch was on hand to offer condolences and emotional support.

"He has helped me out a whole lot," Davis said. "He has been like a father figure to me. And I love him for that. You don't find too many people who are willing to open up the doors to their family and invite you in and really mean it.

"I appreciate him more than he thinks I do. He helps out more than he thinks he does. That type of impact, you can't say enough about.

"In his own right, he is a celebrity. It is amazing how people gravitate toward him. He never forgets anybody he meets. He's humble. He has a great family, a great wife, great kids. They've all treated me like one of their own.

"It's not about black or white or I'm some superstar basketball player. When I go over there, I'm Baron and he's... well, I call him Senator Rauch. Everybody is on a first-name basis. It's a release. You can be who you want to be. The way his family accepted me was just a joy."

The recipients of Rauch's benevolence and support have

Baron Davis, a NBA all-star, and Marshall Rauch prior to a Charlotte Hornets game. Davis calls Rauch a close friend and mentor on financial issues.

obviously realized positive benefits and have seen their lives enhanced. To Rauch, the benefits of giving have equaled, if not surpassed, those of the receiving. "Each person quoted in this chapter is more than just a friend," Rauch said:

Every one of these people is a special and precious part of my life. Space doesn't permit me to talk about the others who are also important to me. Each of these people—who are really extended family—have given me the opportunity to experience some of the greatest joys of life. That has been to see and be a part of their success and to rejoice in it with them as they succeed and transmit their attributes into their own sphere of influence. Their successes have given me great satisfaction and enormous pleasure. I am pleased to have been a part of their lives.

Chapter 20
The Rauch Foundation

Life is not how long you live; life is how well you live.
Life is not how much you made; life is how much you gave.

Marshall Rauch, eulogizing state Senator Jim Ezzell,
February 2, 1991.

Those poignant words spoken by Marshall Rauch for the friend he loved, state Senator Jim Ezzell, accurately depict the life of the late senator who inspired many people with his zest for living and giving of himself. Ezzell was killed in a tragic car wreck on opening night of the 1991 session of the North Carolina General Assembly.

While the words were appropriate for Ezzell's memorial service in Rocky Mount, where approximately 1,000 friends, ranging from the politically powerful to the common laborer, packed Englewood Baptist Church to say farewell in their own personal ways, they were, in a quiet way, also a description of the speaker, Marshall Rauch.

Rauch's life has been one of caring and giving, both of himself and his financial resources, for the benefit of others. His reputation for benevolence is well known among close friends, many who have been recipients of his kindness and counsel. Countless others have benefited through his anonymous gifts or simply been recipients of gentle words of encouragement in a time of need or crisis.

Those acts of kindness by Rauch will surely multiply in years ahead as he focuses his energies in the remainder of his life to expanding the recently established Rauch Family Foundation as a way of expressing his desire to provide help, support, and encouragement to others.

Rauch has been blessed with success and good fortune in his business during a fifty-plus-year career in private industry. He started that career with little more than a strong determination for hard work and a burning desire to succeed. In those early days he had help from many others among family and friends, and their lessons in kindness and caring have not been forgotten. Indeed, they are in part responsible for his desire to carry forth and extend the same kind of good works. The family foundation he feels is the best and most efficient way to help the most people.

Rauch didn't wait until he was financially successful to begin his good works. He has done kind things since he was a teenager growing up in New York, where he worked with younger children in sports and community service. "It's something that I've always done and wanted to do," Rauch said.

"I remember in high school working with younger kids in the neighborhood with sports and encouraging them not to smoke and to do the right things. It was never anything formal. I never woke up one day and suddenly decided that I was going to help people. I do it because I enjoy doing it."

When Rauch first moved to Gastonia, he helped start the city's first Big Brother program with Gilbert Bell and worked with the Gastonia Boys Club and his close friend Rex Edison. He also was involved with other youth programs long before he was financially successful. As his businesses and investments prospered, his willingness and philanthropy grew.

"As time went on and I had more financial means, the more I've been able to do," he said. "Some people are creative in other ways, like being artistic. I'm not gifted that way. But to me nothing is more important than what I have been able to do and hope to do in the future by helping people help themselves. I enjoy seeing people succeed in life, to achieve their maximum potential."

That's where the Rauch Foundation will step forward with future gifts to individuals and community projects. Through the years, Rauch has given away hundreds of thousands of dollars in addition to his time in public service and his counsel and advice to numerous individuals. The foundation will give structure and organization to those expanding philanthropic efforts.

The foundation was created in 1994, when Rauch was in his early seventies and had closed his public career in elective office. He added to it in 1996, when he sold his business and he and his family shared in the proceeds. His goal as the 1900s closed was to build a foundation with at least $10 million in what he calls the "shortest reasonable time," in the twenty-first century. "I believe that's an attainable goal," Rauch said. In coming decades, he would like to see that figure double and triple.

Rauch launched the foundation with an initial contribution of $400,000 of his own money. He and his family have and will add to it each year for the continuing benefit of charitable causes. During the first years the foundation existed, Rauch and his wife Jeanne also have donated sizable amounts of money to educational endeavors independent of their own foundation.

In 1996, the couple gave $1 million to the Gaston Community Foundation for use in what federal laws refer to as "donor recommended" charities. Out of this $1 million, the

Groundbreaking for the Rauch Science Fine Arts Building
at Gaston College on September 8, 1998

269

Rauches designated $700,000 for a new arts and science building at Gaston Community College. The remaining principle and interest will be for other community projects.

Rauch also has donated $233,000 for an endowed professorship at the University of North Carolina at Charlotte. That money will be matched by $167,000 in state funds and another $100,000 from the Spangler Foundation, headed by retired UNC President C.D. Spangler Jr. The professorship, endowed at $500,000, is named the Marshall A. Rauch Distinguished Professorship in Political Science.

Rauch also has an endowed professorship in his name at Elizabeth City State University, given in his honor by friends.

UNC Charlotte Chancellor James H. Woodward is generous in his praise of Rauch, not only for the financial contributions to the Charlotte institution but also for his contribution to the good of the state through public service:

> I have a great admiration for Marshall Rauch because he reminds me of the citizen legislators who played key roles in establishing this country. He achieved tremendous success in business yet chose to contribute his talents to the people by serving in the General Assembly and in other public service capacities. The University of North Carolina and particularly UNC Charlotte have been the direct beneficiaries of his commitment to enhance the well-being of the people of this state through higher education. Marshall has always been supportive of the university system of this state, especially our campus. As a member of the UNC Board of Governors, he had to consider the needs and interests of all sixteen campuses, but I'm confident he has always had a special place in his heart for UNC Charlotte. There is no question in my mind that tens of thousands of North Carolinians have led better lives because of Marshall Rauch's public service. I consider it an honor to know him and have him as a friend.

Rauch also has donated $50,000 for athletic scholarships at UNC Chapel Hill. That money will be used to support the women's tennis program there. As undergraduates, Rauch's two daughters, Ingrid and Stephanie, were members of UNC varsity tennis teams and have contributed another $50,000 to UNC Chapel Hill to pay for the completion of the stadium court at the school's tennis complex near the main campus.

The Rauch Foundation has two specific, ongoing commitments. It has pledged to provide money for two annual scholarships at Gaston Community College. One was established in memory of Rauch's long-time friend and attorney, J. Mack Holland, with preference going to students with an interest in a legal career. Because of Jeanne's lifetime commitment, the other goes to students studying art.

"We really haven't focused on more than a few specific areas of giving for the foundation yet," Rauch said. The highest priorities for the foundation, he said, will be contributions for educational opportunities and various Jewish causes. Another area will be efforts to help people or groups with physical handicaps, partly because of Rauch's friendships with the late Senator Ezzell and his high school friend "Brud" Gamp.

"Right now," Rauch said in early 2004, "our thinking is to allow the Foundation to help with one-time challenge gifts and grants to get projects started with lesser amounts to be contributed in later years as organizations get better established. That way, we will be able to help more groups get started at helping themselves." That philosophy is consistent with the way Rauch has handled individual donations to benefit people or projects in the past.

The mission statement of the Rauch Foundation is specific in its intent: to help people achieve their maximum potential. The foundation's stationery lists the degrees of charity as taught by Jewish philosopher Maimonides. Rauch said:

> I know of nothing as rewarding as being able to help somebody help themselves. In addition to the personal satisfaction and pleasure I get with this, I want my family to have and maintain the teachings of Judaism, including the Eight Degrees of Charity taught by Maimonides. I don't know anything I could leave for my family that would be worth more and be more important than these teachings. My family has always known my views on Maimonides, and they were not at all surprised when I told them I was

going to start the foundation to make contributions to worthy causes. They've all just jumped into it and have already helped.

Each of Rauch's children and grandchildren has made personal voluntary contributions to the foundation. "On occasions, we've stopped giving gifts to each other on holidays and made donations in honor of family members to the foundation instead," Rauch said. All the Rauch children willingly agree that they will contribute to the foundation in any way their father recommends. In years to come, Rauch says he hopes a family member will always be available to run the foundation.

"The tax laws governing private foundation laws require a minimum distribution of 5 percent of the total asset value each year. When we reach a $10 million base, the Rauch Foundation would give away at least $500,000 a year. With that kind of money, we could really do some worthwhile and important things," Rauch stressed.

The foundation's assets will be expanded in stages as Rauch and his family make annual contributions. Rauch hopes others outside the family will see the benefits of the foundation and be willing to make contributions so the principal will grow more quickly.

"The foundation is a name only, and I hope it isn't limited to contributions from within our family," Rauch said. "I hope others will see it as we do, a process for good, and will want to be a part of it and see it grow. That's certainly what our family intends.

"As assets grow, it is most important to study the requests for donations. We want to make sure the money is spent properly where it will do the most good for the most people. We will study each request but will want to keep the rules flexible enough to help as many people as we can. There will likely be times when we give to one area of need at one time and another area the next time. As times and needs change, we want to be able to help in the best and broadest way."

The Rauch Foundation directors are Rauch, his wife, and his children. The family members meet formally as a board at their annual beach reunion and at other times as needed. The board meetings are always all business, but not always tranquil, as family members discuss desires for growing the foundation assets and for distribution.

"We sometimes have rather heated and adversarial discussions on how to distribute the funds and who recipients will be," Rauch said. "The girls are pretty adamant on women's rights efforts, and they make that very clear. The boys don't really oppose those things, but they have said some things that have raised anxieties and caused a few arguments. I just let those things go on in the discussions, because it provokes thought and brings new ideas on what we can do. It stimulates some great debate."

The value and future of the foundation will depend on the uses of its distributed funds. Rauch has adopted a set of disbursement guidelines which he feels will maximize the contributions.

"Grants, which will soon be in the six figures, must be made only after careful research," he said. "Directors should pick only a few categories of need. Otherwise, even with the best intentions, eventually efforts become frustrated because you can't be all things to all people. We should specialize and become a strong force for excellence in situations that are meaningful and important, but never forgetting that Judaism and family is our origin."

Rauch said the majority of the grants, especially large ones, should be to and through responsible and proven institutions because they can best administer such sums.

"In my opinion, developed over more than fifty years of giving, one of the greatest pleasures in life is to see, feel, touch, and participate in success as it happens," he said. "That's what I want the foundation to do. I want my family to have that privilege as I have had. Therefore, a portion of our foundation funds should be used to help individuals on a one-on-one basis.

"As long as we remain a small foundation, we need to consider annual gifts without future pledges. Pledges minimize the possibility of substantial gifts that might prove to be even more important in a future year. To do the most good, we should personally investigate by going and looking at where we are going to give money. We should be risk takers and give money to help start up organizations that can help humanity. While our assets remain small, we should limit ourselves to five or ten grants a year so the grants are meaningful. This is not to say we can't go back to give again, but we should not limit what we might want to do in the future by what we pledge today. We should not contribute to any endowments. We should give to compelling new ideas. A certain percentage of our funds could be allocated to scholarships, because the recipients are the people from whom future ideas can come. New buildings for established institutions could be considered for grants but not operating expenses for established institutions. However, start-up operating expenses might be considered so an institution had a chance to prove itself."

Finally, according to Rauch, it comes down to this: "Making money is fun, but sharing it is pleasure."

He wants the family foundation to be a pleasurable experience for future generations of contributors and beneficiaries. His carefully chosen ground rules for those who come after him are firmly in place. His initial small steps, he hopes, will lead to larger ones so that benevolence will spread and good deeds continue. He believes, he says, in the words of former U.S. Senate Chaplain Peter Marshall, who characterized good works thusly: The measure of one's life is not duration, but donation. That may well be the legacy that Marshall Rauch leaves for those who will follow.

Appendix

Through the years, even in serious debate over serious issues, Marshall Rauch kept a collection of wise and witty colloquialisms from his legislative colleagues and others in public life. He hasn't always recalled the speaker, but he always remembered the phrases. They have been borrowed and stolen from the greats, would be greats, and ingrates, he said. Here is the list that Rauch offers for wit and wisdom.

People are like thumbtacks—they can only go as far as their heads will let them.

When you fail to prepare—you prepare to fail.

He's not wound tight.

His elevator goes up but the light doesn't go on.

He doesn't have both oars in the water.

You can tell he's levelheaded, his tobacco juice drips out of both corners of his mouth.

Sometimes you only see the light after you feel the heat.

You can't miss what you never had.

Diamonds are made under pressure, but so is gas.

Power corrupts, absolute power corrupts absolutely.

To make a fine omelet, you first have to break a few eggs.

Always consider the future, or you will only exist in the past.

You can't come back from a trip you never took.

If it ain't broke, don't fix it.

He who the gods wish to destroy they first make mad.

Keep your options open.

Paralysis by analysis.

Success Is a Team Sport

The measure of one's life is not duration, but donation.

When you have to walk a mile, the hardest thing to do is take the first step.

It's a poor dog that ain't got more than one bone buried.

You can shear a sheep every year but skin it only once.

Ask him what time it is, and he'll tell you how to make a watch.

It's easier to throw a grenade than to catch one.

Things don't just happen. People make them happen.

Blood is thicker than water, but money is thicker than blood.

The horse that pulls the wagon gets the corn.

Thunder is wonder, lightning is frightening,
but soft steady rain gets the job done.

The best time to catch a politician is when he is running.

Bureaucracy is a giant mechanism operated by pygmies.

Success is never final.

Nothing in the world can take the place of persistence. Talent will not;
nothing is more common than unsuccessful men with talent. Genius will not;
unrewarded genius is almost a proverb. Education alone will not; the world
is full of educated derelicts. Persistence and determination
alone are omnipotent.

If I am not for myself, who is; if not now, when?
But if I am only for myself, what am I?

Ninety-five percent of the people in the world don't think, and of the five
percent who do think, half of them think wrong. Of the very small part of the
people who do think right—most of them don't do anything about it.

Ignorance may have its innings but will always lose in the ninth.

Don't let some of the good things in life rob you of the best.

The difference between being involved or committed is illustrated by bacon
and eggs; the chicken is involved, but the pig is committed.

Even a dog knows when he's been kicked or stumbled over.

He got bit by his own dog.

There is no limit to what you can achieve
if you don't care who gets the credit.

Stand for something, or you might fall for anything.

He who hesitates is lost.

You can disagree without being disagreeable.

Winning is never permanent. Losing is never fatal.

Them that can brag without lying, keeps talking.

It's easier to stay out of a trap than to get out of a trap.

Destiny is not a matter of chance but a matter of choice,
not something to be wished for but to be worked for.

Ain't nothing that will make a man a conservative quicker
than marrying a rich woman.

If you don't know your fish, know your fisherman.

The time to kill a snake is when the hoe is in your hand.

Some questions cannot be answered, but they can be decided.

Statistics are like a bikini, revealing what you wish to reveal
but concealing several vital points.

I've got no dog in that fight.

That dog won't hunt.

Don't let the fox guard the hen house.

Never been a horse that couldn't be rode.
Never been a cowboy that couldn't be throwed.

He's a legend in his own mind.

Plan your work and work your plan.

Don't let him find out his throat has been cut 'till he tries to turn his head.

He's no refrigerator; he can't keep nothing.

Every day is a miracle. You can either look for it, look at it,
or be blinded by the light.

If you don't train a young dog early, he'll be a chicken killer all his life.

The world is made up of dreamers, schemers, men of action,
and complaining spectators.

Be sensitive enough to feel supreme tenderness toward others,
and strong enough to show it.

Knowledge is power.

Success Is a Team Sport

Nothing ever gets settled around here. It's not like running a company or even a university. It's a seething debating society in which the debate never stops, in which people never give up, and that's the atmosphere in which we work.

Raleigh is sixty-seven square miles surrounded by reality.

If he had the bill, he wouldn't read it. If he read it, he wouldn't understand it. Let's vote.

A closed mouth gathers no foot.

The less you say, the less you have to take back.

The nice part about living in a small town is that when you don't know what you're doing, someone else does.

Think before you speak and be careful what you put in writing.

Don't get mad, get even.

Like the little boy who lost his bubble gum in the chicken house: He knows what he's looking for but doesn't know whether he's willing to find it.

Most politicians, when they become successful, brag about their early beginnings. I don't see anything wrong with that, as I was born in a log cabin—which I built myself.

Don't ever buy a pit bull from a one armed man.

The squeaky wheel gets the grease.

Nobody loves, or even likes, a lawyer until they need one.

When the elephants fight, it is the grass that suffers.

Free rides die hard.

Any day we go without making a law is a good day.

Show me a good loser; I'll show you a consistent loser.

Do what is right. You will please a few and astonish the rest.

Newspaper editorial writers: Those folks who, when the battle is over, come down from the mountaintop and shoot the wounded.

Before you cross the river, find the bridge.

Old age and treachery will beat youth and talent every time.

If you see a turtle on a stump—someone put him there.

It ain't over, 'till it's over.

Politics is like baseball. If you bat 300, you are in the Hall of Fame.

It's not where you're coming from, but where you're going;
not what your name is, but the name you make for yourself.

If you think education is expensive, try ignorance!

An environmentalist is someone who already has a cabin in the woods.

I've never regretted anything I didn't say.

The early bird gets the worm—but the second mouse gets the cheese.

He's not my dog; I'm just walking him for a friend.

If you can't run with the big dogs, stay up on the porch.

If you're not the lead dog, your view never changes.

We make a living on what we get. We make a life on what we give.

This simple amendment will help your bill. (Translation: "will gut your bill")

It's easier to get forgiveness than permission.

My get up and go has got up and went.

Don't get into an argument with someone who buys ink by the barrel.

It's better to be thought of as a fool than stand up, speak, and
remove all doubt.

Don't screw up on a dull news day.

An ounce of image is worth a pound of performance.

Lead, follow, or step out of the way.

To be silent when we should protest makes us cowards.

He's a hard dog to keep up on the porch.

You are either part of the solution or part of the problem.

Organize, deputize, and supervise.

Lay down with dogs, you get up with fleas.

Tell them what you're going to tell them!

Tell them what you told them!

Everything depends on whose ox is getting gored.

If it is to be, it's up to me.

There are more nuts than there are trees.

Success Is a Team Sport

Those who cannot remember the past are condemned to repeat it.

A good legislator knows the art of negotiating his own compromise.

He not only claims ignorance, he demonstrates it.

Legislators aren't bad to be married to—they aren't home much.

The best executive is the one who has sense enough to pick good people
to do what should be done, and self-restraint enough to keep
from meddling with them while they do it.

I haven't had a chance to study your bill.
(Translation: "I'll kill your bill if I can")

There are two kinds of people—winners and quitters.

You are what you eat.

Take one step at a time.

The hottest places in hell are reserved for those people, who
in times of great moral crisis refuse to take either side.

Sell to the classes, you eat with the masses;
sell to the masses, you eat with the classes.

Hope for the best, prepare for the worst, and take what comes.

Give him one kernel of corn and he will make
a giant sized bag of popcorn out of it.

A society should be judged by the way
that it cares for its most unfortunate citizens.

Index